BRAVE MEN
by Colonel David H. Hackworth
(U.S. Army, Ret.)
and Julie Sherman
A condensed edition of
the *New York Times* bestseller
About Face, praised as:

"Everything a twentieth-century war memoir could possibly be—a daydream of battlefield glory come true."
—*The New York Times*

"[A] colorful, multifaceted man . . . Hackworth is also honest, extremely intelligent and perhaps the best military leader this country has had since General George S. Patton."
—*The Philadelphia Inquirer*

"Startling and important insights on American values in war and peace."
—*San Francisco Chronicle*

"Free-wheeling stories straight out of Ernie Pyle—all of it delivered with glory-boy élan."
—*Newsday*

***About Face* was a Military Book Club Main Selection**

D0032534

"Remarkable . . . well-written, thought provoking."
—*The Washington Times*

"Engrossing . . . passionate autobiography of a fierce and fiercely outspoken warrior."
—*Publishers Weekly*

"The greatest war story ever written—dramatic and thrilling . . . the stuff of legend."
—*Army*

"Outstanding . . . Ernie Pyle and Bill Mauldin told of it their way; Dave Hackworth tells of it his way."
—*Infantry*

"An intelligent and clear-eyed analysis, and a passionate cry from the heart of a man who never stopped loving the Army, even when it stopped loving him back."
—Nicholas Proffitt, author of *Gardens of Stone*

"Swashbuckling . . . a compelling story and a prescription for military reform."
—*Detroit Free Press*

"The most important book to come out of the Vietnam generation."
—*Soldier of Fortune*

BRAVE MEN

Colonel
DAVID H. HACKWORTH
(U.S. Army, Ret.)
and JULIE SHERMAN

POCKET BOOKS
New York   London   Toronto   Sydney   Singapore

POCKET BOOKS, a division of Simon & Schuster, Inc.
1230 Avenue of the Americas, New York, NY 10020

Copyright © 1989, 1993 by David Hackworth and Julie Sherman

ISBN: 0-671-86560-9

First Pocket Books printing June 1993

10 9 8 7 6 5 4 3

POCKET and colophon are registered trademarks of
Simon & Schuster Inc.

Cover art by Gaylord Welker

Printed in the U.S.A.

This is a condensed edition of a previously published work entitled *ABOUT FACE*.

To infantrymen the world over—past, present and future

Contents

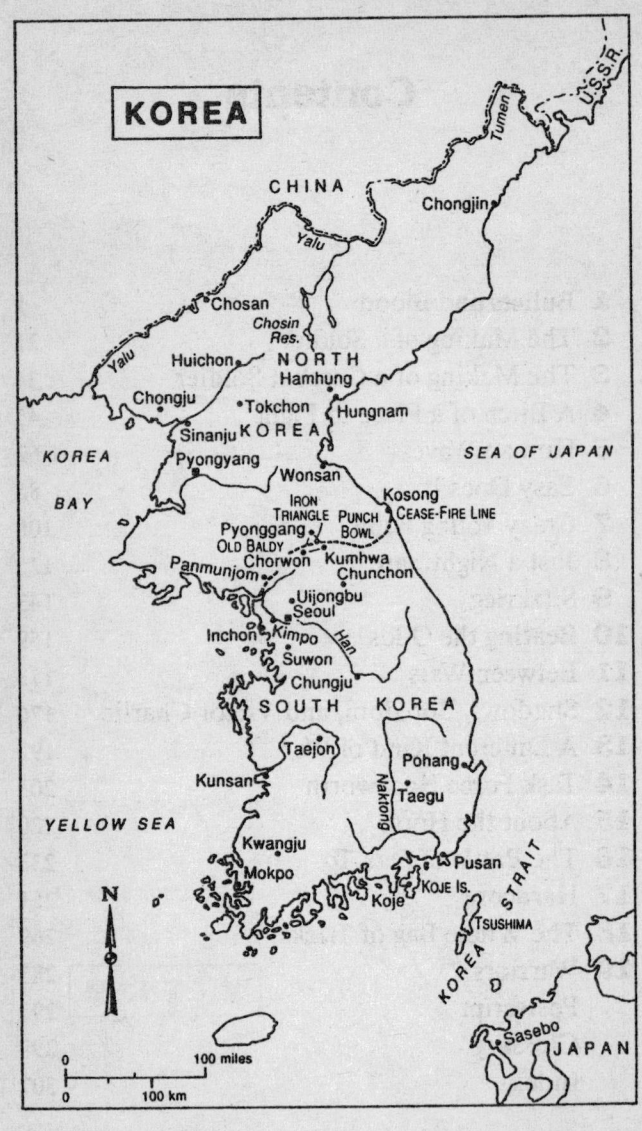

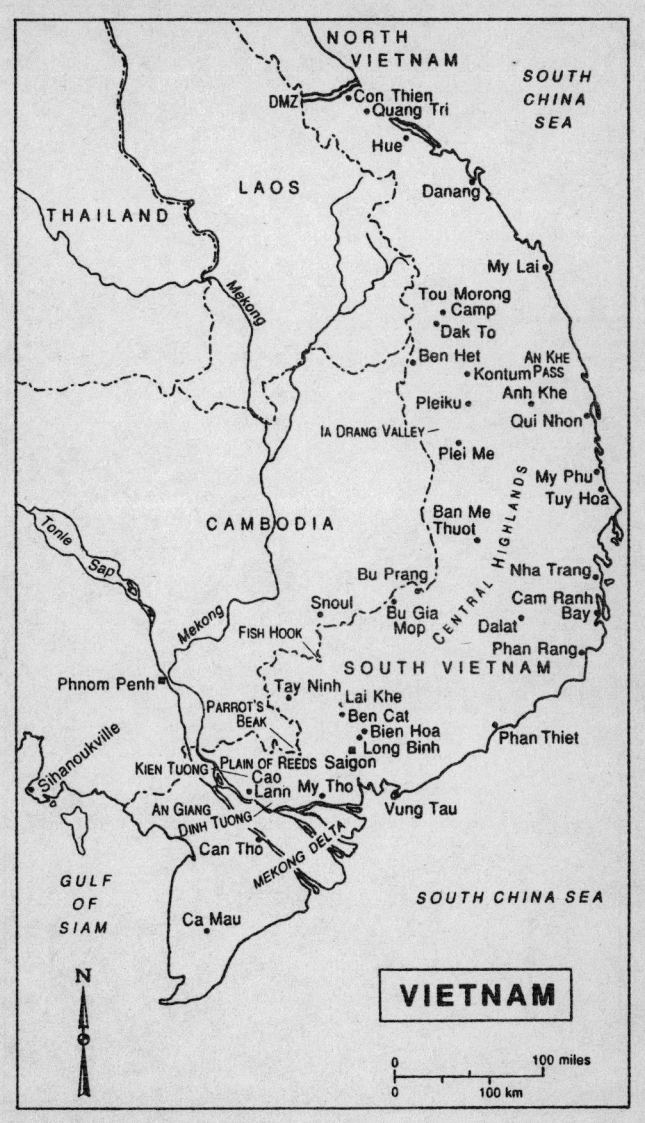

BRAVE
MEN

Chapter 1
Bullets and Blood

★ ★ ★

When I first saw them, about a thousand yards to our front, the enemy looked like little black ants racing from the village toward snow-covered hills. The sixth of February 1951 was a clear, cloudless morning; the temperature hovered around zero as the tanks kept rolling, closing on the ants and the hills set astride the road dead ahead.

My squad was riding piggyback on the lead tank. It was no honor being first in the grim parade. We'd already ravaged the tank's toolbox and knocked off some rations to eat on the way, and now our only comfort was the motor of the M46, which belched welcome heat over our near-frozen bodies.

The tank commander relayed Lieutenant Land's order to dismount. I got the guys off like a shot and hit the ground running as the tank rolled on beside us. But when I looked behind me, I saw that the rest of the 3d Platoon had not dismounted. Maybe I'd heard wrong. Maybe I was just overeager. But it's damn near impossible for infantrymen to reboard a moving tank, so there was no choice but to keep running and hope I hadn't blown it too badly with our platoon leader.

1

I didn't see the ants again for what seemed a lifetime, but I sure as hell knew where they were. In an instant the familiar roar of the tanks was drowned out by the deafening sound of incoming—machine gun, mortar, artillery, and self-propelled antitank (AT) fire.

There were at least a dozen enemy machine guns on the high ground on both sides of the road. Our tanks immediately moved out of the cross fire; my guys were totally shielded as we continued running along the east side of our maneuvering tank. The other squads, on the exposed decks of their tanks, were hard hit— by the time we made it to the side of a rice-paddy wall and set up a base of fire, most of what was left of 3d Platoon was scattered across the frozen ground.

Once the tanks pulled off the road and rolled into position, they froze. Earlier, in the assembly area, a tank commander had told me his unit, the 64th Tank Battalion, hadn't seen much hard combat. I believed him: as soon as they were fired upon, these tankers became paralyzed. They plumb forgot all their training and just sat there in those great big armored hulls while the enemy went on throwing everything at us but the mess hall wok.

I jumped on the back of the tank platoon leader's vehicle and thumped on the hatch with the butt of my rifle. The lieutenant opened the hatch a crack. "Hey, Lieutenant," I yelled, "get some fire going at the enemy! Get the big guns going! Get the machine guns going!"

The tank lieutenant was not with it. It seemed as though he had no comprehension of the fix we were in. Slugs were splatting hard on the side of the tank. The self-propelled AT fire, which was screaming down the valley, dug deep furrows all around us, and yet the tanks still sat there silently, like big, fat clay ducks at a shooting gallery. "Sergeant," the tank lieutenant finally said, in a shell-shocked kind of daze, "look . . . you see that out there on the ice?" Yes, I saw: it was a pile cap, a little fur ball on the ice amid my platoon's dead and wounded, the bullets and the blood. "That's my cap," he said. "Would you get it for me?"

I considered shooting the sorry son of a bitch then and there, climbing inside his tank and taking command. Fortunately, reason prevailed: I just grabbed him and shook him until he looked as if he was back to the real world. Then I instructed him to have three tanks concentrate on the self-propelled AT fire to our front, and use the others to start placing main-gun fire on the hills. To give him a bit of encouragement, I manned the tank's .50-caliber turret machine gun and blasted one of the hills myself, until I'd used up all the ammo and the commander got his men into action.

Once the 90mm guns got going, we were on our way to gaining fire superiority. The amount of incoming decreased as the tankers started to remember why they were there. But the tank commanders stayed buttoned up inside their turrets. No one was using the .50 calibers. I just couldn't believe it—eight inches of steel between them and the chaos outside, yet they didn't have it in them to help the sun come out for the guys stopping slugs with their field jackets. I went from tank to tank, pounding on the hatches and blasting away on each of the .50s until all the ammo was exhausted. This little exercise had its effect; the tank commanders got the word and started doing what they should have been doing all along. When no further spoon-feeding was required, I returned to my platoon.

There were dead and wounded everywhere. Slugs were ricocheting off the ice; we could see sparks where they hit. Jim Parker's 2d Platoon had successfully silenced an enemy machine gun to our left, so the pressure was off enough for us to get our wounded behind the protection of the tanks and paddy walls, where they could be patched up. Our progress was hampered, though, because the tank crews kept moving their tanks. They didn't stop to think they were exposing our wounded all over again; they were too busy trying to save their own armor-coated skins. I told the tank lieutenant, whom I'd come to view—and treat accordingly—as a recruit at Fort Knox, that the next time a tank moved and exposed our guys, I'd fire a 3.5 bazooka right up its ass. There was no more movement.

I saw a soldier prone on the ice. He'd been there a long time; I thought he was dead. But then I saw movement, and rushed out to get him. *My God,* I thought, *it's Deboer*.

Private Henry C. Deboer had been with George Company since early in the war. He was one of the few survivors from the original 3d Platoon, basically because in those first hard months of combat, he had not seen one good firefight. He had an uncanny sixth sense; he could always tell when the platoon was in for a major bloodletting, and invariably he'd find an excuse to be somewhere else. Normally that excuse was going on sick call, which by regulation he was allowed to do, and you couldn't stop him even though you knew the only thing that was wrong with him was a chronic case of cowardice. Deboer himself even admitted he was a coward, and we hated him for it. He was an outcast from the platoon; we even had a little song about him, which we'd all sing in unison: "Out of the dark, dreary Korean countryside comes the call of the Deboer bird: *sick call, sick call, sick call.*" He'd pulled his stunt only yesterday, as we were saddling up for this very operation. He'd sensed the bloodletting, all right, but hadn't figured that the foggy overcast covering the battlefield would not lift and the attack would be postponed. He'd returned from the doc last night (with a clean bill of health) most surprised to see us; the rest of the platoon took great pleasure in the fact that his malingering little ass would be in the thick of things in the morning.

Now Deboer was ashen-faced, hit in the chest or gut—I didn't know, there was a lot of blood—and well into shock. I knew he wasn't going to make it. "Come on, Deboer, you're going to be fine! You'll be all right," I said, giving him the old pep talk as I grabbed his jacket collar and started sliding him across the ice.

But Deboer said, "No, Sarge! Just leave me . . . you're going to get hit! Just leave me, Sarge . . ." Then suddenly he groaned: "Sarge, I shit my pants . . ." and that was it. He was gone. I left him and ran back.

Deboer, in death, became one of the great heroes of our outfit. It was true he'd never been anything in his Army life but a coward, but he'd *died* right—he died like a man. He didn't say, "Take care of me"; he said, "Leave me. Take care of yourself." And when I told the other guys the story, old Deboer became a legend in the platoon.

The road ran north-south, and we were on the east side of it. First and 2d platoons—the balance of G Company—were on the attack, maneuvering to secure the high ground to the north and west. My platoon, or what was left of it, was the "fix 'em" element, tying down the enemy while providing a base of fire for Parker's and Phil Gilchrist's people. After we got organized, I had a moment to look around. I saw my platoon leader, Lieutenant Land, sort of crouched down, leaning against the rice-paddy wall, observing the whole action. John Land was a good man; a WW II vet and former G Company NCO, he was one of the few battlefield commissions in the 27th Infantry Regiment. *Isn't he a cool customer,* I thought to myself now, *just watching this whole thing and taking it all in.* Because really that was about the only thing you could do at a time like this: stay cool, stay down, and establish fire superiority as best you could.

I examined what we had left in terms of a fighting force. "Tennessee" Mitchell, Delbert Bell, old Deboer —there were seven dead altogether, and about a dozen wounded. The platoon sergeant was gone and the assistant platoon sergeant nowhere in sight. It seemed that all that was left of 3d Platoon was the balance of my squad, bits and pieces of the other two, and a light-machine-gun team. I ran over to the Lieutenant to ask for instructions. When I got there, I realized the reason Lieutenant Land was so cool was that he was dead. He'd caught a slug right between the eyes. The blood had poured down his face and chest, filled up the eyepieces of his binoculars and frozen there. I took the binoculars and slipped the radio from his dead radio operator's back. I called Captain Michaely, our company commander, and gave him a situation report ("sitrep"). He said I was now in charge, that we were to continue tying down the enemy and to get the wounded out, in that order of priority.

Lieutenant Gilchrist's 1st Platoon was having a hell of a time. Their attack was being held up by fire from a good number of well-concealed enemy automatic-weapons positions on the high ground west of the road. Meanwhile, just as we'd gotten the wounded under control, one of the 3d Platoon guys who'd been doing some scouting spotted North Korean fighting positions directly in front of our position, just beyond a dike. He motioned me over to have a look. Sure enough, at least a platoon was dug in there, almost in the shadow of the tanks. They were so close that the tanks' main guns couldn't depress low enough to hit them, nor could their antitank weapons elevate high enough to hit our tanks. It was a Mexican standoff, but not for long. "All right, who's going with me?" I asked.

"I will," said Van Mieter, our platoon medic, a stud of a guy who had as great a reputation as a fighter as he did as a doc.

While the rest of 3d Platoon laid down a good base of fire, the doc and I each threw two frag grenades over the dike. When they exploded, we leaped through the smoke, landing front and center of the enemy. It was eyeball-to-eyeball: the two of us facing at least thirty dazed, wounded, or dead Communists. The enemy appeared to be leaderless—they were certainly in a state of shock—and we cleaned up the position with ease, using rifles and bayonets. Then two more enemy soldiers appeared out of the smoke and confusion dragging a .57-caliber antitank "buffalo gun." We were no more than ten feet apart. I leveled my M-1 and was about to shoot when I looked down and saw that the bolt was back—my weapon was empty and it wasn't exactly the time for reloading. I lunged forward with bayonet at on guard, shouting, *"Tao zhong!"* The enemy threw up their hands.

The Chinese word for "surrender" was probably the only one I knew; I'd filed it away in my brain when we were up north. I must admit I learned it thinking that someone would be saying it to *me,* but it didn't matter now—there they stood, with burp guns still hanging around their necks, a buffalo gun at their feet, and me with an empty rifle. The funny thing was that these guys were Korean, not Chinese, and chances were they hadn't understood what I'd said anyway. On the other hand, in combination with that long, razor-sharp bayonet pointed at them, they probably would have surrendered if I'd given the order in Swahili. In any event, we took their weapons and turned the POWs over to our men on the other side of the dike. Then the doc and I continued mopping up. In numbers and in firepower, these guys certainly should have outgunned what was left of 3d Platoon; from the number of bodies, buffalo guns, and other AT weapons we found, we concluded that we'd knocked off an antitank platoon that had been as green and scared as our tankers. The only difference was, of course, that these North Koreans would never tell the story of *their* baptism of fire.

By the time we rejoined the platoon, my guys had looted the two prisoners. The only real treasure was a U.S.-made Waltham pocket watch, which the guys gave to me. It became my 6 February souvenir. None of us spoke Korean, so I tasked PFC Charles to take the POWs back to Captain Michaely for interrogation. I was really pleased we'd nailed them; prisoners are the best source of battlefield information, and with the fight still going on full tilt around us, it'd be useful to find out what the hell was happening in the enemy camp.

The 1st and 2d platoons of George were fighting hard to take the high ground. Navy Corsairs provided close air support (as was their role), working the enemy over with napalm and strafing runs. Cut off between my and Gilchrist's platoons were enemy who'd been bypassed, so I took half a dozen of our guys and we went up the hill to do some hunting.

The North Koreans were in cleverly concealed, well-dug bunkers stuffed with straw for warmth. The pine-covered hill was a maze of seemingly unrelated positions, which we slowly worked through in two-man teams. "Fire in the hole!" was shouted again and again as we grenaded bunker after bunker, one man providing covering fire as the other edged close enough to flip in a frag. The enemy didn't fight back; they stayed in the bottom of their holes like trapped moles. It wasn't long before we ran out of frag grenades. A field expedient was quickly devised: we stripped tracer slugs from the machine-gun belt and clipped them for our M-1s. With one man covering, his partner would slip up to a hole and snap off a tracer or two into the position. The red-hot slugs would ignite the straw inside, and when the defender came up coughing, he'd be shot between the horns.

We moved from hole to hole, systematically burning the enemy out, until the hilltop above us suddenly exploded with gunfire. The Reds were counterattacking. As Gilchrist's platoon fought them off only six feet from the crest of the hill, we beat feet back to the safety of our rice-paddy wall.

Paddy walls, whose purpose in more peaceful times was irrigation control, were dirt walls about a foot thick and about three feet high—perfect cover from most direct-fire weapons. Infantrymen loved them. Now, leaning against my safe paddy wall—even as 1st Platoon fought off another counterattack with the help of the 2d, which could observe the forward slope of Gilchrist's hill and provide warning of the enemy's intention—I realized I was starving. I opened a can of C rations with my trusty P-38 can opener and dug right in.

I started at the top of the can: big chunks of congealed fat, under which lay beef and potatoes, frozen rock-hard. About this time an enemy sniper started firing along the top of the rice-paddy wall. It was harassing fire only; no one got hurt, but it got on all our nerves far more, even, than the larger battle still raging around us. I had just gotten down to the

meat and was about to take my first bite when—
zzzppt!—a slug creased a furrow in the top of the wall
right above my head and showered my rations with
debris. I scooped it out. I was about to try another bite
when—*zzzppt!*—another slug, same place, did the
same thing. By the third time, that was it. I was pissed
off. "I'm going to get that sniper," I said. "Who's
going with me?" Ray Wells, an ace machine gunner
and good old country boy from West Virginia, volunteered.

We followed the paddy wall until we struck a
drainage ditch that took us northeast, behind the
North Korean antitank positions. The plan was simple: to get to the right rear of the sniper, shoot the son
of a bitch, and go back and finish my C's.

The ditch had an L-shaped turn. We stopped just
shy of it, and I inched forward to have a quick peek:
three Koreans manning a machine gun were lying in
the prone about ten feet away, not looking in our
direction. I slipped back to Wells, whispering that I'd
take the first guy, he'd take the third, and we'd double
up on the gunner in the middle. We stepped out in the
ditch. The North Koreans looked up, but Wells and I
were the last thing they ever saw. I knew they were
dead; we were so close that I could hear the slugs
thumping home through their padded jackets. We
jumped over them and continued on our way.

With Wells covering my ass, I came up behind a
little tree at the top of the ditch—ideal concealment
for a quick look-see. After a few seconds' scan, I
spotted the sniper on the hill. He was in a bunker
about a hundred yards away on my left flank, and I
could clearly see the side of his head and his Soviet
SKS rifle. I ducked down. I didn't want to take a
chance on Kentucky windage, so I adjusted my M-1
rifle sights down four clicks and got into a firing

position. I had the sniper's head sitting right on top of my front sight, but just as I was about to squeeze the trigger, I heard machine-gun slugs snapping over my head, and then the weapon's report. *Oh, shit,* I thought, *someone's seen me.* For all I knew, it could have been one of our tankers—the slugs were coming from that direction—maybe they hadn't gotten the word we were out there. So I started to go down. But as I went down I felt the top of my head explode. I'd caught a slug.

I wasn't wearing a helmet—helmets were a pain in the ass unless there was lots of artillery and mortar fire coming in (in which case they became as essential as air). The slug ripped through my fur pile cap and propelled me from the top of the ditch as though I'd been poleaxed by Paul Bunyan. I don't know if I lost consciousness or not, but I do know I was stunned, with four-alarm sirens ringing in both ears. Wells thought I was dead and took off down the ditch. I couldn't blame him—he thought he was all alone out there behind enemy lines. Meanwhile, I tried to focus on what had happened.

Blood, really thick blood, was pumping out of my head. The first thing I did was ask myself my name, rank, and serial number: "David Haskell Hackworth, Sergeant, RA19242907," came the automatic response, which made me decide that my head must still be okay, even if my ass was in the worst crack ever. I started crawling down the ditch. I had to crawl because the North Koreans on the high ground knew they had an intruder in their midst. I stayed low on the enemy's side; slugs were spraying the ditch fast and furious, but thumping up against the other wall. I crawled until I reached the machine-gun crew Wells and I had knocked off.

Now I was faced with a dilemma. If I jumped over

them, I'd become exposed to the enemy fire coming from the hill. If I crawled over them, one of them might still be alive—and the longer I looked, the more my confused head convinced me that one of them *was* alive—and he'd kill me. I couldn't shoot them because when I got hit, I'd dropped my rifle. So I just stared at them, like a dumb recruit, wondering what to do. I pulled my trench knife out of my boot. Very carefully, I crawled over one of them, waiting for him to move. Crawled over the next one, waiting for him to move. Then I crawled over the third guy the same way and slipped on, like a snake, down the ditch until it was high enough for me to crouch, then high enough to stand up and run. And the whole time, I was singing.

Whoever said there aren't any atheists on the battlefield was dead right. Often when we'd be sitting around our little fires, one of the guys in the platoon would play his guitar and we would sing. The songs were all religious ones, like "Down by the Riverside," where we'd be laying down our swords and shields, or "Please, dear Jesus, hear my plea, just a closer walk with Thee"—but they were also songs of great comradeship. And a most magic feeling would always pour out when we sang, a feeling that 3d Platoon, *our* platoon, was our family, our whole life. And somehow, between God and our brothers, we were going to make it through.

So as I pounded down this ditch, I was singing "Just a Closer Walk with Thee," with deep feeling—Ella Fitzgerald, look out. To my mind I was really talking to God. I was talking to The Man. So I'm singing and running, blood's pouring out of my head—and then I remembered I didn't have my rifle. What a rotten example I had set. Good NCOs don't screw up like that; only a dumb-shit of a soldier loses his rifle. So I stopped singing and started chewing my ass as I ran down that ditch.

Maybe it was because I was thinking about my lack of professionalism. Maybe it was just a second-nature thing from my training. Or maybe it was a sixth sense, I don't know. But seconds before I was home free *(Just a few feet more,* I told myself, *just around the corner)*—I stopped. "Hey, Third Platoon! It's Hackworth," I shouted. "I'm coming in!"

Then I turned the corner. I found myself looking down the throat of Corporal Wesley Morgan's mean-looking Browning automatic rifle. "Man, you were so loud coming down that ditch, I thought at least a platoon of gooks was on the march! Wells told me you got it. If you hadn't called out, I would have mowed you down."

The thing that saved my life that day (besides Corporal Morgan's most fortunate restraint) was the very thing I hated most in Korea—the cold. The blood kept pumping, but it froze almost as soon as it came out of my head. After the doc patched me up with a Carlisle bandage, I radioed Captain Michaely and gave him a sitrep. I'd already appointed another NCO to skipper the platoon; Michaely told me to head back for the road where the battle had started, on the west side of which Gilchrist's platoon was still fighting. He would send a litter jeep there to pick me up. The platoon doc, always worried about his flock, wanted to tag along; I told him I'd make it, policed up one of our dead's M-1s, and headed off.

I kept low and used the rice-paddy walls and irrigation ditches for cover. I probably wouldn't have felt it if I'd gotten hit again anyway, because during my run back down the drainage ditch I'd fallen through the ice and been soaked from the waist down. The water and zero-degree weather had turned my lower torso into a block of ice—my head was spinning and my balls were frozen, and I wasn't sure which worried me more.

Then I came upon PFC Charles, the guy I'd earlier tasked to take the two North Korean POWs we'd captured that morning to the Old Man for interrogation. Charles was sitting in a drainage ditch by the road, eating a can of C rations. At his feet were the prisoners stretched out in the ditch—dead, each from a single bullet in the back of the head. I was outraged. "Why'd you kill them?"

"They tried to escape," he said simply, but I didn't believe him. "Besides," he continued, "I wasn't going to risk my ass to get two gooks out of here." There wasn't much I could do; I told him to report back to the platoon.

I continued on. Small-arms and machine-gun fire was skipping down the road. I gave it all a big miss and kept to my little ditch. I headed south until I met Lieutenant Colonel Gordon Murch, our old pro battalion CO, who was controlling the battle from his tactical CP behind a roadside knoll a few hundred yards from the front. There I was placed on a litter in a medical jeep, and as we bumped down the road all I could think was, *Hallelujah, I've got it made. I'm leaving this goddamned place.*

Or so I thought, because just then the jeep's radio crackled on: "First Platoon, George Company . . . got a serious wound . . . real bad . . . Get there fast. He'll be on the side of the road." I couldn't believe it. *Let me out! I'll wait here,* I thought, but I was too weak, too tired, and too cold to get the words out. The jeep spun around and headed back up that fire-swept road, past Colonel Murch, right into the jaws of the whole goddamned Communist army. We stopped. The medics calmly sauntered out to pick up the other casualty.

They took all the time in the world, or so it seemed, while the enemy used the large Red Cross markings on the jeep for target practice. The jeep's canvas sides were being ventilated, the slugs passing above and below my litter; I felt totally helpless, and swore that whoever the wounded guy was, I'd hate him for life (which, from the way things were going, was not going to be long).

It turned out he was a buddy, a handsome Hawaiian named Ray Mendez. I almost kept to my word, though, when I found out his critical wound was a slug in the thigh. When he'd been hit, he'd rolled up in a ball; blood had squirted out of his leg all over the front of his jacket, and someone had concluded he'd taken it in the gut. Oblivious to the fight raging on all sides of our thin-skinned ambulance jeep, Mendez became chirpier and chirpier as we headed out of the battle area. He sang the praises of his million-dollar wound and spun dreams about his imminent return to the Islands—"Me one big war hero, brah," he said.

The regimental collecting station was jammed with casualties. The surgeon who bent over my litter was covered in blood, like a butcher. "We're going to bypass Division Clearing and send you right to MASH at Suwon," he said. "You're on your way home."

The next stop was quick. The Mobile Army Surgical Hospital was near the runway at Suwon; the doc there wrote on my wound tag, "Emergency—Air evac," which somehow scared me, and before I knew it I was strapped down on the deck of a C-47.

We took off, just at dark. *Why don't they close the goddamn door?* I thought—it *had* to have been open, because I'd never been colder. I was shaking like a jackhammer, and I couldn't feel my hands or feet. A flight nurse stayed right with me (another ominous sign); she piled on blanket after blanket, with no effect. Just as I was reaching the point where I didn't know if I could take it anymore, we landed in Pusan, and it was another world. Paradise, in fact. A heated ambulance was waiting, and as they loaded me in, I felt like that old boll weevil who lived in a red-hot fire—"mighty warm, but nice," I'd found a home. I fell asleep and didn't wake again until I was being winched aboard the hospital ship USS *Haven* in Pusan harbor.

I opened my eyes and everything was white, clean, and oh-so-warm. Medics were starched; the nurses all looked like Doris Day. I was stripped, placed in crisp white sheets with soft blue blankets—I was safe, and suddenly starving. A medic came to the immediate rescue with a delicious hot meal; I wolfed it down just in time for the next wonder of wonders to greet my twenty-year-old eyes: a beautiful young nurse in a tight little white outfit who came to clean me up. *Why didn't I join the Navy?* I thought.

I hadn't washed more than once in over two months. I was caked with dried blood, Korean mud, and God only knew what else, and each time the nurse scraped off one filthy layer, she had to change the sheets and start again. It took four sheet changes, with no help from me, because as a "head wound," I wasn't allowed to move at all. Next, the poor girl had to shave off my ratty beard. Bad hygiene and ingrown hairs had covered my face with boillike pimples; it was too terrible to be funny, watching the nurse bobbing and weaving all over the place to avoid the flying debris every time that razor hit one of the antipersonnel mines buried in my cheeks.

The next few days were a haze. Sleep, really hard sleep; people standing over me, having whispered consultations. Blood, IV, X ray after X ray; doctors probing, asking questions—"How many fingers do you see?" I slowly regained my strength. Somebody commandeered my Waltham watch; I never saw it again. The sleep was good; I caught up on months of it lost. But then I started getting restless.

The ward, though spotlessly clean and staffed with talented, dedicated pros, was an extremely depressing place. We were all head wounds, most either terminal or vegetable cases. It was amazing that many—young boys, all of them—were still sucking in air. One guy had tubes running out of everywhere. Like Lieutenant Land, he'd taken one between the eyes—only he hadn't been lucky enough just to die.

I wanted out. I'd had my little vacation. I told the docs, "I'm ready to return to my platoon. There's nothing wrong with me." The doctors probably thought that the bullet had done some pretty serious damage to my brain—nobody wanted to go back to the front. They didn't realize that the guys in the 3d Platoon were my brothers, my family, and I loved them. So I didn't want to leave them out there alone, if by being there I could help keep them alive, keep them out of a head-wound ward. "I want to go back," I kept telling them. "Sure," they'd say, giving one another those *he's-a-little-screwy* looks, and soon they sent me to Osaka General Hospital in Japan.

After a lot more tests, the docs concluded that I was okay. There was no brain damage; the wound had actually been superficial: the bullet had passed under the skin on the left side of my head, grazed along the top of my skull, and then punctured through the skin again in the back. All it had left me with was two buzzing ears, a neat V branded on the back of my head where the slug had come out, and a hankering to get out of the hospital and on with the promised convalescence leave.

A G Company guy told me he had seen Mendez up in the leg ward. The bullet had done a job on him; he was still a bed patient. "Your little scratch almost cost me my life," I joked with him. "If I'd been the doc I would have left you there with a Band-Aid." Mendez and I caught up on where George was, what lumps the company had taken, and all other bits of information we could garner from new arrivals. It turned out that on 6 February we had taken on a reinforced North Korean regiment and really torn its ass: 170 enemy bodies were found on position, with additional killed and wounded estimated at 500 men. Before being ordered to withdraw by battalion CO Colonel Murch, we'd captured five antitank weapons, two 120mm mortars, and nine machine guns. We'd knocked out three artillery pieces, too, and come within two hundred yards of overrunning the enemy unit's regimental CP. (The next day 2d Battalion had continued the attack, but the North Koreans had met their match with gallant George, and bugged out to prevent an encore performance.) Third Platoon, despite the mauling we'd taken in the first moments of battle, had hung on tenaciously; we only now found out that we'd been operating in an area intended for an entire *company*—Fox, which had gotten hung up with a lot of enemy behind us, and which George's tank-infantry task force had "hauled ass and bypassed."

We heard that Captain Michaely had been shot in the ass but kept on fighting; that Lieutenant Land had $3000 of poker winnings in his pocket when he died (but that the guys had left it on him, even though they knew it'd be knocked off at Grave Registration), and that 1st Platoon was putting *me* in for a medal—for saving their ass *after* I was hit! Well, that was news to me. I hadn't done anything of the sort—or if I did, I didn't (nor would I ever) remember it. Still, word of this and the rest of the stuff that happened on 6 February started flashing around Osaka General (though all of it exaggerated to hell and back), and suddenly I found I was Big Man in the Hospital.

An ardent admirer came in the shape of an Army nurse. Her shape, to be exact, was that of a tackle for the Rams, and she would look at me adoringly as she gave me my shots. I was getting penicillin every four hours, in the ass; to this nurse's credit, she was so magic with that dreaded needle that I seldom felt a thing. But I was into cheerleaders, not tackles, and the unhappy day came when she started suggesting that we take leave together. At first I tried the soft line: "Love to . . . but sergeants can't socialize with officers." This tack got me nowhere. If anything, it increased her passion for a little hard scrimmage at some idyllic Japanese hideaway. Finally I had no other recourse but to lay it on the line. "There are only two things in life that interest me," I blurted. "One is sex and the other is adventure, and you don't offer either." I was too young to know about the "woman scorned" bit, but until I escaped a week later, she managed to find needles with square points, which she drilled into my aching cheeks with a vengeance.

On the first day of leave I met a lovely Japanese girl. She was probably a pro—some were, some weren't—but it didn't matter; at the end of your leave you always gave your little girl-san whatever money you had left anyway. She'd made you forget the war for a while, and that was worth something. So maybe she wasn't a pro. In any event, she was gentle and kind and fun, and we had a glorious, roaring two-week party together. And that was all you wanted on leave, convalescence or other. To live as high as you could, which meant good food, good women, lots of booze, and staying blasted all the time; to spend all your money and have a lot of fun, and try not to count the days before you had to go back.

And then, of course, you went back. Such was a soldier's life.

Chapter 2
The Making of a
Soldier

★ ★ ★

On 20 May 1946, I was on the corner of Main and Hill streets in Ocean Park, California, waiting for a bus. Al Hewitt, my best friend and childhood mentor, suddenly came running up, brandishing some magazine, which he breathlessly thrust in my face. "Look at it!" he demanded.

On the cover was an Airborne constabulary soldier in Berlin. The trooper was wearing a knockout of a uniform, complete with a very jazzy yellow scarf around his neck. His helmet had a big "C" painted on the front, and a yellow band around it, which tied in perfectly with the scarf. It was a great uniform, with the whole look made complete by the two beautiful blond frauleins the guy had perched on his knees. Al said, "That's the army of occupation in Germany, Hack! We've got to join up!"

I didn't need any persuading; the only problem as I saw it was where to go to enlist. I'd been trying to get into one service or another for the last three years, and by now the sergeants at the Santa Monica recruiting station knew me on a first-name basis. They also knew that I was still underage (even if Al was not), so we hopped the first bus into Los Angeles to join up there.

Somehow we got separated on the way to the physicals. Armed with phony ID papers, I kept on going, and ended up in a room with an officer and a flag. I pledged allegiance to the flag, and then, kind of before I knew it, I was a soldier in the U.S. Army. The officer asked me when I wanted to start basic training, now or next week. *Now,* I said, remembering with a fifteen-year-old's lust those blond frauleins on another trooper's knees.

There were three or four buses waiting at the ramp outside the L.A. induction center. I checked them all to see if Al had come out yet. He had not, so I got us a couple of seats and squared myself away. Recruits kept trickling out of the building and into the buses; what seemed like a very long time passed, and still Al was nowhere to be seen. He turned up just as the buses were about to pull away. I begged our driver to hold on. "Come on, Al!" I shouted. "We're leaving right now! We're going to Germany!"

"Can't go!" he called back.

"Why not?" I screamed.

"Four-F!" he yelled. "Got a punctured eardrum!"

So long, Al.

Sadly, by the time I finished training, American Airborne troops had been kicked out of Berlin; the word was that occupation U.S. paratrooper style was too much even for a country that had seen its fair share of destruction. My destination was now Italy, and when the troop ship (which wasn't a troop ship at all, but a freighter designed for bulk supplies) finally landed at Leghorn, 2400 troops, who'd been packed in like sardines all the way from New York, spilled onto a beach still studded with mines.

We stayed in a huge warehouse at the water's edge. It was more like an airplane hangar than anything else, and there were probably 2000 guys sleeping in there, in makeshift beds. All the windows in the place had been broken out by the troops we were replacing: the Second Great War's combat men, celebrating because they were finally going home.

Wild parties, wild drinking, and whores everywhere. Whores in the barracks, whores on the beach —even if nobody else did, the whores knew where the mines were buried. And wherever you went, little kids would say, "Hey, GI, you got chewing gum? You got chocolate?" It was just like in the movies.

The outfit I was assigned to, the 752d Tank Battalion, was more of the same, including the whores. The only difference was the vets here were not quite on their way out of town. Everything was loose and everything was wild, but these vets, the majority of whom had fought from Africa to Sicily to Italy, were still lean, mean, combat-ready troops—they just didn't have time for garrison-style discipline. It was not uncommon, for example, to be awakened in the middle of the night by a drunk off-duty trooper running through the barracks firing his weapon, or to hear one of his buddies outside, matching him shot for shot just for the hell of it. All in all, it was some violent world I found myself in—nothing like I'd expected—but with wonderful characters, veterans who could spin drunken tales until the wee hours of the morning about some little way they had beaten the system, or the signorinas they'd conquered as they fought up Italy's rugged spine. They rarely talked about combat, though, and after a very short time we new replacements stopped asking. Maybe it was just part of the role, but the old soldiers went silent on the horrors of war. It was as though they belonged to a secret fraternity, and we, the pink-cheeked unenlightened, were—in a word—outsiders.

Gradually most of the WW II warriors went back to

the States, and the postwar wild-West feeling of lawlessness went, too. It had been great fun for a kid to be part of the hell-for-leather spirit that made up the 752d (the "Seven-Five-Deuce"), but like the tightening of a screw, one turn at a time, each day the unit became more military, the "who gives a damn" attitude of the remaining 752d combat leaders and troopers replaced by the exacting discipline of the peacetime Army.

For the next four years I learned my trade—one year with the recon company of the tank battalion in the Po Valley, and three more with Trieste United States Troops (TRUST), the illustrious unit whose 5000 handpicked members Walter Winchell called "the chrome-plated soldiers of Europe" and whose job was to protect the American zone of the divided Free Territory of Trieste (Italy) from the communists of neighboring Yugoslavia. We worked hard during those years—long, merciless days of training, repeating, repeating, repeating until we got it right—our transformation into soldiers inspired and monitored by those dedicated, battle-savvy NCOs, who well knew that discipline and tactical proficiency on the battlefield were direct results of discipline and combat skills instilled on the parade and training grounds.

Punishment was meted out by a process known as NCO justice: for crimes such as a uniform of less than starched perfection, a bed that didn't bounce a quarter, or even a mildly insubordinate smirk, the sentence could range from fifty push-ups to doubletiming around the parade field holding a 9.5-pound M-1 rifle over your head, yelling, "I'm a shithead! I'm a shithead!" until you collapsed. We rarely saw an officer above our platoon-leader lieutenant (and he was seldom with the troops because of administrative duties), but no one seemed too concerned about it; above and below on the chain of command, it was well-recognized that as fathers, teachers, older brothers, and chief tormentors, in Trieste the NCO corps had no equal.

Sergeant Dillard Oller of Harlan County, Kentucky, for example, was the meanest sergeant in the entire U.S. Army. In TRUST's 15th Tank Company, he commanded the Sherman tank on which I was assigned as assistant driver, and when he wasn't growling out gunner corrections in phrases like "down a crack" and "left a cunt hair," he was kicking my ass until I loved and took care of his tank as though it were my first car. Sergeant Oller's 1947 expectations were actually those of 1930 Regular Army soldierly perfection; the style of discipline required to meet this ideal took some getting used to, however, and until I got into the swing of things, I thought I was in prison. But it was the same throughout the tank company: I knew one trooper who'd spent time in the TRUST stockade, and when he came back, he said that as bad as the stockade was—and it was *bad*—in terms of unrelenting discipline, high standards, and tough soldiering, the 15th was even worse.

Or better, depending on how you looked at it. Over the next eighteen months with the tank company, I became a driver and a gunner corporal—and even then, if I'd missed a 55-gallon drum at 1200 yards on the second shot, it would have been an immediate farewell to those two beautiful stripes. The rationale was simple: mistakes on the training field will be mistakes on the battlefield, and mistakes on the battlefield lead to men's deaths. The tank NCOs, many of whom were pre–WW II Horse Cav Regulars, were like gods—they were perfect, and demanded the same from us, instantly. They cut absolutely no slack as they worked overtime molding us into soldiers, in the process establishing standards that would remain with and in us for years to come. No detail escaped their eyes, and when (inevitably) one of us troops screwed up, we paid dearly for it. But the price was never as high as what we gained as a result: first, a respect and appreciation for details, and second, an incredible boost to our morale when, wonder of wonders, we got it right.

In 1948 I joined TRUST's Intelligence and Reconnaisance (I&R) Platoon. There I met the ultimate taskmaster, our platoon sergeant, Steve Prazenka, who picked up where the tank NCOs left off. "If you learn it right, you'll do it right the rest of your life," Prazenka would growl as the endless repetition of one thing or another took its toll on our tired souls. "If you learn it wrong, you'll do it wrong, and you'll spend the rest of your life trying to learn to do it right."

Thanks to him, we learned it right the first time around. We learned about weapons—ours and the enemy's—how to disassemble, assemble, and fire them. We spent days training in the woods, learning about camouflage, woodcraft, creeping, scouting, and observing; we became experts in what Prazenka called "snooping and pooping," all under his watchful eye. We had an hour's close-order drill every day, using the drills of the thirties, and if Prazenka didn't like the way we did them, he'd turn back to the old field manual (which read, "Close-order drill is the foundation of all discipline") and throw another hour's worth on top of us. Holding a 9.5-pound M-1 rifle at right shoulder arms isn't exactly a breeze at any time, and often by the time the Sergeant got through with us, our right hands would be locked stiff in the M-1 grip position for hours, somehow not getting the word that the weapon wasn't there anymore.

Prazenka made out the training schedule; we marched to the tune he played and loved him for it. He commanded our respect—effortlessly, it seemed. He was twenty-two years old, and to us he'd been through it all. An I&R man from basic training onward, he'd been with the 28th "Bloody Bucket" Division's I&R platoon in WW II, and was captured (after a painful cat-and-mouse game with the Nazis) deep behind the shattered U.S. lines during the Battle of the Bulge. He was just a total pro—the finest, fairest platoon sergeant who ever came down the track—who knew as much about soldiering as an Alabama Bible-bashing preacher knows about the Good Book. He could double-time ten miles first thing in the morning regardless of what he'd drunk the night before; sometimes he'd come roaring into our barracks at 0500, still loaded to the eyeballs from a wild night's partying, shouting, "Out of those sacks, boys—let go of your cocks and grab your socks, it's time to go for a run!" and off we'd go. Usually it was just five or six miles, but on special occasions (if we bugged him enough) we'd run up to the town of Prosecco—about nine miles round-trip—to try to catch a glimpse of his girlfriend Anna. The first time we'd gone up there, Anna had been out in a field tending her cows. She'd waved to us, all blond hair and big tits, shouting, " 'Ello, Stevie!" and Prazenka never heard the end of it from his envious platoon.

Prazenka quickly became my mentor and my hero, and when I finally got my own squad in the I&R, I did everything I could to emulate him, if not to go him one better and become the meanest bastard of an NCO the world had ever seen. If the guys didn't measure up to the standards of spit-and-polish perfection *I* set for them, for example, sometimes I'd just decide that no one was going to go on pass. I'd say, "Gentlemen, I want you to fall out in the company street." Then I would double-time them to the front gate, halt them, and have them stand at parade rest. Then I'd say, "Now, gentlemen, there is the front gate. That front gate is designed for soldiers who are good soldiers. Soldiers who deserve a pass. A pass is a privilege, not a right. You get a pass for making me happy. For having beautiful shoes and beautiful weapons and being motivated and spirited and dedicated. I have found you to be failing in all of these areas. So, none of you is going out on pass. You are not going out until I consider you fit to go out, until you are soldiers who are fit to walk in the streets of Trieste. I am not proud of you men. And the reason you're not going out is *because* I am not proud of you."

Then I'd double-time them back to the barracks and open my locker, where they'd see all their passes thumbtacked under the lid. "There are your passes," I'd say. "There they are and that's where they are going to stay until I'm impressed with you. Now, that may be months, gentlemen. I just don't know how long that's going to be." Newly, proudly perched on the first rung of the leadership ladder, it'd be fair to say I was much hated by my squad; fortunately, the higher-ups of Headquarters Company (to which the I&R Platoon belonged) made sure that my enthusiasm didn't keep my men off the streets of Trieste forever.

Still, the double dose of discipline had our little band working better and better by the day, and soon we were bopping along like a well-oiled machine. To me the proof came on the training field, on a TRUST training exercise for which the I&R was designated the aggressor force. My squad was given the mission of infiltrating behind 1st Battalion lines and capturing a prisoner, preferably an officer. I decided that if we had to get an officer, we might as well get the *commanding* officer, so we set our sights on "The Helmet," Lieutenant Colonel James Muir II, CO of the 1st Batt. We called Muir "The Helmet" because he was very small, and when he put on his steel pot, it seemed to come down to the top of his boots. Capturing him would be a real coup; he was a well-liked, damn good officer who got around, saw his troops, and cared a lot about their welfare, and there seemed little doubt his men would go to any lengths to protect him.

Since I knew our area of operation (AO) just about as well as I knew anything those days, I concluded that Colonel Muir would set up his command post (CP) in one of only two places: in a hollow behind the Red Cross Club or in an orchard by Opicina. Our recon confirmed it was the Red Cross Club; we slipped behind it using side trails, and camouflaged our three recon jeeps on the side of a road nearby. In the darkness and on foot, we got to a place where we were looking down on the "enemy."

Colonel Muir's CP was hidden in a clump of trees. The sun was just rising; we could pick out tents and vehicles, and hear the sound of generators. The Colonel had a rifle company close in for security. As the I&R were the aggressors, we were wearing dark-green Russian-looking uniforms (these being the early Cold War years) with a red triangular patch, as well as "enemy" helmets, so-designated by the wooden block attached on top; it was winter, bitter cold, so we were also wearing heavy parkas with hoods. I instructed my men to wear their hoods over their helmets—that way, when we got into the CP area, 1st Battalion wouldn't be able to tell us from their own.

It was getting light as we infiltrated through the CP. People were getting up; I could hear mess kits clattering and guys moving through a chow line. Even though it was only a maneuver and no one could get hurt, I still had that scared feeling in the pit of my stomach, that prayer that we wouldn't get caught. My fear was wholly unjustified, though, because after we got into the CP, as far as the "enemy" could see we were indeed just some of their guys strolling through the area with our hoods on. We made our way to

Colonel Muir's tent and disarmed and captured the guard outside. Then I went into the tent.

The Colonel was sleeping. I gently shook him awake. "Yes, what is it?" he asked.

"Colonel Muir, I'm Corporal Hackworth from Regimental I&R and you're a prisoner of war." Muir's eyes popped open and he reached under his pillow. He was an old soldier, and I knew he had a pistol there. I had my weapon pointed at him. "Sir, I have the drop on you. If you'll just put on your gear and come with us."

Muir withdrew his hand from under the pillow. "Fair enough, Hackworth," he replied, and got up from his bed.

He could have taken his time. He could have made some noise. He could have pulled rank. But he didn't—he played the game. We left his tent and walked down the road until we got to our jeeps. I put him in the back with two guys, then hopped in the front with the driver. The windshield was down, with canvas (to prevent glare) tied over it on the hood as we drove through Muir's positions. No one suspected us. After all, we were driving out of 1st Batt lines, and besides, the Colonel himself was sitting calmly in the backseat. It was a perfect operation.

The main road from Muir's battalion to our regimental CP was mined with dummy antitank mines. They weren't dug in—just sitting on top of the road as window dressing for the exercise—but as we swerved around them about three miles out of Muir's CP, elements of the 1st Battalion recognized our I&R vehicles and started shooting at us with blanks. We zoomed on as fast as we could, but the windshield on my jeep hadn't been tied down properly and suddenly it flew up, the canvas cover obstructing the driver's vision. *No operation ever goes according to plan,* went the old military axiom, and in my mind's eye I saw the jeep crashing into a tree, killing everyone, including the Colonel (which would have been a bit hard to explain if I'd been unlucky enough to survive). I threw myself onto the windshield and stayed there until we were beyond enemy range. Then we stopped the jeep, blindfolded Colonel Muir, turned him around nine times (by the book, so he wouldn't be able to find our CP when he was released), and drove on to a dismount point near our headquarters.

I reported in to our regimental commander, Colonel Paul W. Caraway, at his CP. Captain Kenneth Eggleston, the HQ Company CO, was there, too, and both were almost as excited as I was about the capture of Colonel Muir (whom I considered my own personal trophy). The I&R got kudos and letters of commendation from Caraway on down for our work on that maneuver. My own reward was getting my ass chewed by someone at the CP because in all the excitement I'd taken off my much-hated aggressor helmet and left it in the jeep outside. But after this maneuver, Colonel Muir never forgot me; every time he saw me he'd say, "I'll get your ass, Hackworth," but good soldier that he was, he always said it with a smile.

By the time I finished my first hitch, I realized I'd found a home in the Army, so at eighteen I reenlisted for three more years. Soon after, I made sergeant. Then Prazenka went back to the States on reenlistment leave, during which time his replacement, Sergeant Charlie Durham, finished his tour and rotated home, and I found myself the acting platoon sergeant of the I&R, responsible for its training.

I took on my new role with great confidence and full enthusiasm, and managed to alienate most of the platoon within days. The older soldiers of the outfit, the combat vets of WW II, resented me most of all: I was playing out the role of Prazenka (and pretty well, I hoped), but with no experience to back me up. The truth was, other than a few brushes with Red guerrillas along the Italian-Yugoslav border, I'd never heard an angry shot, and all I really knew about war was what I'd seen in the movies and read about in manuals and books. The guys had long been calling me "Combat" due to my zealous nature on manuevers; now it became "Sergeant Combat": "Ask Sergeant Combat . . . he'll tell us how to do it," they'd say, to which I'd reply, "You're goddamned right. Field Manual 7–75, paragraph 101, says you'll do it this way, and that's the way I want to see you doing it, right *now!*" I was determined not to let them get to me, but it was hard. I'd been in the Army now for more than three years, yet when it was all shaken out, I was still a greenhorn.

Prazenka came back from leave then, and I went back to my squad. I had no regrets about my decision to re-up, but I was antsy. The guys in the platoon still called me Sergeant Combat, and it frustrated the hell out of me because, after all, it wasn't my fault there wasn't a war going on. But suddenly all that changed when, on 25 June 1950, North Korea crossed the border into the South. U.S. troops around the world went on full alert; we moved to our battle positions, because the word was that the Communists weren't going to stop at South Korea—they were going to bust out all over the globe.

We were ready for them at Trieste. The regiment moved to the border, to await the marching Red Army. Day followed day and they never came. My adrenaline was running fast and I wanted to be where the action was. I couldn't stop talking about it. Every day I'd warn Prazenka to treat me nice—I was going to Korea and I might just give him all my medals when I came back. I was ready to try out my warrior wings. I wanted to prove myself, I wanted to win that Combat Infantryman's Badge (CIB), I just wanted to *go*—so badly it hurt.

During the alert, in that the I&R manned the critical regimental observation posts (OPs), we were frequently visited by regimental commander Colonel Caraway. The Colonel was a stern, no-nonsense, often seemingly unapproachable man, but on one of his visits I got up enough nerve to ask him to help me get over to Korea. He said he'd see what he could do, and within a few weeks I got my orders. Colonel Caraway had even arranged it so that I was to be flown back to the States, unheard of at a time when almost all troop transport out of TRUST was by ship.

I said good-bye to my buddies and hopped on the plane, the first NCO from Trieste on the way to Korea. Many more soon followed, of course, and about 75 percent of the TRUST NCOs who went and lived were destined to be either battlefield-commissioned to lieutenant or to receive high awards, proving that "the chrome-plated soldiers of Europe," of TRUST, trained in the spirit of what was probably an anachronism of an army, were indeed soldiers of the highest caliber.

But in September 1950, on that plane from Italy to the States, I didn't really know that; nor did I know, in general, how much I didn't know—especially in matters of life and death. But I did know that I was hot to trot and ready for whatever came my way, and that if nothing else, I wasn't going to be Sergeant Combat ever again. A month later I was in Korea.

And a month after that, so were the Chinese.

Chapter 3
The Making of a Combat Soldier

★ ★ ★

My first real firefight occurred just before the Chinese came, on a dull, overcast day. Upon my arrival in Korea, I'd been assigned to the 25th Division's Recon Company as a replacement scout section leader; my scout section was set up near a secondary road when we spotted a squad of North Korean soldiers, weapons at sling arms, coming out of the treeline. They were good-looking troops, but asleep at the switch: they didn't see us. It was amazing the sense of power I felt—ultimate power, I suppose—just watching them come and holding that weapon in my hands. We let them get within about thirty yards before we cut loose; I dropped four guys point-blank with my M-1, each dead with a six-o'clock-sight picture in the chest, just like the good book said. I felt no guilt—few of us did; I'd been trained too well, and besides, the enemy had been utterly dehumanized throughout my training. *They aren't men, they're just gooks,** I thought, as the four enemy fell and a fierce firefight began—we'd

---

*The term "gook" is derived from the Korean word *han-guk,* which means Korean person.

knocked off the point element of a much larger enemy force and stirred up a hornet's nest.

Following the lead of a lot of the older veterans, earlier in the day I'd placed several clips of ammo on my rifle sling. I liked the look—it was kind of John Wayneish—and it seemed to make sense, a new clip only seconds away. But when I'd taken up my prone firing position, the sling had flopped on the rain-soaked ground. Now, as the firefight got going, I grabbed for a clip, only to discover that it and the rest of them were clogged with mud. I vaguely remembered an old tale about how well the M-1 worked under any battlefield condition; quickly knocking off the bigger pieces of mud, I oozed the clip into my rifle. I got one round off. The weapon jammed, and for the next few minutes I sat in the ditch, field-stripping, cleaning, and reassembling the thing, while my first real combat went on without me. Our artillery (arty) fire took the starch out of the North Korean advance, and we were able to scoot ass with no friendly casualties—other, that is, than Sergeant Combat's bruised pride.

My first fight had been my first screwup. I didn't know until much later that you generally don't walk away from that one.

A few days later, five of us were on a reconnaissance patrol. It was a black night, save for the U.S. flares that hung eerily over the battlefield; very quiet but for the occasional whine of artillery fire and the odd burst of an automatic weapon. We had moved about a mile into enemy territory when we heard motors. Leaving the patrol, I crawled to a mound near the edge of the road for a firsthand look.

Through the darkness, silhouetted by the artillery flares, I could see four enemy vehicles. A file of infantry was walking on each side of the motor column, with more infantry walking in front. They were so close that I was sure only the vehicles' engines prevented them from hearing my pounding heart. They passed by. I was about to return to the patrol when I saw a lone North Korean soldier, his weapon slung, tracing a telephone wire in one hand, examining it for breaks in the line. As he passed my position, I parted his hair with a submachine-gun magazine and dragged him back to the patrol.

Daylight wasn't far off when we headed home. Progress was slow. Initially we had to pack our zonked-out prize; later he awoke and stumbled along belligerently, but at least under his own steam. Just when we thought we had it made, we ran into a large enemy force moving down the road in formation. They were jabbering excitedly and dragging machine guns behind them on squeaky wheels. We were about six yards from the road; I lay on top of the prisoner, covered his mouth with my hand, and pressed my trench knife hard against his throat. I thought the cold steel would be enough to convince him to be good, but it wasn't. He started squirming around. My hand was muffling his cries to his comrades; when he tried to bite it, I had no choice—I slit his throat, and lay there on top of him for what seemed like a bloody eternity, until the road was clear and we could hotfoot it back to the U.S. lines.

I hadn't wanted to kill him. A live prisoner is worth a thousand dead hombres. But I was probably as scared as he was, and in a millionth of a second I'd had to decide—and it was either him or my patrol.

The night the Chinese came, I was in a foxhole in the center of my scout section's defensive position. The sector was densely covered with screw pines and scrub oaks; my foxhole buddy and I were sitting on the edges of our hole when we saw—and it was like right out of a cartoon—a row of the small trees moving toward us. We chopped them down (along with the little Chinaman creeping along behind each one) with hand grenades, but that was just the beginning. The next thing I saw was what I could only describe as a wave—a human wave—of Chinese crashing over us.

It was yet another dramatic turn in the course of the Korean War since its lightning-fast beginning in June. At the start, U.S. forces, hopelessly outnumbered, outgunned, and undertrained, had been driven back by the North Koreans into the tiniest corner of South Korea, beyond the Naktong River. There the Eighth Army had made its stand, holding what was known as the Pusan Perimeter until September, when MacArthur's amphibious invasion at Inchon severed the North Korean army's lines of communications and chopped its legs out from under it. With the enemy no longer an effective fighting force, our certain defeat along the lines of Dunkirk in 1940 suddenly had appeared to be surefire victory. Units of the Eighth Army had smashed out of the Naktong perimeter and raced north, beyond the 38th parallel, beyond the North Korean capital of Pyongyang, almost to the banks of the Yalu River, the dividing line between North Korea and Manchuria. But as units moved farther north, the weather had worsened and enemy resistance had increased. It had been like compressing a spring, and finally, inevitably, it had sprung: the Chinese presence heralded the start of the largest and most bitter retreat in U.S. Army history.

Now that the Chinese were in the conflict, the Recon Company's mission was to provide a reconnaissance screen in front of the 25th Infantry Division's withdrawal—in other words, to "delay, deceive, and disorganize" the undeniable Communist advance. Exchanging ground for time, the drill went that we would hold a position until the enemy was on our asses; then we would break contact and run like hell, leapfrogging through another recon platoon or a rifle unit that was set up behind us in the same way. It was a dangerous game with no room for error, and we found ourselves playing it day after day after day.

They were strange dudes, the Chinese, seemingly with no sense of personal peril. It was not unusual to see them jump on a U.S. tank, holding grenades, and then scramble around looking for some opening to toss them in. Of course, if the tank was buttoned up, this was impossible, and the tank commander inside would simply call another tank nearby to "scratch my back," at which point the second tank would spray the first with .30-caliber coaxial machine-gun fire and wash the hitchhikers off. But there were always other Chinamen to take the dead ones' places; it was a grim fact we were constantly reminded of as we kept moving south.

Morale dropped with every rearward step of the humiliating retreat. We kept falling back—away from the Yalu, beyond Pyongyang—until soon we'd re-crossed the 38th parallel and were back in South Korea. I think the only things running faster than the Eighth Army were the rumors: the Marines were cut off at a place called Chosen Reservoir in the north and were being zeroed out; the U.S. Army's X Corps had surrendered; boats were waiting at Pusan harbor to take us to Japan. Meanwhile, winter had arrived, but winter gear had not. MacArthur had said we'd be home before Christmas; I guess his supply people believed him, because the Chinese had caught us with our pants down and they were summer trousers. Feet in leather boots froze; gloves and mittens were as scarce as good-looking girls; our field jackets were as thin and protective as page one of a newspaper. We were slowly freezing to death in the bitter below-zero weather, while the Chinese, like Genghis Khan's mighty hordes, marched on, seemingly unstoppable.

The Making of a Combat Soldier

Food was in short supply. All spare time was spent scrounging; one of the most modern armies in the world became an army of days past, foraging and living off the land. We kicked in walls of houses, searching for rice and kimchi (fermented cabbage, a Korean staple) hidden in false walls and secret caches; we cooked what we found in our steel pots. When nothing else was available, we'd take the C-ration packets of sugar, powdered coffee, powdered milk, and chocolate we'd stored for days in the pockets of our fatigues, mash it all together with snow in our helmets, and trick ourselves into believing it was ice cream.

Trying to beat the elements became a war in itself. It was so bitterly cold you couldn't sleep. You had to keep moving, stomping feet and flexing fingers twenty-four hours a day. Those who didn't were saying good-bye to their hands and feet (and in some cases their lives); for a while, every day a couple of men were evacuated because of frostbite—black toes and fingers to be cut off at the hospital. Grenades, knives, and ammo would freeze fast to the foxhole brim. Weapons froze, too—you'd have to kick the bolts of the M-1s and Browning automatic rifles (BARs) to get them back. We seldom had rifle patches to clean our weapons; most of us cut little squares out of our shirts or trousers to do the best we could. Gun oil was a luxury usually beyond our reach; we lubricated our weapons with motor oil or the frozen lard of C rations, and took to keeping them with us in our fart sacks at night. Staying alive became our only concern, and we did.

When we passed through the villages, if a house had lots of wood—doors, window frames, even the most beautiful hand-carved furniture—we'd burn it, one piece at a time, finishing off the job by throwing a thermite grenade on the thatch roof and standing by until the whole structure was burned to the ground. Our orders were to destroy anything the enemy could use; *Gladly,* we thought to ourselves, and we could stay warm while we did it. At night we would carefully —obsessively—bundle, stack, and restack kindling wood, while waiting for daybreak when we could light our fires. The thought of those friendly flames allowed us to make it through the night; instantaneously, at first light thousands of tiny fires would spring up across the front, and around each huddled a cluster of shivering men. It was probably as bad in the Chinese camp, except at least the chinks were prepared with winter gear—down trousers and jackets, long overcoats that blended in with the snow, and down mittens (the latter of which we liberated and wore until our own supply people came through).

It was a frigid, brutal, soul-destroying time; I knew then how the Wehrmacht must have felt during World War II, or how Napoleon's army must have suffered years and years before that, when each made their horrible winter retreat from Russia.

After three months with the division recon company, I left to join the 27th Infantry "Wolfhound" Regiment, specifically the 2d Battalion, 3d Platoon of G (George) Company. The Wolfhounds were a colorful outfit with a long history: they'd gotten their name fighting Communists in Siberia during the Russian Revolution. In Korea the Wolfhounds were known as the "Fire Brigade," because whenever there was trouble, they were sent in to save the day; they weren't a special unit—just a group of guys who *thought* they were good, so they *were* good. And while on one hand that made the Wolfhounds my kind of outfit, on the other, I soon realized that I'd have to pay some dues before the Wolfhounds believed that I was their kind of man.

The Making of a Combat Soldier

It's always a bitch to join a unit (particularly one as tight as the Wolfhounds) as an individual replacement, and for some reason it's even worse when you're an NCO or an officer. You don't know anyone, and no one trusts you until you've proved yourself in battle. You get all the lousy details and only the worst battlefield horror stories; you're just "the new guy," you're just "fresh meat."

I didn't help my cause any that evening, soon after my arrival, when just at dusk I got caught in a rice paddy right smack in the middle of a blistering chink mortar attack. I started to run, but slipped and fell in the paddy. When I finally got back to my foxhole, I discovered that my water-repellent outer trousers were covered with human shit, which the Koreans used for fertilizer. Unsurprisingly, the guy sharing my hole was as unhappy about this as I was. I took the trousers off and made do for the night with the two pairs of long johns and two pairs of OD trousers I had on underneath. Then I sacked out until it was my turn to go on guard, leaving my foxhole partner to contend with the lingering aroma of my "accident."

Guard was a grueling ritual, mainly because everyone was always so tired. Each squad had its own sector, normally four foxholes, each about four yards apart. Two guys shared a hole and took turns throughout the night searching into the darkness. You'd look until you got tired, then glance at your buddy sacked out at the bottom of the hole. Then you'd look a little longer while you thought, *Should I wake him now? Has he had enough sleep?* Few guys had watches—to own a watch in an infantry squad during that first Korean winter was a luxury beyond imagination—so you spelled each other based on the honor system, and you asked for relief only when it was impossible to keep your eyes open any longer. Then your buddy would ask for a sitrep and that was it; you'd be asleep almost before you'd zipped up your feather-down fart sack.

"What's happening?" I asked, when, later that night, my foxhole partner woke me for my turn.

"Not a thing," he replied, and was out cold.

Still inside my sack, I sat in the darkness on the edge of the hole, got my eyeballs unglued, and tried to remember where I was. I was fantasizing about smoking a cigarette, drinking a hot cup of coffee, and eating a charcoal-black rare steak bite by delicious bite, when, to my amazement, I saw a man lying prone to my immediate left rear. I woke up my buddy. "There's a goddamned chink almost on top of us!"

We whispered through our options. We could toss a hand grenade, blast him with a rifle, or crawl out and get him with a knife. We decided on the third alternative, because the guy was right in the middle of our squad position, and rifle fire or a grenade could easily start a firefight among our own guys. The chink wasn't moving and his back was to us. My buddy covered me while I crawled out of the foxhole with my trusty M-1, a ten-inch-long, razor-sharp bayonet attached.

In a crouched position I silently slipped up behind the enemy soldier. When I got within sticking distance, I drew back my rifle and thrust it with full force. Branches crackled and it was over: I'd bayoneted my own frozen-stiff trousers, which I'd earlier hung over a bush behind our foxhole to dry. The next morning I had to put the shitty things back on again (now with a hole in the ass as well), and for some reason the "fresh meat" was the only one in the squad who didn't think it was very funny.

The war seemed lost; at best it was hopelessly confused. I'd thought wars, at least America's wars, had happy endings, like capturing Berlin and Tokyo. All we were doing was yo-yoing across the Korean peninsula—defeat, then victory, then defeat and defeat. G Company, too, was retreating: shuffling along, heading south, colder—sometimes the temperatures were twenty degrees below zero—and more tired than we'd ever been in our lives.

One day a snap thaw had us wading through mud on both sides of a mire that had once been a road. Jeeps and trucks sloshed through it, too, each vehicle trying in vain to miss the rut of the vehicle in front so as not to get bogged down. One jeep stalled and would not restart just as our column was passing by. The driver and his lieutenant passenger unassed the thing; the lieutenant called for help to push it over to the side. But before we could slosh through the quagmire and give him a hand, he whipped out his pistol and aimed it at one of the tires. I figured his daddy must have been an old horse soldier and this guy was going to follow the Cav tradition of shooting his disabled mount, and sure enough: *pow, pow, pow, pow.* But the last shot missed the tire. It glanced off the rim and boomeranged back to strike the lieutenant right between the eyes. We pushed the jeep and the warm, still body off the road and then returned to our column. Soon the temperature dropped, the road turned to ice, and we just kept heading south.

It hadn't meant anything, the lieutenant's death. For openers, what he'd done was dumb. But more than that, we'd become immune. Fighting a war on the ground is like working in a slaughterhouse. At first the blood, the gore, gets to you. But after a while you don't see it, you don't smell it, you don't feel it. *So what's another dead body?* It's almost as if you don't care. In this case, we just leaned forward, kept walking, and tried to ignore the song in our heads, the one the troops called "The Bug-Out Blues."

And then, as if overnight, everything changed. The new Eighth Army commander, Lieutenant General

Matthew Ridgway, had been all over the Eighth Army front, assessing the situation and making new plans. He recognized even before we did that the Chinese offensive was running out of steam, and sought to take advantage of it with deep patrols to the north to find out exactly how stretched the enemy was.

This was another turning point for U.N. Forces, and a turning point for me as well. After the action on 6 February—part of another of Ridgway's morale-boosting reconnaissance-in-force missions, Operation Thunderbolt, which turned into a full-scale attack—I was done paying my Wolfhound dues. When I returned from the hospital a month later, I discovered that the "new guy" had become "Hack"; Hack, the Great Fighter, who'd gotten shot in the head courageously saving lives and inflicting punishment on the enemy. I was actually quite relieved to know that I would not have to prove myself to anyone anymore— but what I didn't know at the time was that the name I made for myself on 6 February 1951 was one I'd have to live up to for the next twenty years.

Chapter 4
A Bitch of a Place to Fight

★ ★ ★

By mid-March the enemy was on the run. As we headed back up the peninsula, my unit was miraculously well-equipped with winter gear and weapons: two Browning automatic rifles (BARs) per squad and two light machine guns (LMGs) in the platoon, well-insulated jackets, cold-weather shoepacks, and hot chow at least once a day. Tactical air support (tac air) and outgoing artillery were plentiful as well; no matter how hard the enemy fought, they couldn't hold us back. Our spirits had never been higher, and it really wasn't until 30 March, when G Company was tasked to seize and hold a high, craggy hill designated Objective Logan, that the good times seemed to come to a screeching halt.

Korea was a bitch of a place to fight, because you weren't just fighting Chinamen and North Koreans. You also fought the hills themselves. Most were steep and razor-backed; many were solid rock, which meant an attacking force had to contend not only with enemy fire raining down from above, but also with rock fragments—as bad news as the flying steel. Objective Logan was one rocky hill. It resembled the top of the Rock of Gibraltar, and was so steep that only one platoon could attack on the company front at a time. After the lead platoon secured a ridgeline about 500 yards from the objective and established a base of fire, the thirty-five men of 3d Platoon, originally tasked as the reserve element, passed through and became the assault force.

We moved along a ridge, concealed by low-lying clouds. But as the sky opened up, so did the enemy, with 75mm pack howitzers, 60mm and 82mm mortars, and wall-to-wall automatic-weapons fire. We had casualties from the first shot, including our new medic, a black sergeant named Brown, who took a slug just below the heart while pulling a wounded kid to safety. We were pinned down, and would have remained so forever but for Phil Gilchrist, late of 1st Platoon, who'd recently taken over as 3d Platoon leader. Gilchrist told us to move out, and we moved out, with him at the point, up Objective Logan with weapons blazing.

On top of the hill, the Chinese were well dug in and fighting a tenacious and determined defense. They were throwing the world at us, and for every inch of ground we gained, they extracted a terrible price. It was tough slugging, not unlike the fighting in Italy in 1944–45—the same sort of determined enemy, the same rough, difficult terrain. The chinks flung grenades at us in barrages of three and four by ringing the pins around their fingers and throwing a handful at a time; we could see their hands rising over the crest of the hill, bedecked with grenades, which an instant later were hurtling toward us. The grenades, bullets, shrapnel, and flying rock fragments took their toll: by the time we reached the top of the hill, only seven effective fighters remained in the platoon. Everyone else was badly wounded or killed.

We etched out a little fingerhold by stacking up

stones around shell craters. It was still broad daylight; we'd crested the hill and now looked down on the reverse slope to see the Chinese leaders below getting their men together for a counterattack. U.S. artillery and mortar fire were adjusted through the company radio net—the stuff was popping in so close it was amazing we had no friendly fire casualties. I'd recently taken over the weapons squad; now I placed our one remaining light machine gun in a 155mm artillery crater, and for a while gunner Ray Wells and his buddy Thacker's blisteringly effective fire kept the enemy at bay. But it was still hot. Very hot. The Chinese concentrated all their fire on our little redoubt. Mortars, artillery, and small arms thundered around us; one round landed so close that it knocked over our LMG and filled that hole with fragments. Amazingly, none of us was hit. A six-inch-long, jagged shard of shrapnel landed an inch from my knee. So close and yet so far from a million-dollar wound, without thinking I picked it up to show to Thacker and Wells, only to burn the hell out of my hand on the red-hot steel.

We stayed low in our crater—even looking over the brim was a guarantee to be blown away—and for a while had to go blind, returning fire by holding our rifles over our heads and pointing downhill. We were so low on grenades that Lieutenant Gilchrist ordered that we get his permission to throw one. I was down to my last when gut feeling told me it was time to unlimber it, right in front of our position. I motioned for Gilchrist to come over. Indicating that we were not alone, I requested permission to pull the pin on the frag. He gave it.

I was lying on my back with my head pointed toward the attackers. When I pulled the pin, I spent a lazy second or so setting the grenade on the crater's edge (which didn't make Gilchrist, still lying beside me, too happy). Then I gave it a little flick with my fingers. It slowly tumbled down and exploded. *Bwam.* The hole shook, debris rained down, and then the air was filled with gently floating feathers. A down-jacketed Chinaman had gotten what he was going to give us—except gut feeling had told me to get there first.

We were quickly running out of ammo. Thacker had no more than a belt and a half for the machine gun, and our rifles were down to a couple of M-1 clips. Strict fire discipline became the rule; we couldn't afford to waste one round. We policed up a case of Chinese potato-masher grenades. They were probably World War I German army vintage and about as effective as cherry bombs, but they made a lot of noise and at least they were something. Funny how a few hours before we'd been a rifle platoon loaded for bear, and now we were on our ass, hurling firecrackers and not making a dent.

As we broke up the last belt of LMG ammo and distributed it for the M-1s and BARs, Gilchrist told us a squad from 2d Platoon had volunteered to join us on the hill. What a great sight it was, moments later, to see their lead element coming up behind us. "Hello, brah," said their point man, Aguda, as his buddies ran past, tossing us bandoliers of M-1 ammo, grenades, and several boxes of machine-gun ammunition. "Big fight here, huh?"

James Aguda had just returned to his platoon a few days before, after having been wounded during a previous operation. When I'd first seen him after he'd gotten back, I'd noticed he was not wearing shoepacks. "Get rid of those leather boots," I'd told him. "You Hawaiian Buddha-heads have enough trouble with the cold. No sense asking for frostbite." I'd given him a pretty hard time—intentionally, because I was trying to find out how much his wound had affected him. Sometimes a man would come back from the hospital and say, "Yeah, Sarge, I'm cool . . . only a scratch," and the next thing you knew he'd crack up. But Aguda had taken everything I dished out, and finally I'd said, "Okay, fine . . . but you better get yourself some shoepacks."

Aguda had just shrugged and said, "I'm not going to be around here long enough to need them."

I'd dismissed the comment; such fatalistic statements were routine, especially before a big fight. I hadn't thought any more about it, nor did I now, on the hill. All I thought was that help had arrived. More ammo, more rifles, the staying power we needed to hold our objective. Now we just needed a little time. Aguda, casually sauntering past with his BAR, gave us that.

The crazy bastard stood up. He didn't go prone like the rest of us. He just walked to the forward slope and started mowing down the attacking Chinese ranks like John Wayne in *The Sands of Iwo Jima*. His BAR was singing as he fired magazine after magazine. And the whole time he was screaming to the Chinese, "Come on, you motherfuckers, come and get me." I yelled, "Get down! For Christ's sake, Aguda, get down!" But he just kept firing and reloading, firing and reloading —the perfect killing machine. Slugs were snapping all around him. I knew he was going to be killed. Then I could see he was getting it. *I could see it.* In the leg, in the arm, then two more in the legs. But he just kept shooting and screaming, and I kept yelling for him to get down. Finally he took one in the chest. It spun him around and he dropped. KIA.

Aguda's action, and similar actions from the other brave volunteers of 2d Platoon, gave us back the fight. They bought us time at perhaps the most critical phase of the battle—time in which the men of 1st and 4th platoons could get into position and start putting down effective fire that completely undid the Chinese counterattack. But the strange thing about Aguda was that he really had known he was going to be killed. It wasn't just his shoepack comment; after the battle, a poem he'd written was found among his personal possessions, predicting he would die in battle on a cold, windswept hill. I guess he knew his number was about to come up, and he just decided to go out fighting.

The Chinese had broken off their attack, and we had time to consolidate our defenses and evacuate our casualties. An ad hoc platoon aid station had been set up in a rocky outcrop near the crest of the hill; at one point in the battle it had been crammed with forty-two casualties, all of whom were cared for by an amazing infantryman named Phil Bender, who, armed with knowledge gleaned from a YMCA first-aid course, had taken Sergeant Brown's aid bag at gunpoint when the severely wounded medic insisted he could still do his job. We couldn't dig—the hill was solid rock—so we modified chink bunkers, stacked rocks in front of our fighting positions, and hunkered down as best we could. The position was still hot, with plenty of incoming mortar and small-arms fire. Our platoon, which was now less than a squad, drew most of it; Thacker's machine gun had been the focal point of the complete battle so far, and we still occupied the high ground in the company center.

I was looking for a better machine-gun position when the enemy launched another attack. I hopped into the nearest hole, a large Chinese foxhole that had probably been a platoon CP. Now its sole occupant was one dead Chinaman, curled up in the bottom. I lay there with him, and whenever there was a lull in the firing, I'd pop up, fire eight rounds, and go back down to reload and wait until I could jump up again. It was kind of like playing human jack-in-the-box, and during one of these routines I caught a slug. *Oh, shit,* I thought, *not again, not in the head.* My helmet, which I had on backward, was ripped off my head and I was propelled to the bottom of the hole.

If someone took a baseball bat and swung it at you—at your arm, your leg, or your head—with all his might, that's what getting hit with a bullet feels like. *Bam!* and then you don't feel anything for about twenty or thirty minutes because of the trauma caused by the speed of the projectile. Only after about half an hour does it really begin to hurt, so when I got it this time, all I knew was it felt just as it had on 6 February.

My head was spinning. I slowly reached up and touched my forehead, and then looked at my hand—no blood. I found my steel pot. It looked as if it had been neatly parted with an ax. The bullet had struck the helmet between the bottom lip of the steel and the liner, but because the back of a steel pot is reasonably oblique, the bullet had skipped along between the liner and the steel before coming out the top. If I hadn't been wearing the thing backward (which was just a habit I'd picked up from a buddy in the weapons squad), I would have been as dead as the chink who was sharing my hole.

The incident took the fire out of me for a bit. Ears ringing and in a daze, I was stuck in the hole and didn't know how long I'd be there. I decided to get to know my Chinese companion a little better. I looked through his pockets and found a wallet full of Chinese money and some pictures of his family. The pictures stung me inside—this dead chink had been a real person. I didn't want him in my hole anymore. I rolled his body up the side with my feet. I got him to the top and was about to tip him out when a Chinese machine gun hosed him down and blew off his head. This scared the hell out of me, and I dropped him. Now I was sharing my hole with a headless Chinaman whom

I liked less with every passing second. It took a dozen tries before I finally rolled him out.

Dusk brought a lull to the fighting, but it brought nothing else—no food, no water, no resupply of ammo. The word was that the Korean *chogi* party,* our human resupply train, had gotten lost. We were so thirsty, all we wanted was water. We'd been in constant hot contact for hours, using up a lot of adrenaline, generating a lot of fear—and fear dries you out. One of the guys found a knocked-out Chinese water-cooled heavy machine gun. We drained the stagnant, filthy water into a steel pot and filtered it through a piece of dirty cloth; it was still oily when we drank it, but to us it tasted beautiful, like a nice cold beer on a stinking hot day.

When you're fighting, you're scared. And it's such an all-pervasive sort of fear that you can't even pinpoint what the feeling is. It's a gnawing, a churning in the gut. You become so afraid that it's as if you're not afraid at all. And that's what bravery is. It's not *fearlessness;* it's the ability to get off your ass and charge even when your mouth is dry, your gut is tight, and your brain is screaming *Stay down!* But even the bravest of men have a breaking point, and on Objective Logan a couple of good men reached theirs. One was one of our best NCOs. He'd been a great fighter and a fearless leader. At the Pusan Perimeter in the bleak, early days of the war, he'd taken a newly issued 3.5 bazooka and destroyed three T-34 tanks single-handedly. So he was not a coward—nor, I discovered, were most men who lost their nerve on the battlefield.

Over time I concluded that a man is like a bottle. On the battlefield, fear is what fills him up and fuels

---

Chogi was our nickname for the Korean laborers who worked for the Eighth Army. In Korean, *chogi* means "over there"—as in "put it over there."

him to perform. But some bottles are smaller than others. When a guy becomes unglued during a firefight, it's just that his bottle has filled up and overflowed; it's time for him to get away and let the fear drain out. But even when it does, there's a catch: from that moment on, the man is like a spent cartridge, and no amount of gunpowder will ever make him a real fighter again.

As darkness fell, the chinks started attacking again, with great enthusiasm. "Hold at all costs" was passed from Company. Ominous words—"all costs" meant die on position. We stacked up more rocks and got ready. I just hoped the chink CO hadn't told his guys to *take* the hill at all costs. A major Chinese breakthrough occurred on the right; we could hear their bugles and see their flares in the valley to our rear. New orders: "Conduct a night withdrawal. First and 2d platoons start pulling back now. Third Platoon hold. You fight the rear guard." To the few men left in our platoon, that sounded even worse than to hold at all costs. But the shake of the dice is never fair in combat, and in retrospect the order was sound. Third Platoon held the high ground and was marginally combat effective; we could delay, and if destroyed, our skipper would still end up with two strong rifle platoons (less 1st Platoon's weapons squad, which was tragically destroyed by an enemy mortar round just moments after it arrived on the hill).

The company's main body slowly pulled back, and by the time the order came for us to withdraw, we were engulfed in Chinamen. I was the last guy down from the few left in my squad; I walked backward, slowly, down our well-reconned escape route, shooting chinks as they crested the hill. When I reached the safety of the saddle, I shagged ass and caught up with the rear of my platoon. I arrived just in time to see a badly wounded Sergeant Connie Moore about to be tipped out of a makeshift poncho litter and over a gorge by the two new men who were packing him down the hill. I jabbed one of them in the ass with my bayonet. "We'll take him back, won't we, guys?" I asked, leveling my M-1. "Sure, Sergeant" was the kids' startled reply. I stuck with them in case they needed more cold-steel encouragement, but they didn't. I never mentioned the incident to either of them again, and both turned out later to be great fighters. They'd just been scared, and ill-prepared for this, their first battle.

Last of all off the hill was Lieutenant Gilchrist, who made his way along the ridge with friendly artillery—his only security—crashing in just fifty yards away. His uniform was caked with blood, his own and that of a boy who'd taken a direct mortar hit and disintegrated to (in Gilchrist's words) "a purplish mush" before dying in the Lieutenant's arms. Now, as he reached the area of the ridge where the fight had begun so many hours before, he heard a voice. "Is that you, Lieutenant?" It was the medic, Sergeant Brown, who'd lain on the ridge all day with a hole in his chest, for the sole purpose of checking the bandages of every casualty that Bender, the first-aid-trained rifleman, had treated on the hill. The medic was new, he was a black man in a white unit, he was grievously wounded, yet he was there. He didn't have to be; common sense would have dictated *Get out while the going's good!* but he'd stayed. And if that didn't epitomize the spirit, the loyalty, and the guts of 3d Platoon and the rest of George as well on this terrible day, then nothing ever could.

We were all dead on our feet by the time we passed through the dug-in 1st and 2d platoons and set up. Soon our topkick arrived with the lost carrying party. We gobbled down yesterday's breakfast (cold pancakes and even colder black coffee); it was delicious.

Then the First Sergeant handed me a stack of mail for 3d Platoon. *Mail call in the pitch-black night,* I thought, and most of the guys already evacuated or dead. I tossed the packet down next to my rock-pile wall and was asleep before I'd stretched out on my stone bed. For once, the mail could wait.

We kept attacking north. Resistance was light, a blessing considering that we had twenty replacements joining the platoon in the wake of our losses on Logan. (It took only a couple of days for a new replacement to become a seasoned veteran; before that, though, in fast-moving, heavy combat like we'd been in, he was a liability—cannon fodder—the first to get hit.) There was a transition on the leadership level as well, when squad leader Walt Schroeder, who'd knocked out two enemy machine guns during the Logan fight, took over as platoon sergeant and I became his assistant. Both Schroeder and I believed training was everything, so we used every spare moment we had to get those replacements into shape. Things were looking good, and I was feeling pretty confident about our future, until the battalion was given the mission of seizing a bleak, craggy hill designated Objective Jake Able.

The only approach to Jake Able was almost vertical, with little concealment and cover. It was a formidable piece of real estate, so steep that even a pastoral walk up the thing looked enough to kill an ordinary man— let alone the fact that there were people up there already, whose sole mission was to shoot us long before we reached the top. All in all, to me it looked like a suicide trip—we'd be easy pickings from the second we crossed the line of departure (LD)—and even though George Company was the reserve unit for the operation, there was little doubt we'd be committed. I was so worried about it that the night before the attack I couldn't sleep. All night, again and again in my mind's eye, I saw 3d Platoon painting the slopes of Jake Able red with its own blood. Finally I got up and went to the company CP to see the topkick.

First Sergeant Maurice Flemings was to me and foot-slogging infantry what Prazenka had been to me and recon—a real mentor. Flemings had fought from Sicily to Germany in WW II, and when the Korean War broke out, he'd been one of a number of battle-hardened senior NCOs who were cleaned out of Fort Benning's Infantry School and sent over to provide some muscle to an otherwise pretty sorry-assed Eighth Army. All in all, he was just a fine old pro to whom I often turned for battleground advice.

Flemings was wide-awake, too, worrying the operation. I told him what I'd been thinking and how anxious I was; we walked to a point where we could observe the ominous hill, and he chalk-talked me through the attack. Then I went back to the platoon assembly area, feeling better but not much. I was still afraid for my unit, and had the clearest premonition that Jake Able was going to be my last attack. I even wrote a letter to my brother Roy, one of those "I don't think I'm going to make it back" numbers that I gave Carroll, the platoon radio-telephone operator (RTO), who was awake on security. He said, "I'll give it back when we get to the top, Sarge." I talked to him about the attack, even though confessing my concerns violated all my leadership training as far back as TRUST *(Leaders do not cry to their men. They are resolute islands in the center of all the insanity)*. But Carroll was older than I; he was a smart, college-graduate draftee replacement, and I felt calmer having talked it through.

The next day, Easy and Fox bore the brunt of the Chinese defense of their hill, both companies losing almost all their officers (wounded and dead) and many men. Their wounded streamed past us to the rear in an endless, bloody line. It was a scene of unimaginable impact for us as we moved forward into the same fray that was gutting their ranks. The Chinese, reinforced in preparation (we later found out) for a major offensive, had cut down trees and bushes to deny any semblance of a covered and concealed avenue of approach; Easy and Fox fought courageously for every inch. Over in E Company, one platoon was pinned down early by a chink firing an automatic weapon from a fighting bunker. Every time the guys fired on him, the Chinaman would bob down, then pop up again and fire on Easy's men. The company commander, a reputedly fine shot named Dell Evans, got into the act, and after three tries the enemy position was silenced. When Evans later went out to check the bunker, he found a pile of three chinks behind a Bren gun, each with a single hole in his forehead.

By the time George was committed on Jake Able's west flank, our sister companies, in concert with the 21st Anti-aircraft Artillery (AA) Battalion (which called itself the Wolfhounds' Fangs), and our direct-support artillery unit, the 8th Field (the Wolfhounds' Bark), had broken the enemy's back. The ridgetop was an erupting volcano of U.S. artillery and quad .50-caliber fire, as well as tac air's napalm, white phosphorus (Willie Peter), and delay bombs. Round after round of Willie Peter pounded in only fifty yards in front of George's advance—tactics right out of World War I that denied the enemy visibility and allowed us to close in. We could almost have caught the shells as they exploded before us in red-hot white plumes. But then I heard one falling short. I heard the shrill whistle, and I knew my name was on that round.

I was with the point—two guys just a few yards ahead, then me, then the rest of the platoon well spread out on the ridgeline. The round exploded in an airburst. The force of it knocked the three of us down.

I rolled and looked up to see burning white phosphorus streaming down—kind of majestic, deathly snow fingers. I thought, *You were right, Hackworth. You're dead. And the thing that killed you isn't even Chinese, but made in the U.S.A.*

I rolled again, and then, for an instant, I was back at home, at Ocean Park Pier. Al Hewitt had gotten us jobs at the amusement park, working on the Waltzer, an incredibly exciting, incredibly dangerous revolving ride that looked kind of like a wagon wheel laying on its side. One morning, before anyone was there, we'd decided to see how fast the thing could go. Al manned the controls and I sat in one of the cars; when he got it to full speed and beyond, he released my car from the couplings that held it onto the wheel's steel frame. That was how the thing worked: as the finale to the ride, when (as judged by the ride operator) the moment was right and the speed great enough, one by one the cars would be completely cut loose from the frame, and by their sheer velocity would go flying up a six-foot ramp, through a darkened tunnel, and thrust out again on the other side, down another steel ramp before coming to a stop. Timing was everything on the Waltzer, and at this accelerated speed Al's timing was off. Instead of entering the tunnel, the car I was in slammed into the iron trestle and I was flung out onto one of the ramps. When I looked up, a ton of steel—the car itself—was screaming down on top of me. I rolled, and kept rolling out of harm's way. The Waltzer car, and now the Willie Peter, didn't touch me. I was alive and unscathed. Both point guys had multiple burns, but they were more scared than hurt. I emptied my canteen in a patch of dirt, made some mud (just like the good book said), and heaped it onto their wounds. Both returned in a couple of weeks.

The men of George were almost at the top of Jake Able before we ran into any serious enemy. And even there, the Chinese were so shaken up from the artillery and mortar fire, the tac air, and E's and F's assaults that they fought badly, and finally didn't fight at all. But they'd certainly made a dent, particularly when they got Spotlight Sims. This fine lieutenant's luck ran out on Jake Able, which was a damn shame; maybe he didn't know that in combat you get only so many passes before you crap out.

Derwood "Spotlight" Sims was F Company's commander. He was a brilliant leader; his troops loved him because he approached the battlefield like a matador, parading around during firefights with a walking stick and acting as if he were invulnerable to bullets and all the other shit that came in. The story on Jake Able was that as F Company made its way up the hill, the lead platoon got pinned down by a chink machine gun and its platoon leader was killed. Hearing this, Sims went to the point. His men shouted, "Stay down, Lieutenant! There's a machine gun here!" But Spotlight said, "Screw the machine gun," walked right into the thick of things and got himself shot in half—not-so-living proof of the old adage: "There are old warriors and there are bold warriors, but there are no old, bold warriors."*

We secured Jake Able, consolidated our positions, and were preparing to dig in when I got into a pissing contest with the platoon sergeant of the 2d Platoon, a Texan named Reeves. It was our second run-in in little more than a week, and the truth was, I dreaded its outcome.

Reeves was in for the Distinguished Service Cross (DSC) for his part in the battle up on Logan. He was a

---

*Given the fog of battle, there ended up being a number of stories about how Sims died. Most likely, in fact, it was a grenade, but legends live on beyond death, and if the Spotlight had to go out, it had to be with a flair.

bold, aggressive, good soldier, but for some reason he'd always bugged me. One evening shortly before Jake Able, the company was in battalion reserve and a squad from 3d Platoon had drawn outpost duty. The chow line had formed and it was a rifle company long; I'd taken the outpost detail to the front so they could eat and be on their way. The next thing I knew, Reeves had come along and put one of his squads in front of my people. "Look, Sergeant," I'd said, "my men are going on outpost duty. That's why they're first."

"So are mine," was his reply. "That's why *they're* first. And nobody is going to get in front of them."

I said, "Oh, yeah? Well, your people are not eating before mine." Words led to fists, and was I ever outgunned. With most of G Company looking on—175 soldiers with ringside seats—Reeves cleaned my clock. I don't think I even got a hit in. It turned out that Reeves was a former division heavyweight champion, and he tore my ass simply because I'd failed to follow an age-old military axiom: know your enemy. Needless to say, his guys ate first.

Now, on top of Jake Able, we could not agree on our Company-assigned platoon boundary. "Look, Sarge, we tie in here," I said.

"No, Sergeant, you're wrong. It's here." He was vying for a shorter line, and so was I; a shorter line meant less area to defend. I thought, *Christ, here we go again. It's going to be another fight on top of this damn hill, and this cocky bastard is going to clean my clock all over again.*

Just as we were getting pretty heated about it, out of the corner of my eye I saw movement in the Chinese bunker we were arguing in front of. There was a Chinaman in there, big as life, holding a weapon. I shoved Reeves aside and flipped a grenade into the position, killing the chink and sending a small shard of shrapnel from the grenade flying into Reeves's

A Bitch of a Place to Fight

hand. For a long moment we just looked at each other—he was stunned—and then we both doubled up with laughter. I told him I was sorry he got hit, but couldn't resist commenting on what a lousy job his guys had done clearing their positions. For once, he didn't fight back. We quickly agreed on the boundary, but I don't remember who got the shorter line.

Then Carroll came up and handed me the letter I'd given him the night before. Jake Able was secure, and I was still here. He smiled and walked away without a word.

61

Chapter 5
Human Waves

★ ★ ★

After Jake Able came Jake Baker, Jake Charlie, and Jake Dog, each just another objective, another "critical" hill to take "at all costs." The Eighth Army offensive, which had been roaring along since 25 January, was running out of gas. I'm not sure the generals knew this, but we at the cutting edge damn well did. The Chinese were getting stronger. We were facing good-looking, well-equipped Chinese troops who had plenty of ammo and lots of fighting spirit. The feeling among the 3d Platoon's old-timers was that we'd be hard-pressed to continue the attack much farther north. The situation was beginning to feel eerily like November 1950 all over again.

For the 2d Battalion of the Wolfhounds, the Chinese Spring Offensive began at 0230 hours, 23 April, when our positions along a railroad line in the Chorwan Valley were blistered by savage mortar and artillery fire. In the darkness we could hear the unnerving, unmistakable sound of enemy tanks moving toward us, and the whistle-bang of our own tanks' 76mm main-gun fire. Next came bugles and flares, and then waves of Chinese infantry, who struck simultaneously across the battalion front. For two and a half hours the Wolfhounds' 2d Batt held like a stone wall in well-prepared positions against an estimated enemy regiment. Then, like a curtain coming down in a theater, exactly at 0500 hours the battlefield became quiet. In the early light of dawn we could see the ground to our front littered with enemy dead and knocked-out tanks. In George Company we counted forty-two enemy dead within hand-grenade distance of our holes alone. Regiment later estimated that the battalion had inflicted more than 700 casualties on our Chinese attackers that night (George's losses were amazingly light for this total—just two KIA and four WIA); we'd chopped up a force three times our size, and stood ready to do it again.

But word soon came down from Captain Michaely at Company that there would be no second show on this bloody ground. The units on our flanks had collapsed, and we had to get moving south quick or be cut off. At 1030 hours we carefully leapfrogged down the valley. Just as we were thinking we were home free, a U.S. Air Force B-26 bomber came swooping over us, all twelve forward-firing .50-caliber machine guns blazing. The pilot did a couple of enthusiastic strafing runs down the valley before someone gave him the word he was firing on his own people; we unscrewed ourselves from the ground and flipped him the bird in unison while he flew off into the early-morning light.

We continued fighting a delaying action south through the Chorwan Valley until we received the welcome word that we were going into reserve. Instantly high spirits charged bone-tired feet; all of us looked forward to a few days off, to sleep, take hot showers, sing, and drink booze. In reserve we'd pay a hundred dollars for a bottle of shit whiskey, ten bucks for a can of beer, and whatever the going price was for the 190-proof alcohol that the docs got through their black-market medical outlets, which, even mixed with pineapple juice, was so powerful that it made the insides of our canteen cups look like they'd been chromed. The purpose of it all was, of course, to get drunk as we relaxed around our fires, and then, without the pressures of our everyday survival, we could talk about the war.

But not this time. This time reserve was not the few days that we'd expected; in fact, it was only a few hours. At 0245 the following morning we were roused with the news that elements of the 24th "Deuce-Four," one of our two sister regiments (the 35th "Cacti" was the other), had been overrun by Chinese. It was a real emergency, and the Wolfhounds' 1st and 2d battalions were tasked with restoring the 24th's positions.

H (How) Company jeeps shuttled us toward the scene, the infantrymen literally stuffed into the heavy-weapons unit's vehicles, a squad to each jeep, more squads standing upright in the attached trailers, or hanging on all sides around How's own equipment. Finally we reached the base of a mountain ridge; the 3d of George was in the lead as we started climbing a hill far steeper than Logan—it was steeper than any hill I'd encountered in Korea, and covered with boulders. The winter had passed now; frostbite casualties had given way to those of heat exhaustion, and despite much pushing, dragging, and cajoling, our out-of-shape replacements began to fall out in droves.

The seven of us who reached the top of the hill first had a chance to rest; the enemy was nowhere in sight. Soon we saw another unit, Fox Company, coming down toward us from an adjacent, slightly higher hill. We lazily watched them come, and it wasn't until they were about 300 yards away that we realized it wasn't

Fox Company at all, but three or four hundred Chinamen, many wearing abandoned Deuce-Four steel pots, who, with bloodcurdling screams, started steamrolling down the hill in a mass, like an avalanche. We were in shock, and with only two BARs and five rifles to take them on, we were also in very serious trouble.

I heard Lieutenant Bell, George Company's artillery forward observer (FO), before I saw him. How he'd gotten to the top of our hill with that bulky arty radio I'll never know, but he was there, calmly calling for fire. "Fire mission . . . battery one round . . . rifle company in the open. Fire for effect."

The whole salvo fell short. It hit behind us, and sounded as though it landed right on the finger the rest of the company was climbing. It wouldn't make the trek any easier. Bell, standing there without a helmet, his long hair blowing in the breeze, didn't blink; instead, he made one of the boldest adjustments I'd seen in a long while. "Add four hundred, left two hundred, battalion six rounds," I heard him say through his huge handlebar mustache. "Fire for effect."

One hundred eight rounds of 105mm high-explosive (HE) shells flew through the air. They landed right smack in the center of the wave of Chinese attackers; their ranks simply disappeared from earth as bits and pieces of arms, legs, heads, and bodies flew skyward. *Iron on target,* I thought. *Thank God for Lieutenant Bell and the 8th Field,* a unit so good that Chinese POWs often swore we'd been firing automatic artillery.

The last of our herd of disenchanted mountain goats finally stumbled onto the top of the hill, with word that no one had been hit by the opening short rounds. With that, George Company dug in and hunkered down for a battle that raged all afternoon. With the help of Fox Company, we stopped a three-battalion Chinese counterattack force dead in its tracks, but it was hard, hard fighting all the way. Then, just before dark, somebody somewhere must have decided the best course of action would be to blast holy shit out of the enemy force with every bit of firepower we had. And for the only time in my life, I thought my bottle was going to overflow.

P-51s and Navy Corsairs strafed and bombed from the air; artillery, half-tracks, and tanks boomed from the valley floor, and it felt as if all this friendly fire was going directly over 3d Platoon. We were being showered with spent shards of U.S. shell fire and hot brass from the fighter-aircraft machine guns. Rounds were bursting so close that every one of them seemed to have our names on it. We couldn't dig in on our solid crag, so we squeezed into cracks and crevices, and I wanted to stand up and scream, *"For God's sake, shut it off!"* The noise was incredible—whining, whistling, zinging sounds as plummeting bits of steel ricocheted against the boulders all around us. The longer it went on without my being hit, the worse it became; every near miss brought the odds down, and I was more sure than I'd ever been that soon some tank gunner would screw up and I'd be one dead hombre, with a 76mm round right through my ass. *Well, get it over with, goddamnit!*

The inferno blazed forever, or so it seemed, until blessed darkness came and all was quiet. Well, not all. Although the U.S. war machine had dampened it, it had not put out the enemy's fire, but our M-1s and automatic weapons sounded like pop guns after the thundering hell of the last couple of hours.

The fight continued, and in the dark we could see and hear Easy and Fox engaged as well. The Chinese kept coming, and so did the word from Company: "Hold at all costs . . . hold at all costs." But the problem was that the word was not coming from Captain Michaely (who'd gone on R&R that very morning), but from a new CO, Lieutenant Peterson.* The fact was that all of us had been shaking since the first short rounds were delivered more than twelve hours before. Add to that the fire storm we'd just survived, and Peterson's inability to hide his anxiety had us scared stiff. We were stuck on this boulder of a hill while the enemy pushed south, and by the time we got permission to withdraw "as best you can," it was midnight and we were cut off well within enemy territory.

We had some trouble getting out. When the word came to withdraw, we'd been told to pull out one platoon at a time, with 3d Platoon last off the hill. I'd tasked Sposito, a reliable corporal in our platoon, to follow 4th Platoon down and then come back to guide us out. This he'd done, but now, as the 3d reached a particular junction on the ridge, Sposito had forgotten whether the 4th had gone right or left. It was pitch-black; we couldn't see a trail, nor could we feel a track on the sheer rock path. With fifty-fifty odds we took a guess—it was the wrong one—and ended up on the valley floor with jabbering chinks to our east and southwest. Not a little unnerving, and only made worse by the bugles the enemy blew incessantly (as part of their communications system, which had the fringe benefit of driving the U.S. troops nuts) and their eerie flares, which were popping to our front, flanks, and rear. Schroeder and I got the men into a perimeter around a dry creekbed, then squad leader Fred "Chris" Crispino and I went out looking for

---

*A pseudonym

some English-speaking comrades. When we finally found H Company's 81mm mortar platoon merrily firing away, we crept back to the creekbed to lead our guys out.

I could not believe my eyes when we arrived at the perimeter. With Crispino out with me, and Schroeder holed up on the other side of the position, a few of Chris's new replacement troopers were openly smoking cigarettes, as if they were at a downtown bus stop, not in the middle of enemy territory. Crispino and I exploded; that madness on the hill was nothing compared to what the smokers experienced with our flying feet and fists as we hissed under our breath the rules about smoking on the line. The cigarettes went out in a big hurry; luckily neither they nor the ass-kicking compromised our location, and we slipped on silently to the H Company positions, and then on to rejoin George.

The next day, as the regiment continued south with the entire Eighth Army front, exchanging ground with the Chinese attackers for huge mounds of their dead, Chris continued punishing the smokers in his squad with as much dirty work as he could find. (And he could be pretty imaginative: Crispino's military career had started in Italy at the age of six, when he became—and remained, until he and his parents wised up and fled to the U.S.—a member of Mussolini's Black Shirts.) Meanwhile, the kids tried to defend themselves by complaining that in basic training no one had told them they couldn't smoke in the field. *Shit,* I thought to myself, *what else didn't they learn?*

Any hope of reserve was lost when orders came down that we were to set up in a delaying position on the east side of the Chorwan Valley and execute delaying actions across yet another mountain range. The Spring Offensive had the Chinese attacking on a broad front; "Spring is here, wish we weren't," cracked the jokers. And if there was any comfort in knowing that at least we were not fighting in subzero temperatures this time around, the feeling was more than offset by the fact that the warming weather held torments of its own.

As the ground thawed out and the spring rains came, the battlefield became a sea of thick, oozing mud. It built up on the bottom of our boots and made them as heavy as lead. Movement was not just putting one boot in front of the next; it was slipping and sliding and damn hard work. The mud fouled our weapons and equipment. It stuck to our shovels, making the daily foxhole-digging ritual a nightmare. Then the rains filled the foxholes. The roads became quagmires. The rivers and the creeks were swollen and hard to ford. The two things that we had going for us over the Chinese were mobility and firepower, but they were advantages greatly reduced in the conditions we now faced. Even so, there was none of the panic that had marked those hard winter days. Ridgway had left his mark on the Eighth Army—he'd recently been promoted to Supreme Commander of all U.N. forces in Korea, in the wake of General MacArthur's snap relief by President Truman—and mud and rain, big numbers and all, we were set for Joe Chink.

We arrived on position at midday. G Company was deployed with 2d Platoon on the valley floor, tied in with 1st Platoon, whose position crossed the north-south road to tie in with my platoon on a small rise leading up to a little piece of high ground 3d Platoon held west of the road. The battlefield was quiet, less the occasional rumble of a firefight to our front. But as darkness came, the outpost line (consisting of the 5th Ranger Company, the 25th Recon Company, and B

Company, 89th Tank) started passing through us with word that the chinks—"millions of them"—were right on their ass. This rearguard force had been in heavy contact all day, and they'd had a hard time breaking contact. "They'll be here soon," they warned of the Chinese. "Good luck."

Schroeder and I made it a policy that almost to a man each rifleman in the platoon carried two extra (250-round) boxes of .30-caliber machine-gun ammo in addition to his basic load. When the men sat down, the ammo sat down; when they walked, the ammo walked. We all hated the extra weight, but it meant the ammo was always there when we needed it for our LMGs, and when things got really bad, we could break it out for our M-1s and BARs. Now, in light of the latest word from the outpost line, we had a good look at our ammunition level and then sent our scroungers out for more. And as the rearguard force rolled through, they tossed us stacks of hand flares, grenades, and even more machine-gun ammo, so by 1700 hours the platoon was loaded for bear and well dug in, with good fields of fire for our two light machine guns and our one captured Chinese Bren gun.

Schroeder sent a two-man outpost out with instructions not to get engaged, but bug back when they heard the enemy coming. There was a big gap between 3d Platoon and Fox Company to the west, but a platoon from the 5th Ranger Company was now on the move. They would fill in the gap, making the main battle line complete.

We picked out three great positions for the section of tanks we were getting. They'd be able to put flanking fire right down Company G's front, and cover in front of G Company, 35th Regiment, whom George was tied into on the right. The tanks would also be able to cover the north-south road that ran smack into

George's position and was a good high-speed enemy-tank approach, plus they'd be able to pummel the hell out of anyone coming directly at 3d Platoon. We were going to be tougher than the Germans' WW II Siegfried Line.

But when the tanks appeared on the scene, we could not get them up the muddy hill leading to 3d Platoon's positions. Hard as we tried, after an hour the tank commander had no choice but to pull back and laager for the night behind us. Mud had led to Napoleon's defeat at Waterloo; now, 136 years later, it had just played a significant role on a small piece of Eighth Army's tumultuous western front, and specifically in the fate of George Company. But as I watched the M4s with their mighty 76mm guns disappear down the road, I didn't know that yet.

Schroeder told Lieutenant Peterson about the tanks. The CO assigned the company's 57mm recoilless rifle section to replace the armor, and reported that the Ranger platoon would be in position within the hour. With that, I went back to the platoon CP to enjoy the sheer luxury of my new air mattress. I'd just gotten it that morning. Maybe it was someone's way of saying "I'm sorry" for cheating us out of reserve. All in all, our supply tail was indeed wagging—a lot of creature-comfort goodies were coming our way these days. In general I liked to think it was a grateful thanks from the stateside war machine, which was running along again at full bore (even if no one seemed to know that by the time a trooper dug a hole big enough to fit his 5'7" x 2' air mattress and then inflated the thing by mouth, he'd probably be too bushed to fight the enemy).

At 2015 hours, just as I was beginning to think the rearguard force had either overreacted or had been bullshitting about all the Chinese, several green flares popped about 500 yards in front of our positions. The outpost was back in a flash, with reports of countless enemy out there.

It remained deathly quiet. Peterson was informed of the situation, and we requested max harassment and interdictory (H&I) defensive artillery fire and flares. *Bam, bam, bam*—the 8th Field Artillery barked obligingly, and simultaneously our front lit up and shook with the impact of outgoing rounds. Then, under the cold, ghostly light of slowly descending parachute flares and the WW II antiaircraft searchlights we'd asked for (the beams of which, bouncing off the clouds, lit up the battlefield), we saw the enemy. They were marching in column. Neat formations as far as the eye could see, each at least a company in strength, marching down the north-south road, one after another. They were not firing. They weren't even in battle formation. It was more like a pass in review.

Schroeder called in an artillery fire mission with his report to Peterson, and told the recoilless rifles, who had a good supply of canister shot, to start blasting. The 8th Field plus all available artillery pounded rounds in front of us and turned the valley into an inferno of high-explosive geysers. FO Lieutenant Bell said later he'd had all the American artillery going in the 25th Division's sector—fifteen battalions, the second-largest barrage of the Korean War—yet all this fire did not seem to put a dent in the Chinese mass attack. The enemy just continued to march, like mechanical robots.

More Chinese signal flares lit up the cloudy, starless sky. Bugles, whistles, and high-pitched Chinese screams were interspersed with the dull thud of high explosives thumping down in ugly red-black fireballs all along our front, and the steady tap of our machine guns, BARs, and rifles. The Ranger platoon was right behind us now, on its way to fill the gap between us and Fox Company. But it got caught. It couldn't get in position between us and the steadily advancing Chinese, who walked right over their dead and, from the high ground, played taps on their bugles to signal "objective taken." We shifted a light machine gun to cover the open flank. The Rangers withdrew and the Chinese kept coming. Where they were going, I didn't know, but wherever it was, they'd been tasked to get there *at all costs*.

Third Platoon had three Chinese columns marching toward us, on parallel axes. Ironically, each was headed directly into the field of fire of one of our automatic weapons. We cut their ranks to pieces; enemy dead were strewn all along the platoon front. Our LMGs were red-hot, firing longer and longer bursts of grazing fire from point-blank range. I thought the machine guns would melt before we ran out of ammo, and that, I felt sure, would happen before the columns ran out of chinks. But it was impossible to enforce any fire control as long as they kept coming.

But then they stopped. Suddenly the Chinese broke off their attack on our well-armed position, leaving only their dead to litter our front in scattered mounds of broken, twisted bodies. Like a rich man down to his last million, I guessed even these bastards finally realized that some things cost too much.

Not so in the valley below, where the main battle raged on. The Chinese left us alone. We were still putting down fire, but we became more like spectators, watching a ball game from the fifty-yard line. From our high perch I could see the tracers from our machine guns pouring rounds upon rounds onto the enemy; I could see the Chinese controlling their formations with flares. It was really quite spectacular, in a nightmarish kind of way: in the dark, the artillery, recoilless rifles, and machine guns firing; the chinks' whistles and their screaming; the silhouettes of both friend and foe moving through the half light of flares and searchlights and exploding shells; the huge mounds—four to five feet high—of enemy dead mounting in front of 2d and 1st platoons' positions.

I checked the squads. We had three U.S. wounded and one dead KATUSA (Korean Augmentation Troops, U.S. Army). Our light-machine-gun crew had vanished from the left flank and no one could account for it. We redistributed ammo and reconfigured our defense into a tight perimeter ringing the top of our perch. And then we heard the most incredible sound.

As if someone had blown a whistle to stop the game, suddenly there was no shooting in the valley at all. For a split second there was no firing, no artillery, no flares. Then, in their place, was a hum—a drone—as the Chinese yelled in terrible, bloodcurdling unison and steamrolled their way through our 1st and 2d platoons, like a great wave washing over the battlefield. They smashed the position in half, creating a gap of five or six hundred yards. The floodgate was open and the enemy was pouring through. From the high ground we could see them rushing behind us, flattening everything in their path. They washed down the valley, guiding on the north-south road. George's mortars were firing; we could see white sparks as the rounds left the tubes. Then the flood hit them and the little sparks were submerged. No more mortar section.

The 5th Ranger Company (less the platoon originally tasked to fill in the gap on the main line) had set up a blocking position on the valley floor behind George Company. Their plan was to let George pass through them and then meet the Chinese attackers head-on.

But the 1st and 2d of George did not come back as an organized force, platoon leapfrogging through platoon. According to Ranger witnesses, the men came back as a "panic-stricken mob," and right behind them were the chinks. The Rangers could not tell the friendly from the enemy. They held their fire as George Company people ran through their position, screaming, "Don't shoot. Don't shoot. George Company," but the enemy was mixed among George's people and some got behind the Rangers. It was bedlam. Captain John Scagnelli, the Rangers' fine CO, had no choice but to pull back and try to regain control of his unit, which had unavoidably been split up and intermingled with George guys and Chinese.

Before long the penetration was at least a mile behind us. We could hear chink bugles and whistles deep to the south, far beyond where the battalion CP, the Rangers, and other isolated units were somehow hanging on. The Chinese were still all around our little knob, but they ignored us as if we were not there. U.S. artillery was blistering George's vacated positions in the valley, and now we were starting to catch a few rounds of this friendly (but no less lethal) fire. The arty had long since cut our sound-power line—a problem at any time, but disastrous now because our SCR-300 radio (which had been acting up all night) was dead. Schroeder, grumbling that "the damn thing only seems to work when you don't need it," had me try to call Peterson. "George 6, this is George 3–5, over." Nothing. "George 6, this is George 3–5, do you read me? Over." Nothing.

I was about to give up when I heard my radio break squelch and the faint whisper, "George 3–5, this is George 6 Able."

I had connected with Peterson's RTO. "Let me speak to the Six," I said, referring to the commanding officer. The RTO whispered back, in a tearful voice choked with fear, "He's gone. I'm lost. There're chinks all around. I'm alone."

There was no way I could help him. "Keep moving south, and keep cool. Destroy your radio. Good luck . . . Out."

By midnight our area was reasonably quiet. The Chinese were pouring down the road past where our 1st and 2d platoons had been dug in. Their medics were picking up the dead and wounded. It was pretty obvious they thought our hill had been taken. We were cut off.

I had learned three things about being cut off: keep a cool head, maintain tight discipline and an even tighter perimeter, and don't let the troops panic. Walt Schroeder had won a Silver Star in September in a situation like we were in—only then the whole battalion had been cut off, and Schroeder had saved George from certain annihilation when he pretty well single-handedly intercepted and destroyed a North Korean force moving directly toward the company perimeter. Now, 3d Platoon was cool; over the winter months we'd all become pros at being cut off. Danny Abella said, "Call Eddie at Battalion. He'll give us the skinny."

Eddie Abella, Danny's brother, had been in G Company until he became the 2d Battalion Operations sergeant. Danny was still a squad leader in our platoon, and on calmer nights the Abella brothers always checked in with each other. If trouble was brewing, Eddie was on the horn to let us know; if one shot was fired anywhere near the vicinity of the 3d Platoon of G, Eddie called up to see if Danny and the rest of us were okay. It was great to have a private line into Battalion Operations and Intelligence—there was nothing like being informed.

Eddie reported that the Chinese main attack had

bypassed the battalion CP and raced southward. He said the CP had been hit by a couple of half-assed probes, but that a scratch force of cooks, clerks, and George and Ranger company stragglers had driven off the enemy with the unexpected help of the tank section that had been earmarked for us (which had roared into the CP perimeter seemingly out of nowhere). I thought to myself that if *we'd* had those tanks, none of this would have happened at all. The only guidance Eddie could give me was "Hang on, and get the guys out the best way you can." He said that F Company, on the high ground to our left, was quiet, and gave me their radio frequencies. "Look after Danny," he said, "and good luck."

Our withdrawal route to the south was a sea of Chinamen. We had to link up with Fox, but after all the trouble that Ranger platoon had run into, we couldn't chance going directly up the ridge to their position. So Schroeder and I talked about it, and decided to go north, parallel to the Chinese axis of advance, and then double back along the high ground leading to F Company's front. We had all the guys throw their steel pots away—the Chinese didn't wear helmets—and went down the hill into enemy lines, hoping we looked like Chinese medics toting out wounded. We hadn't gone fifty yards when the radio crackled with the most welcome voice we'd heard all night. It was Captain Michaely, back from R&R. In a whisper, Schroeder explained the mess we were in and the course of action we'd chosen. Michaely agreed, and on we went.

We snaked across the valley floor, dodging medics and stragglers, U.S. artillery, and the Chinese columns still moving south. Once on the ridge directly in front of F Company, we contacted Fox's CO. In the middle of outlining our situation, the SCR-300 radio went dead again, and we spent agonizing minutes reestablishing communication (commo). When we finally did, we got a fix on the company position and started moving toward it. From that moment on, our big worry was not the Chinese; it was that we'd get ironed out by our own artillery (which was still slamming through the valley), or a friendly-but-nervous trigger finger. There are few more dangerous movements than entering a friendly front line when a fight is going on.

We were received by Fox with open arms, and we stayed there until first light, when 3d Battalion's K (King) Company arrived. King's was not a happy lot. The whole 3d Batt had been on the move as the regimental fire brigade for more than a week already, and everyone was flat worn-out. Most recently, after George and the Rangers got brushed aside, the 3d Batt had taken the Chinese attackers head-on in their blocking position deep in the valley behind our battalion CP and stopped them cold. Then K Company was attached to 2d Batt and sent on a sixteen-mile hike in the dark back over the rugged terrain the enemy had steamrolled through, with the mission of sliding behind F Company and then fighting through and sealing the initial penetration by occupying G Company's holes. It was all standard procedure, but to the guys in King, there had to be an easier way to fight a war.

So K slid down through F, just before first light. The company commander was not in a good mood. He didn't want to go down in the valley. It was *very* bad down there—a lot of Chinese, a lot of artillery (both chink and American) blasting the hell out of everything on the valley floor. He asked for a sitrep. A Fox lieutenant said, "Talk to Hackworth, he's from G Company." I thought, *No, no! Don't let him know I'm from G Company! Don't tell him!*

Too late. King's CO said to me, "You'll lead the way."

"Like hell we will. You've got the job of closing the hole—it's not our job."

"Yeah, but you're the bastards who bugged out."

"We didn't bug out, we were overrun. And no way are we going to be your point into that valley. No fucking way." I quickly added, "Lieutenant," realizing that this little bantam was bone-tired, pissed off, and would not take much more from me. He looked as if he was just angry enough to blow me away.

Still, I felt guilty. My company had caused this mess. Maybe we did bug. Maybe we were just a bunch of "yellow-bellied bastards," as the King Company lieutenant went on to say. And now, with him bad-mouthing my unit, it became a point of honor. I told him we'd go down with him. "You take the Second and First platoons' holes—Third Platoon will occupy its own positions."

Down we went. King successfully sealed the penetration, and the Chinese were caught in a net. As the dawn was breaking, from our old positions I could see the complete battlefield. The Chinese were like headless chickens in a slaughterhouse yard, running in circles while P-51s darted down from overcast skies, bombing and strafing anything that moved, and artillery kept pounding in.

"The Rangers have been given the mission of sweeping and clearing the valley," the CO of King informed us. "Your platoon is attached to them. I'm squatting in G Company's holes. Good luck." In that at least two-thirds of George had been scattered to the winds, and for all practical purposes we were no longer an effective combat force, it was logical to follow King's CO's orders. We joined what was left of the Rangers, under Captain Scagnelli's command.

John Scagnelli was a soldier's soldier, and his 5th Airborne Rangers were among the finest fighting men in the U.S. Army—strictly professional. "You'll sweep on the right of the valley. Tie in on line with my First Platoon," snapped The Scag.

We formed a skirmish line (soldiers lined up abreast, ten yards apart) that stretched across the valley floor—a moving wall of weapons on the hunt for human beings. Soon we came across the body of a Ranger lieutenant; it was a gruesome sight. Fred Lang was a huge guy, an ex–Oklahoma A&M football star. The lieutenant had been hit in the legs earlier, and the story—as I gathered from the Rangers' shorthand discussions over his body—was that Lang, who was far too heavy to carry, had told his men to prop him up by a trail with a bunch of ammo and grenades and get the hell out of there. Lang had done a Custer's Last Stand, blowing away Chinamen until they blew away him. But apparently that wasn't enough for the chinks. They'd gotten him with their bayonets, too.

The Chinese bayonet on the Soviet SKS rifle was only about eight inches long. It was not so much a bayonet as a large and lethal three-pronged leather punch. It didn't make a clean cut—it made more like a rip—and the dead Ranger officer was just ripped to pieces. With jagged punctures all over his body, he was just a mound of shredded, bloody flesh; it seemed to us that every Chinese trooper had administered his own coup de grace as he filed past the lieutenant's body. This pissed the Rangers off. It got to all of us. The word went out: no prisoners. The Rangers were like NYPD cops when one of their own was shot down—vengeance, swift and without mercy.

What followed that day, walking through the valley, was not a sweep but a bloodbath. Chinks were coming at us and we just mowed them down. Many played possum, lying motionless on the ground, pretending they were dead; when this was discovered, every single "corpse" got a slug in the head—if blood pumped out, you knew you'd gotten a live one. It'd be fair to say that we were all a little in shock by the time the "mop-up" was over. Regiment would later estimate that 722 casualties were inflicted on the enemy throughout the battle, but all we knew at the time was the valley floor was blood-red and littered with dead Chinese.

And then there was nothing more to do. We headed south, the platoon passing through the 3d Batt positions where they'd stopped the chinks the night before. "Hey, boys, here comes G Company, the cowards," someone shouted.

"Yeah, 'G' for Guys Who Bugged."

"You rotten sons of bitches."

We all hung our heads and walked as fast as we could, trying to ignore the jeers. "Bug out" was an officially forbidden phrase in the Wolfhounds; its use, even in a whisper, tended to cause panic on the battlefield. Now that the whole thing was over, though, it was open season on old George, and it was humiliating. We were a proud company, and—despite the apparent flight of 1st and 2d platoons the night before—not the kind that bugged. Still, 3d Platoon had had a machine-gun team disappear in the middle of the battle and no one had seen it since. In the heat of a firefight, a platoon leader can't be everywhere. Neither can a platoon sergeant. Somehow, as the battle warmed up, neither Schroeder nor I got over to the left-flank light machine gun, and by the time I did, it was gone—vanished.

Fortunately we soon found the team, holding court at the 8th Field's gun positions, with an incredible story to tell. It seemed that the night before, when the

Ranger platoon—which happened to be the Rangers' 3d Platoon—got hit going into position between us and Fox Company, a Ranger had yelled to his people, "Third Platoon, let's go," and our gun crew, thinking I was the one doing the yelling, had automatically saddled up and gone with them. Then, when the Rangers got into more trouble down on the valley floor, my guys split for safer ground, and walked until they found the 8th Field.

We kept heading south, leapfrogging through other units. At 1600, when the column halted and the battalion dug in, George Company was tasked as battalion reserve and reorganized behind the new front in an abandoned village. In a cluster of Korean mud-walled huts we found many tired, familiar faces—G Company brothers from the other platoons who'd straggled in a few at a time—and huge mounds of new gear. The company had almost nothing except its rifles and what we had on our backs. Everything else had been abandoned in the battle—our asses in exchange for our equipment.

Everyone was still bad-mouthing us. No one had a good word for George:

"Watch out . . . there's Bug-out George!"

"When they said 'push on,' George heard 'Pusan,' and they've been heading south ever since."

But G Company had not run. As we gathered our unit together and started swapping stories around our ubiquitous campfires, it became clear that 1st and 2d platoons couldn't have fought more valiantly. The Chinese had just poured through. Regiment reported that two reinforced battalions had blasted through the positions; to those on the ground, two reinforced regiments—perhaps even a division—was closer to a true figure. "Lefty" Unumura, a Hawaiian guy who was a machine gunner in the 2d Platoon, told me he'd been firing long bursts of machine-gun fire—twenty or thirty slugs a hit—into the advancing Chinese ranks. The chinks didn't even try to knock out the gun. They just kept coming, until in the end the machine gun got so hot it wouldn't fire. Then Lefty whipped out his .45-caliber pistol and started blasting away with that. Eight dead chinks later, he found himself sharing his hole with an empty pistol and a live Chinaman. He beat that guy to death with the butt of the pistol, and it was only then that he decided he'd better get his ass out of there.

There really wasn't anything more he, or any of the guys in those two platoons, could have done. The Chinese had steamrolled right through. Meanwhile, Lieutenant Peterson (who showed up in the village to a few choice words from Schroeder) said he'd withdrawn the company under pressure, and swore he'd tried to get the word to 3d Platoon that the rest of the unit was hightailing the scene. When he couldn't raise us on the radio, he said he'd sent up a runner; it was pretty damn apparent the kid never got there, and we went on blaming Peterson even though Lieutenant Bell took full responsibility for the decision to withdraw in the first place, *and* for leaving 3d Platoon behind. From his FO perch on the northeastern slope of our little hill, he'd watched the whole battle, knew the company could never survive the massive onslaught, and felt the rest of the unit would be zeroed out if they stayed until we got the word. Bell's decision had been the right one, but it was not easy to convince any of us in 3d Platoon.

The guys continued straggling in, and after a good night's sleep and a packet of new replacements to fill our ranks, we headed south again as part of the regiment's rearguard action. As April drew to a close, the Wolfhounds' official Operations (S–3) summary for the month reported the result of the Chinese Spring Offensive and this period of the most intense fighting I would ever experience: "Offensively, the [27th] Regimental Combat Team (RCT) . . . advanced for a period of forty-five days from the Han River; defensively the RCT withdrew approximately the same distance in six days."

Chapter 6
Easy Does It

★ ★ ★

I was battlefield-commissioned to lieutenant on 5 May 1951. It was a great honor; the criterion for a battlefield commission was simply proven combat leadership—the ability to get the job done and to inspire fellow troopers to do the same—and in ten months of Korean combat, only eight men in the 27th Infantry Regiment had been commissioned in the field. I was proud to be considered worthy of inclusion among this distinguished group of warriors—the only problem was that I really didn't want to be an officer.

"I want to be a platoon sergeant like I am now, and just run my platoon," I'd pleaded with First Sergeant Flemings when he told me I was wanted at Division. "Then one day maybe be a master sergeant. I'll be happy as shit when I've got three stripes up and three stripes down. I don't want to be a lieutenant."

"And what if you don't make master sergeant?" Flemings had asked. "Look, Hack, if you don't take the commission, one day some second balloon* might

---

*Second lieutenant

come in and take over your platoon. He also might get a lot of your people killed. Then how would you feel? You've got to take the promotion and look after your troops."

The First Sergeant had had a point. And when he told me that even as a lieutenant I'd be able to return to my platoon in George Company, I'd made tracks to Division Rear to join the officer world. Unfortunately, in this important detail the topkick proved to be wrong: the minute I got my bar, I was taken out of George and reassigned to the 3d Platoon of Easy Company, the glamor-boy outfit of the Wolfhounds.

It was a great disappointment—I hadn't even said good-bye to my brothers in the 3d of G—but I couldn't let on. In fact, I decided not even to tell the Easy guys I'd come from George. I'd scrounged a new set of fatigues at Division when I was commissioned, and with my shiny second lieutenant's bar, I looked like a brand-new replacement officer, fresh off the boat. I played out the new-guy role, and the war stories of the Thirsty Third—"bloodthirsty, that is"—came, one more impressive than the last, from the "Bowling Alley" at Taegu to the Yalu and back. It was small wonder that any other units were needed in Korea at all, judging from Easy's own accounts of their derring-do, but I actually enjoyed the little game. As these bad hombres of Easy tried to run me, or at least scare me, out of town, I had time to take the measure of my new outfit, and I was pleased with what I found. They were a spirited, proud company (unsurprisingly, with two Medal of Honor winners and one DSC winner among their most recent skippers), and besides, most of their stories—to some degree, anyway—were true.

The platoon I inherited was a strong, solid outfit that knew what it was doing. It was full of characters, too, like PFC "Red" Smalling, a freckle-faced kid and brilliant combat soldier from Arkansas, who'd walk up and down the line at night making sure the guys on guard were all awake. If one wasn't, Smalling would hold his .45 against the side of the transgressor's head and fire off a round. And as if that wasn't enough to wake the kid up and teach him a lesson, the next day Red would follow him to chow and beat the shit out of him, with the First Sergeant making sure the fight wasn't broken up until Red had done a good job. This particular routine was explained to me by weapons squad leader Bobby Stokes, who also introduced me to the machine-gun duo of John Lipka and Richard Sovereign, two gunners who knew their weapons as well as a guy knows every curve of the body of his first great love. They practiced night and day, and had down pat a "shave and a haircut, two bits" duet, which they'd play on the machine guns during enemy attacks so Bobby would know their positions hadn't been overrun. It was a brilliant idea, and it worked.

Our company commander, Lieutenant Dell Evans, was a brave and distinguished soldier, a great leader who also became a great friend as he helped me negotiate my first steps in the officer world. Only once did his one-step-forward approach almost send me two steps back, and that was when, shortly after my arrival at Easy, the 2d Battalion went into corps reserve at Uijongbu—the Chinese Spring Offensive now petering out and the U.N. forces preparing to attack north—and one of Dell's ROTC buddies from college days, a guy by the name of Lieutenant Lloyd Leslie "Scooter" Burke, came to visit.

Scooter Burke did not look like a big war hero. He was of small build, with metal-rimmed glasses; he was Clark Kent, not Superman. But by May 1951 he was well on his way to becoming a legend in his own time. He'd already won a Bronze Star, Silver Star, and, in November of '50, the DSC for almost single-handedly stopping a large Chinese force from destroying his 1st

Cav unit. By the time he'd leave Korea in November 1951, he would earn three Purple Hearts and the Medal of Honor, too, the latter as company executive officer (XO), just about to rotate home—when he'd hear his battalion was in deep shit on the line, he would lead about thirty-five men left in his company in a final attack, catching live chink grenades and tossing them back on the enemy, killing or capturing about a hundred Chinese, and generally playing Audie Murphy on his way to successfully securing the battalion objective.

So Scooter came to visit, and one night, with nothing better to do, he, Dell, Captain Eugene Snedeker (CO of H Company), a couple of other guys, and I decided to reliberate recently liberated Seoul. We jumped into Dell's jeep and drove down the road; the first stop in our quest for excitement was the Fifth Air Force Officers' Club. The place was dim and garish inside, but plush compared to where we'd come from. We were wearing our Sunday-best field gear, and it got us a lot of heavy looks from the Wild Blue Yonder gang in their Class A's. They acted as if we were savages invading their territory, and it pissed us off—these fly-boys had the world by the ass while we lived like rats in the field, yet they resented our being in their club. *Screw 'em,* we thought, and sat down anyway.

The chips on our shoulders grew larger by the drink. We became more antagonistic, more obnoxious, more profane. There were a number of complaints about our conduct, and the more complaints, the grosser and badder we got. Before long, the club officer, a big fat major, came over: "You people are not authorized. You're in the wrong uniform, and your conduct is unbecoming to officers." Scooter, who was the baddest of us all, grabbed him. He put a .45 against the major's belly and looked at Dell.

"Say the word and I'll blow him away."

Dell gently convinced him that greasing this guy would ruin our party, so Scooter just pushed the petrified pilot away and we left. We jumped into our jeep and headed home, taking potshots at passing street lamps just to entertain ourselves. An MP jeep gave chase (we were driving in a blackout zone with our headlights on): "Turn those lights off!" we heard. Paratrooper Gene Snedeker whipped out his .45 and shot a hole through the instrument panel of our jeep. Somehow that kind of sobered us up, and we started concentrating on avoiding the MPs until we successfully cruised into the reserve area and crashed into our beds.

By the end of May, U.N. forces in the east really had the enemy on the run, and now the 25th Division was ready to put the squeeze on the Chinese from the other side. The Wolfhound and Cacti regiments were to lead this assault from the west, jumping through the Deuce-Four to attack into the Kumhwa Valley. The day before the operation, 31 May, our unit was trucked from Uijongbu down a dry creekbed which was to serve as our main road. Easy Company's assembly area was a ridge running down about ninety degrees behind the front line, with the company CP located at the bottom.

It was payday, traditionally the peacetime Army's day off, that wonderful, lazy day once a month when you put aside soldiering for the roll of the dice and the snap of the cards. We were still in reserve (which was as close to peacetime as anything in a war zone), so we spent the hours pretending we were in Las Vegas. I'd learned to play poker in Trieste, the same place I learned the basics of just about everything. I don't know whether I'd read it in a book or seen it in a film, but at some stage early in life I'd concluded that great warriors were usually great poker players, so it was only natural for me to feel compelled to be the best poker player on the block. And generally speaking, except when Dell Evans, a truly brilliant gambler, was around, I was.

As we waited to jump off into the Kumhwa, I was on a bona fide winning streak. We played all day, and one by one all my opponents fell out. At nightfall we continued by the light of our campfire, but by then I'd pretty well cleaned out the gamblers of the platoon, so we decided it was time to quit. I must have won at least two grand; I didn't bother counting it, just stuffed the loot into my fatigue jacket, feeling a bit disappointed that I had nowhere to blow it.

Throughout the day we'd taken light incoming, but nothing close and nothing big. Our platoon CP was in a draw, and since we hadn't taken any incoming in our area, we hadn't bothered digging in. I'd made the platoon dig for sure, but not the CP, and now that it was dark, it seemed pretty pointless to get carried away scratching out a hole, since we were jumping off first thing in the morning. The rest of my CP group— the doc, RTO Lee Livesay, assistant platoon sergeant Whitey Snyder, and platoon sergeant Charlie Greer— agreed, so we snapped together our ponchos and made a big lean-to, which we hunkered down under solely to keep out the drizzling rain.

Soon after we'd settled in, the Chinese artillery got serious, blasting all over E Company's position. Then our guns got into the act, and the next thing we knew, a big artillery duel was raging between the good guys and the bad guys. The only problem was that our lean-to was right in the middle, getting the overs and shorts from both. For some reason, it didn't bother me. The guys were saying, "Shit, we should dig," and I kept telling them not to worry about it, that we had a great position here in this draw. "Natural protection," I said.

But then I heard the son of a bitch coming. I could hear the incoming whistle, loud and clear in the dark. And it started coming in louder and louder. We flopped onto our bellies and hugged the ground. Greer was next to me; he flung his arm across my back as the incoming round kept screaming. It was going to land right on top of us, I knew it—and it did, right at the edge of the goddamned poncho, with an earsplitting roar.

"Everybody here? Anybody here?" I asked when the dust settled and the ringing stopped.

The doc, Lee, and Whitey all said they were okay, and then Greer said, "I'm hit."

Greer had just returned from a wound he'd gotten up north. A .50-cal slug had torn through the muscle and tissue of one of his arms, just missing the bone. He had an incredible scar from it, and now the poor guy told me he'd gotten it again, this time in the other arm.

The rest of the CP group, in the meantime, were beginning to sit up, checking out all the places where mud, debris, and equipment had slammed against them when the round exploded, to see if they'd been wounded. Amazingly, Greer was the only one. I was still prone, waiting for Greer to move his injured arm. When he finally tried, I felt blood, and a lot of pain. "Wait a minute," I said. "I think I'm hit, too." At first we couldn't work out the connection. Then we discovered that Greer's arm was nailed to my back.

A shard of shrapnel, about eight inches long and half an inch thick, had pierced his arm in exactly the same way the bullet had. It had missed the bone, gone the whole way through the muscle and tissue, then out the other side and into my back. If Greer hadn't been such a big guy, if he hadn't had such huge arms, and if he hadn't thrown one of them across me, I would have been dead. But as it was, I was essentially intact, with a good wound and a kit full of money; as we pried Greer's arm off my back, all I could think was *Japan, here I come.* With great delight I flipped on my radio and called Dell. "I'm hit, Greer's hit, and Whitey's taking over."

"How bad are you guys hit?"

"I think it's pretty bad. In the back for me. Greer got it in the arm. We're going down to the aid station now. I'll see you on the way out."

Greer and I started down the draw, hindered by thorny bushes and scrub trees growing on the ridge, as well as by the artillery that was still popping all around us. We got to Dell's CP. He was concerned about our wounds, and about losing a platoon leader and platoon sergeant just before jump-off. I took his mind off it—first of all, I reminded him, Whitey had been a WW II combat platoon sergeant and he could handle the platoon better than Greer and I put together, and second, I was going to Japan and I was loaded with dough, "So you're not going to get a goddamned cent of it!" (The thing was, if I hadn't gotten hit, the next big game would have been the play-offs down at Company, and Dell would most likely have cleaned me out.) I really rubbed it in, but my poker-playing nemesis wasn't even ruffled. He knew there'd be a next time.

The battalion aid station was overflowing with wounded. *Screw this,* I thought; *we'll wait in line forever.* A medical litter jeep was parked outside; we piled in and the jeep slowly rocked its way down the creekbed road. Much heavier chink artillery was coming in now; fires blazed in the darkness— American artillery pieces that had taken direct hits. It was a scary scene: rounds were smacking all around the jeep, and there we were, well outside the battalion area, traveling about three miles an hour with the headlights off. I told the driver to flip on his lights and make tracks. No can do, he said, we were beyond the light line. I said, "Fuck the light line. We're talking about our asses!"

He flipped on the lights and we buzzed down the creekbed at a fast clip, leaving all that incoming behind. A few miles down the road an MP stopped the jeep. "GET THOSE LIGHTS OFF!"

"Battalion surgeon!" I called out. He shot his flashlight at my bar, which I'd pinned onto my steel pot. "Got some critically wounded here, got to get them out!"

"Yes, sir!" he said with a smart salute. We tore off.

The regimental aid facilities had taken a direct hit; there were wounded everywhere. Some of the medics were in worse shape than their patients. They were brave men, the docs, patching people, ignoring their own wounds. An aid man came along. "Where're you hit?"

"The back," I said.

"Does it hurt when you breathe?"

As a matter of fact, it didn't. But I was glad he asked the question; it was the million-dollar question, which —if I answered correctly—would be my magic ticket to Japan. "Yeah, Doc," I replied. "A lot."

A surgeon came up next, had a look, and asked if it hurt when I breathed. I felt really guilty bullshitting this guy, because he looked a lot worse off than I did—he'd gotten it in the back, too. But I kept thinking of the bright lights of Japan, and all this dough I had burning a hole in my pocket. "Oh, shit, Doc, yes. Yes! Like daggers, every time I breathe."

Both Greer and I were evacuated to Division Clearing. A splinter of shrapnel was still in my back, and the medics suspected that my left lung was collapsed.

By this time it was morning, and I was a litter case marked "Critical." I still hadn't been X-rayed, but again came the million-dollar question: did it hurt when I breathed. My response, which was getting better all the time—"It's killing me! Doc, do you think I'm going to make it?"—got me back to MASH, and from there onto a hospital train back to Pusan.

Litters were stacked three high on both sides of the crowded ambulance train. The wounded composed a fair slice of the United Nations forces fighting in Korea: Turks, English, French, Greeks, Australians, and Yanks. Most were noncritical—leg, arm, and back wounds that didn't require intensive care—which was all for the best, because our nurse was a bulldog. No compassion and strictly business. She thumped a needle in my ass and lectured me about staying put, lest the shrapnel splinter lacerate my collapsed lung further. I moaned and groaned and nodded, all the while keeping my eye on the hot crap game that was roaring in the aisle at the foot of my litter. "You must keep on your left side!" she barked. *I want into that game,* I thought.

The minute the Iron Florence Nightingale went on to the next car, I was in, knee deep. I still had two grand of 3d Platoon's loot, and with that kind of backing, I could almost buy my luck. And I was hot—red-hot. On one occasion I made seven straight passes. The bucks were rolling in, in U.S. Military Payment Certificates (MPCs), lire, drachmas, pounds, and francs; my left hand could barely wrap itself around the wad of United Nations funny money I was collecting, as my right hand went on making pass after pass. Just as I lost the dice and faded into the crowd, Florence marched back into our car. I slipped back into my litter and was following orders by the time Her Sternness came by. Trying to ignore the resentful glares of my fellow gamblers (who'd lost the chance to win back their money), I concentrated on sorting and counting my loot—now close to four grand—and daydreaming about Japan.

The train pulled into the station at Taijon. Delayed for four hours, we were told. Walking wounded could visit a nearby Red Cross Club, but litter patients had to stay on board. *Shit.* But then dear Florence was replaced by a laid-back medical corpsman who, not knowing about my "lung condition," told me he'd look the other way "if you want to stretch your legs, Lieutenant."

The Army sergeant who ran the train depot was wearing the Wolfhound crest. I hadn't known him; he'd been badly hit, placed on limited duty, and was now a railroad man. "Come over to my place," he offered. "Got a bottle of Daniel's there." The guy's "place" turned out to be a railway car that he'd converted into a plush—at least by an infantryman's standards—mobile apartment. One corner was stacked with loot. "I take what I need from the supply trains and a little extra for swapping," he said. "Sure beats climbing hills and getting shot at."

I readily agreed, especially as I looked over the fine body of his little Korean mama-san. The railroad man caught my hungry stare. "She's yours, old buddy." He told her he was "going out to check my trains—take care of my friend here," and he left. The girl and I cracked open another bottle of whiskey and hopped into the sack; she wasn't much to look at, but I didn't spend a lot of time looking.

There's a thing about combat soldiers and sex. On one hand, it's the most important activity in the world. On the other, it means nothing at all. Sure, sometimes it was a love thing, but most times it was just a good, hard screw. You were always horny and never discriminating; you weren't looking for love, you were looking for pussy. *Pussy.* One word. And no matter who it was or how it was, that's what it came down to in that all-male, ultramasculine world of the Army. You'd come back from leave and the first question your buddies would ask was, "Did you get some pussy?" "Yeah, it was great," you'd reply, even if you'd struck out. "Best pussy I've had in a long time."

"I want some pussy" rolled off a soldier's tongue as easily as "I want a drink." Getting as much pussy as you could was part of the role: proving yourself in the cot was as important as proving yourself on the battlefield. Tribal behavior, I guess—the great warrior, the great conqueror of all lands and all broads—or some deep psychological thing: knowing you might get killed and wanting to plant the old seed before you went. Or maybe it started in Hollywood. Who knows? Who cares? All I know is we talked about it a hell of a lot more than we got it—but when we got it, it was pretty damn good.

"Train's leaving in twenty minutes, old buddy," said the railroad man when he returned to find an exhausted, drunk, but well-screwed trooper. He walked me to the train; I thanked him for his hospitality. "We Wolfhounds gotta stick together," he said. "Hope you get to Japan. Take care, ya' hear?" I'd known the guy less than a few hours, yet he treated me like a brother—the Wolfhounds were a very special fraternity. We said good-bye. I got back on the train, slipped into my litter, and dutifully laid down on my left side to take the pressure off my poor overworked lung.

The 3d Station Hospital was the main attraction in the Pusan shantytown that surrounded it. What a terrible place for my journey to end. The doc who examined my wound said, "Good news, son. No lung damage whatsoever. You'll be back with your unit in no time." It hit me like a death sentence. No lung damage meant no Japan. No Land of the Rising Sun. No place decent to spend my money.

Pusan really was the asshole of the universe: a drab, dirty war town where the sun didn't shine. The train ticket was open; it was an unstated hospital policy that a guy could lose himself in the city for a few days before returning to the front. But I couldn't stand the place, so I took the next train north, thinking I might hop off and visit my railroad buddy and his girlfriend in Taijon. Before I left I bought a case of Southern Comfort from a PX sergeant for fifty dollars a bottle. The stuff sold legally for three bucks, but I didn't care. What else was I going to spend my loot on? At least I could get the boys drunk, and besides, they really bought it with their own dough.

On the train I got drunk with a young 187th Airborne squad leader. He had Shirley Temple dimples, which he'd gotten catching a slug. "Went in one cheek and right out the other," he said. "I was hollering at my squad. Didn't even know I was hit till I tasted the blood." We toasted his Rakkasan para-troopers,* and then we toasted the Wolfhounds; we even toasted the Chinese, and got so drunk that I slept right through Taijon.

The division had been on the attack since the day after I got hit. Easy had spearheaded the breakthrough and led the way ever since; now we continued north through the bitching terrain of the Kumhwa Valley— straight up and straight down, with no roads and few trails in our sector. It took nine hours to pack wounded to Battalion, and about the same time to bring up ammo and supplies; it was no fun, with the only redeeming feature being that the Chinese were

---

*The men of the 187th Airborne were the Rakkasans just as the men of the 27th Infantry were the Wolfhounds. *Rakkasan* is Japanese for parachute.

struggling even more than we were. Enemy resistance was virtually nonexistent. Had someone given us the word, we could have marched right on to the Yalu. As it happened, we did get the word, but the message was entirely different from the one we'd expected to hear.

In late June, after one year's hard fighting, the U.S. Eighth Army started digging in deep on some high ground north of the recently restored 38th parallel. We built sandbagged bunkers and installed barbed-wire barriers, with plenty of mines and booby traps. The chinks were nowhere in sight—if ever there was a time to keep moving, this was it—but the word was *stop*. There were rumors of peace talks, though, which was good news for everyone; we all shared the hope that we would soon see a cease-fire. All things considered, it was probably for the best that our youthful naiveté prevented us from recognizing the enemy's real intention—to fuel the peace flame only to gain time to rebuild its gutted forces—and once the heavy field fortification work was over, we started enjoying the sitzkrieg life in the quiet western sector of the Kumhwa Valley.

That is, until we boarded trucks and headed south after forty-five straight days on the line, only to find that rather than being relieved, as we had expected, the Wolfhounds were in fact being shifted from our quiet western sector to the red-hot eastern side.

Here, to our north, the enemy held the high ground; from the towering slopes of "Papasan," Hill 1062, the Chinese had commanding views of the entire valley. And as well as having such brilliant observation, the enemy had plenty of indirect mortar and artillery support. This was not going to be fun.

That evening we conducted a night relief without incident, but when the fog lifted in the morning, we found ourselves looking straight into enemy guns on the higher ground across the valley. For the first two days we followed the schedule of the relieved unit so the Chinese wouldn't get wind of the switch until we were set. We stayed in our holes and dug even deeper. Just at dusk on the second day, the chinks clobbered the company front with a stiff barrage of mortar fire. This was followed by a PA announcement from the Chinese trenches: "Welcome, Wolfhounds. We kill all of you." So much for military security and our clandestine relief. This message was repeated over and over, until a crazy little Hawaiian in my platoon, Takashi Maki, jumped out of his hole, stood in the open, and screamed back, "Fuck you, Chinamen. Fuck you! Come and get us, you lousy sons of bitches!" Chink psychological warfare couldn't faze a Hawaiian, especially the likes of Maki, who attacked up hills shouting, "Yea, Wolfhounds!"

Just before our move, Dell Evans had left the company to become the battalion Intelligence officer. Now he needed a prisoner—a POW could tell him who we faced on Hill 1062 and what their intentions were. It was only natural for him to call on his old comrades for help. "Hack, you should conduct this raid," he said. "If you volunteer, I'll fix it so the operation comes directly under Battalion control. You can plan it yourself, however you want, and I'll get your platoon off the line for a few days to get ready." Bored with just sitting there day after day on the receiving end of Chinese incoming, and with the assurance that 3d Platoon would get a break, I said yes. We were moved off the line and were given three days to plan, rehearse, and execute the raid.

We set up at E Company's supply trains. It was the first time 3d Platoon had been off the line in more than two months, and immediately one of our scroungers went out to get some steaks. While the other guys cleaned up and rested, Dell, a few key leaders, and I planned the operation in detail. What we devised was simple, bold, and maximized shock and surprise.

I decided on a lightning tank-infantry daylight strike that would put us into the Chinese positions before they knew what hit them; shock action and speed would be the key to the chinks' front door. We'd go with a stripped-down platoon—only rifles, BARs, and fighters—the heavier stuff and the timid could stay home. The surprise would come from our daring (no one in his right mind would ever attack a Chinese main battle position of at least a couple of regiments with one platoon in broad daylight) and our timing (we'd jump off at 1700, that is, five o'clock P.M., which was unheard of—the Americans had been attacking at dawn since Washington was the Main Man).

Surprise through stealth was impossible—we'd be crossing a wide-open field of no-man's land—but I figured we could still catch the Chinese napping, hit them while they were dazed, and run before they got their act together. We laid on a fire plan that included every artillery tube in the corps area that could strike Hill 1062 and its adjoining hills. A maximum mix of smoke, Willie Peter, and high explosives would be used to blind and shock the defenders—it would slam down on the enemy in a wall of smoking steel from the moment we jumped off until we got home.

The first night behind the lines we ate steaks, sang around a big bonfire, and got knee-knocking drunk on the last six bottles of Southern Comfort I'd bought in Pusan, augmented by a gallon or two of scrounged medical alcohol. The next day, with heads slightly the worse for wear, we conducted rehearsals with the tank and M16 half-track platoon that composed our little task force, on terrain similar to our objective.

That night, while the platoon finished up the medical alcohol in a halfhearted attempt to recapture the

fun of the night before, I took two NCOs for a recon.
We started at the LD and carefully probed with trench
knives, clearing out a dozen cake-sized U.S. antitank
mines as we marked a path for our track vehicles with
small pieces of white engineer tape. A bomb-damaged
bridge spanned the north-south main road; I looked at
it carefully but concluded it probably wouldn't take
the weight of a Sherman, so we probed a big looping
path to the east around the bridge through a fordable
creek, then across an open rice paddy and back to the
road.

The map showed the road forming a lazy S, and the
contours indicated a slight slope at the top end. This
was the ridge where we planned to dismount and
commence our assault into the rear of the Chinese
positions, so I wanted to have a look at it. We carefully
slipped along the side of the road, our movements
masked by darkness and the whoosh and impact of
U.S. artillery H&I fire.

U.S. flares were popping in the valley to our west.
We had coordinated our patrol and asked that no
flares be used in the 2d Battalion's area during our
recon, but in battle at least ten percent never get the
word. Tonight it was a welcome snafu. One came in
close and we hit the ground, only to see in its surreal
light a Chinese sentry on the road about twenty-five
yards away. We couldn't chance getting around him,
and knocking him off would risk blowing tomorrow's
raid. *Live and let live,* I thought as I signaled to
withdraw.

August eighth dawned, overcast and rainy. It was a
perfect day for the mission; the chinks would be like
us, all hunkered down in their positions, trying to stay
dry. We made final preparations for the attack: test-
firing and cleaning weapons, last-minute briefings,
and organizing a forward aid station just behind the
LD. We married up with the tanks and tracks, and at

1700 hours we shot up the road to the north like an express train, to the deafening roar of massed artillery fire. The tanks, with the stripped-down 3d Platoon riding piggyback, quickly and easily rolled through the lanes we'd cut in the mine field and swung behind the enemy positions. The operation was going exactly to plan. Hill 1062 and all key enemy terrain around our objective were simultaneously being blistered with high explosives, Willie Peter, and smoke. The enemy was blind and surprise was ours. We dismounted the tanks and rushed to the base of the hill. And stopped. I could not believe what my eyes were telling my head.

The gradual slope we'd expected from the map was absolutely vertical. *The best-laid plans of mice and men . . . and one goddamned Chinese sentry.* "You can read all kinds of books you want and you can make all kinds of plans you want," Steve Prazenka had said, "but when you get out in the field, those books and those plans might not meet the eye of the situation you find there. So you just have to roll with it." *Right, Steve. Let's roll . . .* I thought as I slung my M-1 across my back and started climbing hand over hand, straight up. My guys followed. No orders were given; the men in the 3d Platoon were a magnificent team—they'd stayed loose, flexible, and above all, cool. Meanwhile, the tanks had pulled back off the road and joined the tracks in the cleared lane through the open rice paddy east of the road; together they were laying down welcome, murderous overhead support fire.

When I got to the top, I jumped into a trench, almost on top of two enemy soldiers. I shot them both, then started blasting stunned Chinamen on my left and right. Meanwhile my guys poured into the trench. We fanned out through the intricate, mazelike trench system, knocking the Chinese defenders off as we went. When we crested the ridge, we looked down onto the enemy's main battle positions. They were manned only by a light security force, but behind the main positions, in a deep draw, was what looked like a complete rifle company. They'd been eating; now they scurried for cover while our point-blank plunging fire took a heavy toll.

Our artillery was still slamming in. We were now in complete control of the ridge and had captured three prisoners—it was time to withdraw. We quickly slid back the way we had come while the tanks returned to the base of the hill to pick us up. I sent the wounded down first with two squads and the prisoners, and stayed with a couple men to hold the chink positions until the WIA were loaded and our task force ready to split. Artillery, quad .50, and tank fire kept the stunned Chinese at bay when we, too, finally slid down the hill.

After I'd given the order to withdraw, one of the tracks had panicked, left the cleared lane in the rice paddy, and hit a mine. Now the disabled vehicle was sitting right across the lane itself, blocking our only escape through the mine field. Meanwhile, the Chinese were getting themselves together. They started putting down a lot of fire—small arms, mortar, artillery, and self-propelled antitank. As yet they didn't have our range, but even with their lousy commo, it wouldn't take long. There was only one alternative. I shouted to the tank platoon leader, "Let's try one tank over that bridge, and if the son of a bitch holds, we'll go out that way."

The thirty-six-ton Sherman gingerly rolled across the semicollapsed bridge. The bridge sagged, swayed, but held. I radioed the crew of the damaged track to abandon their vehicle, load on other tracks, and follow the lead Sherman's trail to get the hell out of there. Once my own tank had crossed the bridge, I ordered the tank platoon leader to fire a couple of armor-piercing rounds into the disabled track. No way was I going to have those four .50-calibers dismounted by the enemy and remounted on the hill facing my platoon. The rounds split the thin-skinned vehicle in half, and it burst into flames.

We made it back—sixteen wounded and nobody badly hurt, no friendly dead, and three prisoners. Not a bad show. I got off my tank and was making sure our wounded were being looked after when a lieutenant colonel raced up, bellowing like a bull. "Who's in charge here?"

"I am, sir. Second Lieutenant Hackworth."

"And who gave the order for destroying my track?"

"I did, sir."

"Well, I'm going to have you pay for it! That's $120,000! You do not have the authority to destroy my vehicles!" Lieutenant Colonel Henry, CO of the 21st AA Battalion, raged on, chewing my ass for not going into the mine field with a tank and winching his damn track out. I tried to explain that it was so hot out there that no infantry soldier would have lived, that we'd barely gotten his crew out alive. He did not want to hear. Finally I got pissed off. *Very* pissed off. I told him that no way was I going to risk one infantryman for a rotten piece of twisted steel, that my people's lives were more important than his goddamned burned-out track, and that if I had to make the same decision again, I would do it "in spades."

Colonel Henry was livid. *"You will pay for this!"* he screamed. A jeep screeched up, and out of it jumped my regimental commander, Colonel George B. Sloan; the divisional commander, Major General Ira P. Swift; and the corps commander, Major General John "Iron Mike" O'Daniel—all three great combat leaders of World War II. General O'Daniel boomed out, "Where is the platoon leader?"

Oh, shit, I really must be in trouble now, I thought. "Sir, Second Lieutenant Hackworth," I reported.

"Second Lieutenant, you are a first lieutenant as of now. And," O'Daniel said, thumping a Silver Star on my chest, "I'm also recommending you for the Distinguished Service Cross. I watched the complete attack from the regimental OP and it was outstanding. Outstanding! It was one of the finest demonstrations of professionalism and leadership I have seen in combat. Your platoon operated as a perfect military force. I want you to tell me which soldiers you want me to decorate."

"All of them, sir!" I said, and right then and there, every man of my platoon who went on that raid was given a Bronze or Silver Star by this fine fighting corps commander. Easy.

And then the outraged Colonel Henry crawled away, never to be heard from again.

Chapter 7
Crazy Young Fools

★ ★ ★

As the peace talks went on, the U.N.'s "Police Action" in Korea settled into the trench war it would remain until its end almost two years later. But sitzkrieg or not, the conflict did go on, and the need arose for small units to gather intelligence and conduct patrols all along the front—in general, to take up where large units had left off fighting a moving war. But, as Colonel George B. Sloan, the Wolfhounds' regimental commander at the time, explained, "It's not a simple matter to get a company of infantry and say, 'You guys are going out on a patrol tonight to capture some Chinese prisoners' "—the average military unit didn't have the skills necessary to conduct successful night operations against an entrenched enemy. In the Wolfhounds it was decided to establish an ad hoc platoon to fill this gap; in the wake of the successful 8 August mission, three months short of my twenty-first birthday I was given command of this specialized unit, dubbed the 27th Wolfhound Raiders, and told to handpick, organize, and train it as I saw fit.

I put out the word, and Crispino came over from George Company to be the Raider platoon sergeant.

He brought a bunch of my old platoon with him, and a fair few from the 3d of Easy joined up as well. Hundreds of other volunteers came from throughout the regiment; on a short fuse to get ready, we trained hard and culled the ranks simultaneously.

Other than the guys from G and E, the volunteers were of all kinds: super gung-ho types who did not like trench warfare, eight-ball losers a cunning topkick was trying to unload, bored troops just looking for adventure. I relied on a few of the former E and G NCOs who knew what we were looking for to conduct the initial interviews; they quickly sent the jerks and thrill seekers marching and sent the best and bravest to me. Crispino sat in on my sessions with these "first-cut" candidates; between the two of us it was usually easy to assess a man's mettle. And for the times when it wasn't, Chris had devised a brilliant screening technique.

He'd taken the powder out of a frag grenade and fired the primer cap separately. Then he'd reassembled the thing, and as I interviewed potential Raiders, Chris would sit there playing with this dummy grenade. Near the end of the session, if I still wasn't sure about a man, I'd give Chris a wink and he'd "accidentally" drop the grenade. The safety pin would fall out and we'd jump back—horror and shock on our faces —meanwhile studying the guy's response to this "live" grenade spinning around on the floor. If the volunteer froze, we knew we didn't want him. If he threw himself on the grenade, we thought he was nuts, or at least suicidal, and we didn't want him, either. But if he grabbed the thing and threw it out of the tent, or if he cut a trail out of the place himself, we knew he had good sense—he was a cool hombre, and real Raider material. Using this approach (along with intensive, only-the-strong-survive training), by the end of three weeks we'd bottomed out at forty-seven lean, mean, proud and ready Raiders. And then we went to work.

The Raiders' first mission was kind of a crawl-before-you-walk thing. Chinese snipers were coming down from the hills before dawn and setting up in the flat ground facing B Company of the 27th. By first light they'd be in position and masterfully concealed; they used smokeless, flashless ammunition, making them impossible to spot. The men of B Company were afraid to stick their heads up, and rightfully so. Our job was to eliminate the snipers and try to snag a prisoner.

We assembled behind B Company, where I had a chance to talk to Lieutenant Jerome "Jim" Sudut, whose platoon we'd go through at dark. Sudut's people were dug in along a raised railroad line that ran east-west through the Kumhwa Valley. Fortunately, the position's rear slopes provided good cover from the sniper fire, and relative ease of movement as long as you kept your tail down and moved fast. Unfortunately, there was no patrol path going out. Earlier another U.S. unit had seeded the area knee deep in antipersonnel mines without keeping a record of where they were buried. Their short-term protection meant only long-term agony for subsequent units, who had to find uncharted mines the hard way. It was a problem that had confronted infantry since the introduction of mines, and now it was ours.

When it was dark, Sudut guided us to the edge of his wire and wished us good luck. It had turned cold; I hadn't brought my field jacket, and Sudut took off his, insisting that I wear it. "There'll be coffee waiting for you in the morning," he added. I gratefully slipped on the jacket and eased out into the darkness.

Crispino and I swapped turns at the lead. It was good to work with him again. I hadn't realized how much I'd missed him since I'd gone to Easy three months before. Chris was about five years older than I, but we had a great affinity. Destined to win two DSCs, two Silver Stars, and five Purple Hearts over two tours of Korea, Chris was a first-class fighter and, from our experience in the 3d of G, one of the finest point men I'd ever seen. If I had to be creeping along in the dark, playing point man and probing through mine fields, I couldn't think of anyone I'd rather have been doing it with.

The first mine disarmed was a Bouncing Betty on a trip wire. But there were others to contend with, too—pressure types, which were the worst, those mean little bastards with small pins barely sticking out of the ground. We crawled on hands and knees, clearing the area to our direct front and then carefully sweeping one hand in a long, slow arc. If a wire was found, it would be followed to the mine; the mine would be disarmed and set aside. If no wire was found, then we'd probe with trench knives. Anything solid would be dug up; sometimes we'd sweat out a rock and sometimes it was the real thing. After "all clear," we would crawl another yard and repeat the process. It took three hours to clear ten mines, and my gut ached as if I'd done a thousand sit-ups. It wasn't work to keep you young.

We high-stepped through tall grass—a silent, single file of ghostly night marauders, now a mile behind Chinese lines—toward the ambush site, a spot where the path up the hill from which the snipers were operating intersected a well-used north-south trail. As we set up our killing zone on the east side of the trail, we found horseshit, no more than twenty-four hours old. It was a good sign. The Chinese used horses for resupply.

We waited—forty-seven men, including rear and flank security—lying prone in a killing zone about

100 yards long. Our weapons were set on full automatic with safeties off; grenade pins were straightened, too. All the Raiders were connected to one another by way of a thin wire running from hand to hand. Three quick pulls on the wire meant *enemy,* then one pull for each joker entering the gauntlet. I was in the center of the ambush. I'd trigger it with a blast from my submachine gun only when the fish were well into the net, with Don Neary, my RTO, simultaneously firing a hand flare. Our SOP then called for each Raider to fire one mag, toss two grenades, and pour in another mag.

After three hours of waiting, the only blood drawn was our own: the ambush site was in mosquito country—big mosquito country. None of us used repellent (chinks could smell it as easily as after-shave, soap, tobacco, and toothpaste); we couldn't slap at them (noises traveled loud and far at night). So we waited and reluctantly contributed our blood. I was well-protected. Jim Sudut was a giant of a man, and his jacket was like a tent. I could almost crawl up into it. A lot of the guys who, like me, hadn't thought they'd need their field jackets were not so lucky, but just as they'd set up the ambush, now they were maintaining it like pros, despite the thousands of little stinging bites on hands, faces, and necks. We made no contact. The mosquitoes finally won by a TKO—we had to get home by daybreak.

We saddled up and took a different route back to avoid the possibility of a chink ambush along the path we had taken out. We had about 400 yards to go when the sun started to peek its nose out of the eastern sky. Chris was leading and I told him to pick up the pace. Instead, suddenly, he stopped. He slowly turned and whispered in my ear, "I smell gooks."

I took a long sniff. "Chris, you're hallucinating. There are no gooks here."

He insisted, "No, I smell them. They're around here somewhere."

The sun was really starting to make its move now. I had the monkey on my back—we had to return to our lines in a hurry or we'd get the shit chopped out of us in the middle of no-man's land. No one had told me the Raiders' maiden voyage was code-named "Titanic."

"Let's get the hell out of here," I whispered.

Good soldier Crispino started off again with me breathing fire down his neck. He took one more step. "Look, Hack, they're here. I smell 'em . . . no shit."

"Chris, get behind me, I'll take the point."

I had taken no more than five steps when I heard a metallic click. I knew the sound: a bolt going back on a weapon. A fraction of a second later little red flames licked out of the darkness from a distance of five feet—slugs leaving a Chinese burp gun. I felt the slugs smashing into my stomach even before I heard the report. I hosed down the flames with a long burst of .45-caliber slugs, simultaneously jumping to the right and hitting the deck. The Raiders took up their antiambush positions automatically, as I tossed two grenades while spraying another mag. After one more grenade, I charged the ambush, blasting away. Steve Prazenka, look out—you taught me well. Moments later six dead Chinamen were stretched out in the tall grass. But Chris was also down, and very still, about five feet away. It was light enough now that I could see his head was covered with blood.

I felt sick as I slowly turned him over. Chris looked up at me with vacant eyes. Then, slowly, a sly, mischievous grin crossed his face. "See, Hack, I told you I smelled 'em," he said.

When I realized Chris wasn't dead and there was no chance of his dying, I had another look at the dead chinks. They looked like a forward observer team, but a number of them were armed with Soviet SKS carbines. They had not set up yet, but it looked as though they were just going into position when we surprised them by coming up from behind. Their mission had probably been to put a little heat on the main line with some well-directed H&I fire and selective sniping. *Well, not this time,* I thought. It was broad daylight by the time we scooped up their radio, weapons, and papers and made tracks to the cut in B Company's wire. When we arrived, the Raiders loaded onto our waiting trucks and went home, while Sudut took Chris and me to his CP so the doc could go to work.

I felt no pain. *Hell, I should be dying with multiple slugs in the gut,* I thought, but except for my hands, which were covered with small wounds and swelling to the size of mini–baseball gloves, there was no blood gushing from anywhere. Doc Brakeman said, "Lie down here, Lieutenant, and let me have a look."

I glanced over at Chris. He was kneeling a few feet away, drinking the steaming hot coffee Jim had promised (and which I wasn't allowed to have with my gut wound). He was a casting director's dream, old Crispino—the wounded warrior, blood still dripping down the side of his face. "No, no, Doc, don't worry about me. Take care of Crispino. Take care of the enlisted swine."

The doc went over to Crispino. Chris said, "Oh, no, Doc! I'm just a lowly enlisted man. Take care of the officer. The officer is far more important. We EM can always be replaced." We continued playing the game, ricocheting poor, confused Doc Brakeman back and forth. The doc didn't really know us yet and couldn't understand our warped sense of humor. Finally he gave up trying, and took care of Chris.

It turned out his wounds were not serious—they

just bled like hell. One slug had clipped his earlobe and the other had grazed his skull like a razor slash. By the looks of things, the Chinese gunner must have panicked. He hadn't held his weapon down, and the recoil had lifted the fire from my gut to Chris's head to the stars. But we were just damn lucky the Chinaman wasn't a pro. He could have cut both of us in half and done some serious damage to the Raider column, too.

Then it was my turn. But when the doc laid me down and cut open the side of my jacket, he found no wound. He unbuttoned the jacket and pulled back the other clothes. There was no blood, no nothing. I had small cuts and lots of steel splinters all over my face, neck, chest, and the backs of my hands, but no bullet holes. But I'd been hit in the gut—I *knew* it—unless I was the one who'd been hallucinating.

It was time to call it a night. We said good-bye to Sudut and his gang, and gave them a couple of SKS rifles for their hospitality. Between my blood and Doc Brakeman's knife, the jacket Sudut had loaned me was pretty well done for; I promised to send him a new one with something fluid in the pocket. But I never saw him again. He was killed two weeks later leading a platoon attack against a firmly entrenched enemy position. When his body was found, there were half a dozen or so enemy dead scattered all around him in the trench. The lieutenant had run out of ammo but not out of fight: the last of the enemy defenders had been killed with Sudut's trench knife.*

The doc at the regimental aid station patched us up properly. Chris would be down for a few weeks, but my wounds were superficial, nothing that couldn't be fixed with a few shots of penicillin, Tennessee whiskey, and some deft strokes with a scalpel to get the

---

*Sudut was awarded the Medal of Honor, posthumously, for this action.

steel out. An easy Purple Heart, but I still couldn't understand it.

My next stop was Regimental S-2. The Intelligence shop was set up in a large, sandbagged general-purpose (GP) tent surrounded by concertina wire. I placed my weapon on the table out front, following SOP—magazine out, bolt back, weapon on safety (too many well-armed clerks had blasted each other with "unloaded" firearms inside tents)—and went inside. I made my report on the mission and the contact, and at the end, in passing, I told Major Stambaugh, the S-2, how certain I was about getting hit in the gut. Stambaugh jokingly suggested that I'd "gone Asiatic," whatever that meant, and I left, picking up my weapon on the way out. But when I flipped the grease gun over to close the bolt and insert the magazine, there, staring up at me, was a jagged hole the size of a fifty-cent piece. So I wasn't crazy; I *had* been hit, and the steel splinters were bits and pieces from my all-metal M-3. I couldn't resist running back into Major Stambaugh's tent so he could have a look at it. He told me to go home and get some sleep.

Dell Evans heard I'd been hit, and he came to visit the Raider camp later that morning, to check on friends and get the full scoop. He disassembled my damaged weapon, and upon examination we saw that three slugs had ripped through the trigger housing assembly. The slugs had gone through the oil thong case, then through the bolt retracting mechanism, and smashed into, but not penetrated, the other wall—the wall that was up against my gut. My weapon was an M-3 A1, modified with a recess in the bolt to draw it back; the retracting mechanism had been made redundant by this modification and shouldn't even have been there. So it was almost as though some thoughtful Ordnance man had left it in, somehow knowing that it would be perfect to slow down three 9mm Communist slugs, and thus save my life.

By the time Chris got back from the hospital, the Raiders had completed six successful missions with no casualties, save on the first one. The tasks had been varied, and chosen by Major Stambaugh according to intelligence needs; all required stealth and skill, but not every one required the full Raider force. We took only as many men as needed to do the job, be it taking a prisoner for interrogation, getting enemy uniforms for line crossers, raiding an outpost—whatever the S-2 assigned to us—and from each raid we learned more and got better. The missions gradually became more difficult, taking us farther and farther behind enemy lines, or into territory so hot it might take five hours to crawl a hundred yards.

Raider basic training had consisted of ambush and counterambush techniques, repeated and repeated until the men could do them in their sleep (as well as more specific skills for operating behind enemy lines, such as how to cut throats, toss a hand ax with pinpoint accuracy, and use a garrote); as time passed, advanced training was dictated by mission requirements, and anyone with experience shared in the teaching. At one point or another that included just about everyone; the Raiders had a strong foundation of seasoned combat veterans: Crispino, Costello (both combat Rangers), and Wells from George Company; Smalling, Ropele, Lipka, Sovereign, Bill Hearn, and Jimmie Mayamura from Easy; not to mention McLain (who, in some hard Pacific fighting, had taken shrapnel from a Jap round right in the face) and his fellow Texan, "Tex" Garvin, who were both WW II ex-Marines. My own "snooping and pooping" I&R experience was invaluable, too, and we'd all sit around and discuss techniques, the old pros adding much to the ever-growing repertoire of Raider tricks.

With Chris's return came a mission to destroy four caves burrowed into the side of a hill deep behind enemy lines—what aerial photos and the intelligence "experts" suspected to be a supply depot. Artillery had already tried to close the place down, with zero effect; tac air couldn't get in there at all because the Chinese had too many automatic weapons on Hill 1062, which fired on the aircraft. Our mission was simply to blow the caves and return. It sounded easy, but it wasn't—few of them were. We had to slip through the main Chinese defensive line, make it through real bandit country before we even got to the caves, then blow them up and get out as if nothing had happened—all in exactly ten hours.

We registered artillery concentrations along our route, and for two nights before the raid the gunners hammered away. We'd use them during the raid, too. The noise would help cover our movement, and the flying steel might encourage the enemy to stay in their holes. Another benefit was that the guns would be warm and gunners ready in case we needed their magic punch to get our asses out of a crack.

At 1600 hours, Raid Day, everyone was standing tall. The Raiders' standard uniform was fatigues or coveralls, and black knit caps and sneakers. Black was the order of the day as much as possible—our faces and hands, too, smeared liberally with the end of a burned cork. Loose clothes, dog tags, and anything that made noise were tied down with OD tape or held tight with rubber strips cut from inner tubes. Chris conducted the inspection, which by now was SOP: each Raider had to run in place, hit the ground, and roll without making one sound before he could board the truck.

We slipped through friendly lines at dark, and by

2000 hours we were behind the main enemy line. I'd decided to take only two squads into the objective area: Mayamura's scouts to get us there, and David Forte's demolitions people to do the job itself. We moved fast, with Mayamura and two of his scouts far to our front. About 100 yards from our objective we halted and formed a tight defensive perimeter. Jimmie insisted that he go alone for a look at the caves.

There was no point in debating the issue; Jimmie Mayamura was like a cat at night—totally unafraid. We'd been together for four months in Easy, and by now I was used to his little midnight walks through enemy lines. I loved Jimmie. We all did. He was a no-bullshit gunfighter, a samurai warrior who preferred operating by himself. But he was also a quiet, unassuming first-generation Japanese-American, and he had this strange thing about rank. Jimmie was a PFC when he joined the Raiders, and every time I tried to promote him, he wouldn't accept it. He was ready and willing to do any job (as it was, his role as squad leader called for the rank of E-6), but he just didn't want to be an NCO. It didn't matter to me, but somehow I really felt that after he went home (which was in only a couple of months) and got out of the Army, the time would come when he'd regret his attitude about not wanting rank. So without telling him, I decided to promote him anyway, one stripe at a time, and little did he know, but PFC Jimmie Mayamura was already a staff sergeant.

An hour after he had gone, Jimmie returned with the word that there was nothing in the caves, that they hadn't been used in a long time. There was also no sign of Chinese, but the main track was well-used (with horseshit all over it), and north of the caves there was a rough wooden bridge that spanned the creek we had come up. Jimmie suggested we blow the bridge. It seemed like a good idea (we had enough demo to blow up the Golden Gate anyway, and it was crazy taking the stuff back), and besides, it was good training. Jimmie provided security while Forte wired the bridge to explode when we were sixty minutes down the track; we hustled out of there, and an hour later the bridge blew with a thundering roar.

Whether or not we made contact with the enemy, it was near impossible to relax, much less sleep, after a raid. It took a long time for the adrenaline to stop pumping; you couldn't just flop down and switch off. Most of us would go for a good swim in the river that flowed right by our little camp (the position of which I'd personally chosen, as far as possible from any other unit, so my guys could cut loose without complaints from sleepless rear-echelon folk in the wee hours of the morning); we'd play on the beach and in the water, just to let off some steam, and slowly, slowly unwind. Afterward, we'd pick the raid apart—lessons learned, screwups, and who should get his walking papers (the scrutiny never let up)—over a mighty breakfast of steak and eggs washed down with beer. Then we might play some softball, and only around noon would we crap out and sleep for ten or twelve hours. By midnight most guys were up again and a party would be rocking the Raider camp, complete with open kitchen, 190-proof on the rocks, and, weather permitting, midnight swims. It wasn't bad duty. We raided one night and had the next three off. It sure beat the hell out of hiding in the bottom of a hole on the front and having HE dumped on you twenty-four hours a day.

Another night the Raiders set up an ambush on a track in front of the 1st Battalion, about a mile and a half behind enemy lines. My guys set up on a small, four-foot-high ledge that paralleled and overlooked the track, on the other side of which was an orchard enclosed by a long, rectangular rock wall. It was a perfect ambush site, and with Jimmie covering our rear with his element (on a small knob to the south overlooking the track), anyone coming down the track or through the orchard would have nowhere to run.

As soon as we were in position, we saw a Chinese squad carefully picking its way through the orchard. A larger force was following this point element, and another enemy squad, much closer to us, was moving in single file down the track as flank security for them all. The Chinese were careful, and well spread out.

We let the complete group enter the orchard. Just before their point cleared the southern rock wall, thirty automatic Raider weapons began to blast as our ambush force poured magazine after magazine of lethal fire into the orchard area. Chris called in artillery and we had some harvest; the chinks had no cover other than behind the small trees, and we splintered them with grenades.

Suddenly, we started taking machine-gun fire from behind the northern rock wall. It peppered along the ridge but snapped far over our heads. At the same time, Jimmie radioed: "Got an enemy force, size unknown, moving between us and your rear. What's happening over there?" I gave him the details of the ambush and directed him to take the force under fire—we were about to be outflanked. I told him we were going to head down the track and into his position as soon as we could shut down the machine-gun fire; Chris adjusted the artillery, and when it was on target, we moved. We joined Jimmie's perimeter and waited. The force he'd engaged took off to the northwest, which was fortunate, because Raider enthusiasm and all automatic weapons had just about gobbled up our basic load of ammo.

Chris scattered artillery along the enemy's probable routes of withdrawal. We kept it crashing down around us, a warm (if somewhat noisy) security blanket, while Jimmie went to have a look at our own withdrawal route tó make sure it wasn't blocked. Meanwhile Chris, a few other guys, and I snuck back to the ambush site to see if anything of interest could be scrounged from the enemy dead. Not even Superman could have escaped the amount of fire we'd poured into the ambush area, and we figured we'd net a couple of Thompsons, if nothing else.

The battlefield was dead quiet except for the friendly incoming. Only a couple of hours had passed since we'd sprung the ambush, but now, to look at the orchard, it might have been days. There was not one dead Chinaman to be seen. Not one. There were plenty of pools of blood, a lot of spent brass, but no fallen warriors. *Shit,* I thought to myself, *maybe it didn't happen.* The Chinese had responded that quickly to the task of pulling out their dead, wounded, and weapons. Our final report: one bloodstained, well-pruned orchard. No corpus delicti. The Chinese were pretty slick.

As time passed, the raiding business began to get very serious. Before long it wasn't easy to slip through the front lines and disappear behind enemy positions: the Chinese had wised up to Raider activity and were countering with raiders of their own, as well as with damn good ambushing and observation teams. In the larger picture, while there were limited major attacks by both sides "to keep the pressure on" at the peace table at Panmunjom, for the main our regular units were slowly atrophying in long windy trenches that snaked from one side of the Korean peninsula to the other, while the enemy—fast-digging primitives who had little but numbers on their side—hugged the Allied positions with siegelike trenches of their own to avoid superior U.S. firepower. In some places the lines were within hand-grenade range. More and more, the load of day-to-day fighting fell on the shoulders of special units like the Raiders; because I trusted Colonel Sloan and his regimental staff not to use us as a kamikaze force, I didn't even flinch the day my guys were tasked to take our first hill.

The Chinese had dug a virtual siege line only a couple of hundred yards from 3d Batt's K Company, with manned spider holes that made it impossible for anyone in King to stick his head up during the day without drawing a sniper shot between the horns. When my Raiders fell out, checked gear, loaded trucks, and moved, it was with the mission of taking the Chinese position and getting rid of the whole shebang.

Jimmie and crew slipped through King's wire at first dark. It was more like an ominous twilight, really—the full moon was so bright I would have canceled the raid except for the fog. McLain went with them to try out our newest acquisition, an infrared night device. He'd mounted it on a carbine and assured me that it was accurate to at least forty yards. We needed it; artillery would cover the noise of the shots, and we'd be hard-pressed to get past the Chinese observation post otherwise on a bright night like this.

Three rounds of artillery smashed into the top of the hill; I didn't hear the carbine fire even though I was only fifty yards away. Sure enough, Mac had neutralized the two-man OP with two clean shots between the eyes.

The hill was steep and void of all vegetation. We inched our way forward, slithering along like snakes, carefully shifting loose rocks out of our path. One careless move, one tumbling rock down this artillery-battered hill, could mean serious trouble; it would alert the defenders to forty very exposed and vulnerable Raiders right in their killing zone.

When we got to the first Chinese trench, no one was in sight. Our artillery had driven the defenders underground. I covered Red Smalling, my old friend from 3d/Easy, as he poked his head into a bunker. At the same time, two chinks came down the trench. Smalling gave both a short burst from his stripped-down BAR, and the battle was in full swing. But the chinks had been had—Raiders were all over their positions—and the fight was almost over by the time the enemy at the top of the hill began their usual barrage of potato-masher grenades.

While we were mopping up, Smalling got into a jack-in-the-box duel with one die-hard, burp-gun–toting Chinaman. They went at it for a while—one popping up, firing, and going down, and then the other—until finally both of them popped up at the same time. Smalling cut the guy in half, but the Chinaman's last burst stitched Red right up his left side with half a dozen slugs. "Hack," he said (with Arkansan understatement), "ah'm hit." His left leg was virtually shattered, but he was still mobile, so I told him to go down the hill and Doc Brakeman would patch him up. "What about my weapon?" he asked. SOP in Easy was if you were hit you passed your automatic rifle on to some able-bodied guy (you don't want to lose that kind of firepower on a hill). But we Raiders had plenty, and besides, we were almost through up there. I told him to keep it.

The cleanup continued. We had a few casualties, mostly from grenades being thrown by a couple of hardcore jokers in a bunker on the reverse slope of the hill. Johnny "S'koshi" Watkins,* a young kid of about seventeen who was the size of a jockey with the heart of a lion, got a chunk of his ass blown away, and dear old Ropele had the tip of his generous Roman nose sliced off by a shard of grenade steel. I was especially sorry about Ropele's wound. He owed me about five hundred bucks from jawbone poker, and it was a Raider rule that if you got hit you were cleared of local gambling debts. I always hated to see good money bleeding off a hill.

Suddenly Smalling reappeared. "I thought you'd gotten the hell out of here, Red."

"Yeah, Hack," he drawled in his lazy kind of way, "but I bumped into some gooks on the way out. I thought you should know." He went on to tell me that after Brakeman patched him up, he'd been heading back toward King Company's position when he'd run into six Chinese setting up a machine gun to our rear, along our withdrawal route. He'd killed them all, but then, despite the fact his left side was almost paralyzed, had felt he should come back to tell me. What a good man. After I sent Chris to deal with the threat—his force knocked off another dozen enemy and left a squad behind to secure our withdrawal route—I turned my attention back to the reverse-slope bunker where those potato mashers were coming from.

We couldn't use artillery because we were too close. Our own grenades, thrown blind, seemed to be having little effect. The only answer was one of Forte's bunker busters.† We'd just have to keep the enemy down and stop the incoming grenades long enough for the charge man to toss the thing in. McLain, that tall, brave

---

Sukoshi is Japanese for little.

†A satchel charge, composed of C-4 explosive and a short-fuse detonation cord

Semper Fi Texan, volunteered for the job. Just before he walked up the hill, he hung his patrol cap over the end of his weapon and thrust it far out in front of him. The cap dangled down like a Lone Star flag. Mac turned to me. "Right out of *The Sands of Iwo Jima,* huh, Hack? Sit down, John Wayne!" Grenades—ours and theirs—popped all around him as McLain made his way up the hill. He set his weapon down, armed the charge, and spun it around his head like a lasso. *Yahoo.* He flung it over the top. Good-bye, bunker. Good-bye, Chinamen with your piss-weak grenades.

An infantry platoon from King replaced us before dawn. It had been another good Raider show—mission accomplished, four friendly wounded and no dead. Statistics say that for every three Purple Hearts there's one dead. God was keeping his eye on us crazy young fools.

Chapter 8
Just a Nightmare

★ ★ ★

Hill 400 was what the Infantry School would have called *key terrain*. It was a rocky, volcano-shaped hill that sat astride the left boundary of the Wolfhound Regiment, dominating the battlefield like a Spanish hilltop fortress. The enemy had occupied it for a long time. According to Intelligence, there were no more than fifty Chinamen up there, but the enemy had burrowed deep into the hill's rocky slopes, and despite all tactics used or vast firepower employed, the Wolfhounds could not secure that piece of ground.

When the Raiders were given the mission, we were assured it was not a kamikaze attack. Instead we were told that it was critical, and an operation perfectly tailored for our special team. Though I might have mentioned that this perfectly tailored operation had only been designed for the Raiders after two or three different units of infantry had assaulted the hill (taking extreme casualties in the process), I accepted the mission without comment. But my gut started to churn; 400 was that Jake Able feeling all over again.

We'd jump off in three days. On the morning of the first day, key Raider leaders and I conducted a visual reconnaissance of Hill 400 from Item Company's forward outpost position on Hill 275. The OP was set on a gray knob a mile from the front, with our objective about one-half mile farther north along the ridgeline. "Shit," said Tennessee wheeler-dealer Jack Speed. "This one won't be so goddamn tough." I wasn't sure I agreed. For one thing, there were the ubiquitous mines and booby traps to be disarmed before we even got near. For another, our objective was a formidable piece of real estate, with steep sides and a rear anchored securely by the Chinese main battle positions on Hill 419 to the north. And the third thing was there was only one avenue of approach: it would be hi-diddle-diddle, right up the middle.

That night, Jimmie, Chris, and I left Item's outpost for a closer look at the Chinese defensive positions on Hill 400. We'd been all around that fortress on previous operations and had never been able to find a weak point; now we were up there on it for almost six hours. Item Company guys who'd previously attacked the hill warned of accurate 82mm and 120mm mortar fire and a damn tight defensive system. We disarmed a few mines (but nothing to get too excited about), found three outposts on the hill's southern nose, and behind that a trench bunker system. But that was all. We still couldn't find Hill 400's Achilles' heel.

We returned to our camp and worked out the plans. On request, the artillery people had been punching the shit out of 400 with heavy eight-inch delay stuff since we'd gotten the warning order (causing big sections of the enemy's breastworks to crumble in), but on the night itself there would be no artillery preparation or illumination. Our initial attack would be by stealth: we'd knock off the OPs, move to our deployment position, and, after forming a line of skirmishers, hit the trenchworks. Only when the shooting started would supporting fires be brought in to clobber the Chinese reverse slopes, reinforcement routes, and likely mortar and artillery positions.

Sloan approved the plan. He also told me he'd have a regimental forward aid station set up behind Item's outpost, a comforting thought, but one that did little to assuage my concern about the operation.

We briefed the troops. Every man knew exactly where he was to go and what he was to do when he got there. I guess Chris and I were snapping out orders and carrying on like real bad-ass Regulars—in the hospital, a thousand years later, the guys said that's how they had known we were in for some deep shit.

We moved up behind Item under the cover of darkness the night before the raid. I didn't want to tip our hand, but I wanted my guys up there in the morning so they could get a good look at 400 during daylight, then be rested and set to go at first dark. They had their look and then, spread out among Item's reverse slope bunkers, caught some shut-eye. A number of the guys wrote letters—some in earnest, some in jest, the latter group wrinkling them up and rubbing them in the dirt, so that if they got zapped, whoever was on the receiving end would know that life in the trenches was tough and war was hell. After a last look at foreboding 400, I sacked out for the rest of the day. Unlike Jake Able, I slept like a bear.

The sun dropped out of the sky like an incoming round. Suddenly it was pitch-black—the perfect night to attack—no moon and a thick blanket of fog that settled over the battlefield. Jimmie moved first; his scout section was through the wire and gone without a sound. Jack Speed's squad was next, followed by me and Don Neary with his radio. Next were Bill Smith's and Tex Garvin's people. All was going just like rehearsals. For once everyone seemed to have gotten the word. No one fired at us from Item; no flares were sent up to compromise us in the middle of no-man's land.

The inevitable first hitch occurred just as I'd cleared Item's wire. Word was passed up that a Raider in Smith's squad was refusing to go a step farther. I had Neary halt the infiltrating column, and I went back to find this guy hunkered down in the patrol path like a mule. Until then he'd been a good man—he had at least a dozen raids under his belt—but now he wouldn't budge. He said he'd had it; he couldn't go on. I told him that his timing was off—he should have turned in his quit slip before we left home—and that his ass was going up that hill. Sobbing, he told me to get screwed. I hit him on both sides of his face with my pistol and said that there wasn't a Raider out there who wanted to go, but they'd all made the commitment when they'd gone through the wire. The boy wouldn't be moved. I pulled my trench knife out of my boot and laid it against his throat. "I'd just as soon cut your throat as fuck with you," I said. "You either go on this raid or die. If I kill you, I'll report that you bought the farm in a big burst of glory. Make up your mind." After a few seconds, between muffled sobs, he said he'd go.

The crews of the three enemy OPs must have forgotten the old soldiers' creed: *Stay alert and stay alive*—Jimmie and his gang knocked them off with ease. We moved up to the deployment line, then crept forward, one slow, quiet step after another: toe down, then heel; crush, not snap—taking more care than in a mine field.

All the Raiders around me were now in, or entering, the trench. A short way down, Tex Garvin made the first kill. He'd just finished putting his men into their attack positions and was standing just above the trench when an enemy soldier came strolling by.

Garvin reached down, splattered the Chinaman's head with the butt of his weapon, and rolled him into an empty bunker. Meanwhile, I checked with Speed to see how his guys were doing—everything was okay. Neary and I started creeping down the enemy trench line to where Speed's and Smith's squads were tying in. Then I saw a chink not more than four feet away. I froze. The guy was standing in the trench, looking downhill with only his head sticking out, a difficult target for a knife or a garrote, and I didn't want to shoot him until we were really ready to go. But I couldn't see how I could get at him, or past him, silently. Neary covered me. I slipped my pistol out of its holster, laid my Thompson down, and started bellying along the top of the trench line. Definite heart-in-mouth stuff. I was about a foot away from him when I came to the interesting realization that Chinese sentries were no different from a lot of Americans I knew. He was fast asleep.

He never knew what happened. I grabbed him with one arm, covered his mouth, snapped his head back and cut his throat. Neary, who was at least six feet four and built like a fullback, moved up behind me and pulled the sentry out of the trench as if he were a feather pillow. He dragged him down the hill and stuffed him into a shell crater.

Everyone was in place, and Forte's satchel charges were ready and waiting at the doors of sleeping bunkers. "Let's get this show on the road" was the word from Jack Speed. Jimmie Mayamura appeared in front of me. He whispered, "Hack, I think we're going to have to change the plan." He reported that there were some additional, heavily fortified positions between the trench we were in and the top of the hill. We hadn't found them on our reconnaissance (it would have been too risky to have gone beyond the trench; we could have blown the operation). Now

Jimmie, roaming around as if he were on a Sunday picnic, had stumbled across them. They were unoccupied, but another scout, Bobby Evans, had gone into one large bunker in the area and estimated at least ten men in there. He'd set a trip-wire grenade booby trap to nail them when they came out.

Before I could reassess my battle plan, Hill 400 exploded. Evans dispatched four Chinamen who were moving down a connecting trench into the one we occupied. His BAR had barely started singing when every weapon on the line started hammering away. Forte ignited his satchel charges and an earth-shattering roar shook the trench line as bunkers blew across the position. The remaining chinks in the immediate area didn't have a chance. If they were not trapped underground, then Raider grenades blew them sky-high. Farther up the hill, the enemy were wide-awake now and frantically firing in every direction. They hit nothing. We'd cracked their main line, and not a casualty reported so far. Me and my premonitions. This one, like the one on Jake Able, was a false alarm: Hill 400 was going to be a piece of cake.

I told the boys to use regular daylight assault procedures: we'd fire and maneuver and blast our way up. Cordite hung heavily in the air as Chris formed a reserve of Forte's and Mayamura's people and took over our positions with the mission of guarding our ass. The prearranged artillery fire blistered the top of the ridge as Scaglion kicked off our attack with two fiery blasts of his flamethrower. The Raiders started slugging, but then the world fell in.

The chinks always relied heavily on potato-masher grenades. Already we'd policed up what looked like enough to give each enemy soldier on 400 his own monogrammed case. But even when they threw them at us in bunches—as they had on Objective Logan, ringing the pins of each around their fingers or on little sticks—potato mashers, which were mainly concussion-type grenades, didn't pack much punch in the open. They were virtually harmless firecrackers we'd learned to dance around and (more or less) ignore. The problem on Hill 400, though, was that the defenders weren't just throwing potato mashers. They were also hurling frags. We hadn't counted on that, and the sky was black with them.

Many rolled down the hill and exploded out of range behind us, but many found a Raider target. Smith's guys had a hard time; they took a number of casualties and couldn't gain an inch of ground until Speed's fighters thundered forward in a wild attack. These men overwhelmed one of the unexpected positions, and now Speed's complete force was in there, mopping up. The price filtered back to me: we'd taken three dead and more than twenty wounded. *It's just a nightmare,* the words bubbled up in my brain.

Almost to a man, the wounded Raiders refused to leave the hill. Doc Brakeman was performing miracles in his ever-growing "field hospital" in a shell hole behind the trench below us; the kids determinedly returned to the fighting the minute they got patched up. Some, like Jimmie (who'd already gotten shot in the ass and the arm), didn't even bother with the patching—everyone knew we were a lean outfit and that every gun counted. It was that family bonding again: no one was going to let his brothers down, especially in a fight like this. Even at the cost of his life.

I called for Chris and Forte to bring up their people. We needed everybody on line. Fuck a lot of rear security—if you're losing the fight, a strong rear won't do you any good. We were running low on ammo and grenades so we took all we could from enemy dead. I told the leaders to let me know when they were rearmed, reorganized, and set to go. We had to *banzai* the shit out of the hilltop in a hurry. It was the only way we'd take it, and if we didn't jump off soon, we'd be nickeled and dimed to death by what seemed like ever-increasing scores of frags bouncing down from above.

Green tracers from a machine gun raked our position. It was set up in a rocky outcrop near the top of the hill, firing right down Speed's throat. No way could he get his people through that. The way it stood now, they couldn't even return fire. The gun had to go.

Brave Raiders Smith and Salazar, on the left, took on the deadly challenge. There was little cover and no concealed approaches to the gun, just a fold in the ground in the center of Smith's front, which the machine gun could not depress low enough to cover. Raider weapons laid down good covering fire as the two volunteers crawled up the hill. I liked these men. Especially Smith, an Alabamian whom I initially hadn't been sure was Raider material, because he'd gotten his stripes the National Guard "weekend warrior" way. The funny thing was that Smith didn't think he deserved those stripes either. He was embarrassed about them, and always seemed to go out of his way to prove himself, even when it was no longer necessary. Maybe it still riled him a bit when we called him "NG" (due to his National Guard origins); still, by now he did know it was just a loving nickname for a brave and trusted comrade-in-arms.

Now, under our fire, he and Salazar snaked through the dead space toward the gun. About twenty yards from their objective, Salazar blasted with his weapon and Smith rushed forward, screaming as he unleashed two large Chinese antitank grenades. Both hit home, exploding on impact. The machine gun and crew were blown to a million pieces. The two Raiders turned and started back toward us. Then a Chinaman jumped up on the outcrop and fired a long, long burst. Both men fell, their momentum sending them tumbling into our position. Smith died in my arms. I cried as I held him; *It's just a nightmare,* I thought. And then I swore we'd take that fucking hill.

Speed had jumped off as soon as the machine gun blew. Garvin, picking up the reins from Smith, attacked on the left. Item Company put 60mm mortar fire all over the top of the hill; we came up right under it. Speed's people hit the top like a bulldozer, closely followed by Garvin's squad. The die-hard chinks were making a determined last stand as Raiders fanned out; savage close-in fighting and hand-to-hand combat were the bloody order of the day.

"Shift the mortar fire to the back of the hill!" I yelled to Neary.

"Grenade!" shouted Raider Mendoza, who was kneeling about three feet away from me. We went for cover. Mendoza and Neary hit the ground. I spun, but tripped and rolled down the slope. I stopped rolling about the same time as the grenade. The same place as the grenade. It was under me when it exploded—the blast propelled me into the air like a rocket. Moments later a 160-pound rag doll fell to the ground with a heavy thud.

I could not get any air. I was choking and gasping. Horrible sucking sounds were coming out of my chest. *Fire,* I thought, my chest and left side were on fire. I groaned and tried to breathe. I figured my lungs had burst. Then I stopped moaning. It took too much energy. "Hackworth's done for . . ." the words floated down. "The Old Man's dead." *No, Speed, no. I'm not dead.*

I moaned again, louder, but Jack was gone. *Fuck you, Jack Speed, I'm not dead, and I ain't gonna die, not on this goddamn hill.*

I dragged myself to my feet and headed for the doc. He checked me out and got me breathing while I sent word to Chris to take command and get a prisoner. My left arm was broken and hanging from my shoulder by ripped flesh and torn muscle; scores of shrapnel wounds covered my burned chest. But I would live, and for the second time a submachine gun had saved my life. A submachine gun, and good TRUST training. When I'd rolled down that hill, I'd tucked my Thompson into my gut as I'd been trained, and rolled with it under me; the weapon, not I, had taken the full impact of the explosion.

Johnny Watkins drifted in. A grenade had blown the shit out of him. He said things were heating up, that Chris had been hit in the leg and Speed had assumed command. I could hear the increased fire above, and after a shot of morphine and a little Brakeman bedside manner (he wrapped my arm in a heavy Carlisle bandage and made a sling out of an empty M-1 bandolier), I headed back to the fight. It was almost dawn.

The Chinese had been counterattacking since I'd been hit. Only now was the assault beginning to falter. Raiders, all wounded, had been pushed back; they lay near the crest of the hill and cut the enemy down as they came over the top. I picked up a little M-2 carbine. It was nothing like my Thompson (now a black and twisted mess), but I could fire it like a pistol with my one good hand, and I joined in the fray.

It was getting light enough to see now. To my right lay Chief Denny and ex–Easy trooper Hearn. Both had been hit: Denny in both arms, and Hearn down from a head wound. Hearn couldn't see and Denny couldn't shoot, so the Oklahoma cowboy and the Arizona Indian brave had formed a posse of one: Denny gave directions while Hearn fired the weapon. *Red man, white man, kill 'um yellow man.* Tex Garvin was over to the left, both legs badly blasted by shot. He couldn't move, but he put down effective fire as calmly and deliberately as if he were at the known-distance range at Camp Pendleton, striking for a USMC Expert's Badge.

Neary crawled over to me with a message from Colonel Sloan: *Put Crispino in command and get yourself down to Item.* "You never got that message, Neary," I snapped.

"But Hack, he was serious."

"Shut off the radio."

All colonels are serious. But there was nothing Sloan or anyone could have done for us right then. We needed to know what the hell was happening. It seemed as if we'd already wiped out the whole Chinese army, and the bastards were still coming. I asked Neary if the guys had gotten a prisoner yet. He replied in the negative and slipped into the cordite dawn, while I backed off from the top of the hill to take a moment to examine the situation. All but a handful of Raiders had been hit. Most, twice and more. More than twenty-five wounded and, at last count, five dead, including the boy who'd tried to quit at the LD. *Had he known something I hadn't?* Most of our leaders were down. Speed had taken a shot in the belly and was shooting with one hand, holding his guts in with the other. We were totally dependent on captured weapons. Our ammo supply was gone. We were in a fish-or-cut-bait situation.

Neary appeared again, this time carrying an unconscious little Chinaman. I found out later that after I'd told him we needed a prisoner, he'd taken it as a personal assignment. He'd charged up the hill and stormed the top unarmed. Once in the enemy position, he'd smashed this chink on the head with his fist and hotfooted it back to me. Unfortunately, the POW died before we got the skinny—he'd kept trying to pull one of the grenades off Neary's belt on the way back, and Neary had stomped him, obviously a little too hard. So we got another prisoner, but then, just when we needed him most, our interpreter, Kim Upsu, decided to bug out. Speed saw him running down the hill. He stopped him. "I go, I go," said Kim, and edged away. Jack didn't know what to do. He was good and ready to waste him; instead he leveled his weapon and shot off Kim's hand. This persuasive little tactic worked, and as we bandaged him up, Kim decided he liked our company after all.

The word from the POW was just what we wanted to hear: our artillery had clobbered the enemy reinforcing unit (Intelligence had been off by about 300 men in terms of enemy strength on Hill 400; the chinks were reinforcing through a tunnel-trench network on the reverse slope, which ran through to Hill 419 behind), and no one on the hill had any fight left in him. I told Jimmie and the others to round up every gun that could walk, limp, or crawl. We were going to storm the top.

Twenty bloodied and battered Raiders soon crested the hill. Its surface was covered with enemy dead. The Chinese defenders who hadn't been killed on position had chanced running the gauntlet of artillery shot (which continued to blast the back of the hill); judging from the carnage on the reverse slope, few had made it. But an intact Bren-gun crew was still raising hell among our tired band. There were more casualties, until Jimmie and Evans went on the attack. They killed the crew, but paid the price.

Jimmie lay like a broken reed next to the gun. He'd taken a shot in the face that ripped through his right eye and lower jaw. Evans lay nearby, staring at Jimmie with wide, lifeless eyes and a satisfied look on his heavily mustached face. It was the look of a winner. He'd probably just said to Jimmie, "Well, we got the son of a bitch," before a burst of enemy fire, most likely the last of the fight, hit him full in the chest and ripped the life out of him.

Neary switched on his radio to report the capture of Hill 400. Relief was en route, he was told, dispatched by a worried Colonel Sloan when we went off the air. *"Oh, say can you see,"* I thought, as in the dull light of morning we collected our scattered and broken fighters from the blood-soaked, *American*-held hill. The inexhaustible Brakeman was kneeling over Jimmie, pumping life into him with a container of albumin. Some piece of cake: we had seven KIA, twenty-nine WIA, and one Raider, Salazar, missing. The only two Raiders who were not hit were Lipka and Sovereign, the two gunners. Their machine guns had been out of range of the frags that had depleted our ranks. It was a strange turnaround—normally the gunners ride in the death seat.

We turned the hill over to the relieving Wolfhound unit and continued looking for Salazar. We wouldn't leave the hill without him, and any man who could walk joined in the search. He'd been patched up after he and Smith had knocked out the machine gun, but no one had seen him since he'd returned to the fight. A faint moan was heard in a draw on the steep left-hand side of 400. It was Salazar, more dead than alive; he'd been blown off the hill by a grenade, and somehow, with twenty-nine slugs or shrapnel wounds in his body, that tough Texan hombre was still sucking in air. The doc got some blood into him, and we started down the hill.

We carried all our dead and the wounded who could not make it on their own. Speed and I brought Jimmie's broken body down in a poncho while Brakeman kept the albumin going. Regimental medics took over and carried the litter cases down by stretcher. Chink 82mm and 120mm mortar fire continued to smash in around us, but it was ignored by all. After what we'd been through, it didn't mean a thing.

Colonel Sloan had walked alone to meet us on Hill 400's forward slopes. He, too, ignored the incoming as he went from Raider to Raider, helping, comforting, praising. Tears streamed from his eyes in that early morning light as he helped us down. He led us to the aid station, and there I saw seven figures, all lined up, each covered with a poncho. *It's just a nightmare,* I thought, but I didn't believe myself at all. I went to each body and pulled the sheet back off the face. One by one I cradled those men and rocked them in my arms, crying and mumbling and damning God because he had let me down.

Now that the curtain had fallen, the shock of it all came on. Suddenly I felt empty. Every part of me ached. My mouth was dry as a beachful of sand. Sloan helped me to my feet. He was a fine, caring man and a great commander. A medic came up, looked at my wounds, and hit me with another Syrette of morphine. It dulled the pain, but not enough; he told me to lie down in a litter so I could be evacuated. But I was not about to go anywhere. The welfare of my men was not a responsibility that could be delegated. Until everyone had been cared for, I'd stay right there.

I walked into the small tent that had been set up to act as a temporary surgery. Jimmie was on the table. He was bad—ashen white, almost no blood pressure, and little sign of breathing. He was about to check out. The medical officer could not get blood into him. He kept saying that Jimmie had lost too much, that all his veins were deflated. But Doc Brakeman had gotten a needle into Jimmie's arm up there on top of the hill, in the dark, and *he* was being shot at. I couldn't understand why this surgeon was jabbing everywhere but where it counted. Then I realized he was drunk, or that he'd been on a big binge the night before. He smelled like a barroom rag and his hands were shaking as he frantically stabbed that needle into Jimmie's arm. I pulled my pistol out and put it against his head. "Man, if you don't get that thing in the next time, you're one dead doctor." The needle went in next round, and the grim death mask Jimmie wore slowly began to fade.

Steady, brave Doc Brakeman gently led me outside the tent. He said everyone was fine and he wanted me to rest on a stretcher. Combat medics are mountains of courage and wisdom; Brakeman stood out as the ultimate among these fine men.

I lay down. The shot was taking effect—I was so sleepy. There were faces: Colonel Sloan, Major Stambaugh, Dell Evans from 2d Batt, and then Phil Gilchrist, who'd come the whole way down from Division Forward to lend a hand to his old George and Easy buddies. Then I was being lifted and swung in the air. And then a motor and hard bumps, like knives, sending sharp pains throughout my body. And God hadn't yet explained why he'd forgotten us.

I woke up thinking I was in the Raider camp. Eyes closed, familiar voices were all around. Laughing. Bullshitting. Talking about 400, talking about the fight. *The fight.* I opened my eyes. I was in a long tent ward at a MASH. The bed next to mine was occupied by Chris, and then as far as I could see were Raiders, carrying on as though they were at a Boy Scout jamboree. I turned to Chris. "What is the status of the unit, Master Sergeant Crispino?"

"Raiders! Listen up!" Chris shouted down the row of beds, and the roll call began: Beasey, Denny, Evans, Hearn—the wounded and the dead, all present and accounted for.

Jimmie and Jack fell into the heading of "accounted for." Neither was in our wing; they were down in intensive care. We found Speed first. He was as white as his sheet and filled with tubes. His belly was swollen and painted a bright, ugly orange color. His spleen had been removed. He'd lost a massive amount of blood and there was a good chance of infection. But Jack was a gambler—he dug the challenge of long odds—and I knew he was going to make it. He was talking now, and in my mind's eye he was already sitting on the edge of my bed in the morning with a bottle of Jack Daniel's. *"Now, son,"* he'd be saying in that slow Tennessee drawl, *"take a slug of this, 'cuz ah'm 'bout to taeell you the goddamnedest story 'bout a leetle heel called 400."*

Except for his mouth and one eye, Jimmie's face and head were completely covered in bandages. So was the rest of his body. In addition to any other wounds, it seemed that a grenade must have exploded on top of him and filled him with shrapnel. He lapsed in and out of consciousness; he twisted and tried to turn, and muttered in Japanese. Chris and I tried to talk to him, but he was far away. We talked to him anyway, and somehow our voices brought him back for a moment. "The chinks . . ." he said. "Evans, get down." Then he came off 400 and moved back in time. "I got pineapple, man." Poor, crushed Jimmie was back with Easy, where the practice was to carry your C-ration cans inside your fatigue jacket over your belly. Fruit was a C-ration prize. It could slow or stop a slug with the best of them, and tasted far better than most.

"Jimmie . . ." I said. Then I stopped. What do you say to your friend when he's dying? I loved him. I wanted him to make it. I wanted him to fight harder. Maybe if we could bring him around he'd zero in and concentrate on staying alive. "Jimmie," I said, "you're a sergeant . . . a sergeant first class!"

His good eye fluttered and slowly opened. He

seemed to focus in on me for a second. "Aw, shit, man . . . why'd you do that?" Then he slipped back into his deep, dark coma. He died within a week.

Over the next few days, one, two, and three at a time, medics wheeled us into surgery. *"If you don't make it, I'll have your watch"* . . . *"If you don't make it, I'll be on top of your woman before you hit the slab"*—the same, great Raider spirit followed Chris and me as we went down that long hall together. The injected pre-op cocktail had stung, but it took away most of the pain, and some of the fright.

An arm that was somehow familiar was strapped to a board under the watchful eyes of masked people in green clothes. A glaring spotlight beamed overhead. It seemed even brighter with the second needle, as if someone had brought the sun inside. A gloved hand holding a forceps skillfully probed around the ripped flesh of the restrained arm. The instrument went in empty and came out holding shards of steel. *Like pulling a rabbit out of a hat,* I thought. A scalpel went in next and carved a doughnut around the jagged hole. Debridement, it's called, I found out later. The chunk of meat was extracted. The gloved hand balanced it deftly on the end of the scalpel. With a flip of the wrist the meat sailed through the air into a bucket of blood and other discarded chunks of damaged government property. *They should empty that thing,* I thought, as blood slopped out of the brimming pail and slowly dripped down the white surgery wall.

A voice behind a green mask said there were no complications and to leave it open to drain. "Lieutenant Hackworth," the same voice said, "do you want the shrapnel as a souvenir?" I climbed back through the looking glass. The arm was my arm. The bucket held my blood. And Jimmie's, and Jack's, and all that flowed down 400. And now this man with gloved hands was asking me if I wanted a souvenir. As if I

were a tourist, as if in my old age I'd want something
—need something—to remind me of that terrible
hill, this stinking tent hospital, all the wounded and
all the dead. I tried to tell the skillful hand what he
could do with his fucking souvenir, and for that
matter the whole fucking war, when another gloved
hand administered another needle and I drifted away.
They cleaned up my chest. But I didn't watch.

Chapter 9
Sitzkrieg

★ ★ ★

Hill 400 was abandoned by U.S. forces soon after the Raiders took it. The Raiders themselves were disbanded early in the new year (1952), and after sixteen months in Korea I was sent home, to the Infantry School at Fort Benning, Georgia, to attend my first course in how to be an officer in the U.S. Army. Throughout my stateside assignment, however, I suffered what could only be described as a postcombat hangover: nothing felt *real* in the world I was moving through, and all I wanted was to return to the front. My friends, especially the WW II vets, tried like older brothers to talk me out of volunteering for a second tour. But, *Do as I say, not as I've done,* I thought of these men who'd slugged it out in the tough campaigns of Europe and the Pacific without R&R, without benefit of rotation—who'd stayed *for the duration* —and submitted my application to go back to war.

The 40th Division was deployed on the east coast of Korea, near a large valley called the Punch Bowl. The defensive sector of the 40th's F ("Fighter") Company/ 223d Infantry Regiment, the unit to which I was assigned as company commander upon my return to the theater, started on a high hill where we tied in with Easy of the 223d. An east-west running ridgeline swept up from the valley floor on this edge of our position; it was a company-sized enemy avenue of approach, running from the north right into my 3d Platoon.

Our own east-west running sector ran downhill into a draw, then up another hill about a hundred yards, where we tied in with the 223d's George Company. The draw, which we called the Gap, led into the valley, widening as it went, and by the time it hit the valley floor, it was wide enough to take almost two enemy battalions abreast. It was a most dangerous regimental avenue of approach, and it didn't take much to see—and it was recognized the whole way from Army to Corps to Division, Regiment, Battalion, and especially to me—that Fighter held the critical ground. To overrun the Punch Bowl, the enemy—who were just a thousand meters to the north, on a parallel east-west ridgeline that dominated our immediate battle area in the form of the North Korean–held No Name Hill—would have to strike through my position. If they secured the high knob (my left flank), it would be smooth sailing, walking, or rolling (the draw was also a good tank avenue of approach) from there right through the Gap to the flatlands of the Punch Bowl behind.

It was not a great place for a green regiment. But that was exactly what we were in this, the third year of the war—a green regiment in a green division (the former 40th California National Guard Division), phasing out the Guard and assimilating new replacements more or less on the hoof.

I was lucky; my new unit had talent, albeit untried, and I knew that with a lot of hard work Fighter Company had the makings of a formidable team. The only wrinkle was that the hard work could not be focused solely on the men; besides inheriting the critical ground at the Gap, Fighter inherited a position in shocking repair, with badly laid out fighting positions, exposed bunkers collapsing from age and enemy shell hits, and a broken-down wire barrier of stakes, mines, and concertina wire (upon which bits and pieces of rat-gnawed enemy dead in bloody khaki were featured), that had been thrown up and haphazardly reinforced by one generation of defenders after another. The whole thing had to be untangled and rebuilt.

I woke up on 4 November 1952, thinking that a year had passed since that terrible night on Hill 400. *What had it been for?* I wondered. As the peace talks dragged on and on, U.S. casualties mounted. From the moment we went on line, Fighter was taking a couple of wounded every day, mostly from direct artillery hits that ripped through our underground bunkers. Incoming was as regular as breathing in this trench war—on average, about one round every three minutes across the company front. But on the tenth of November, 3d Platoon received a bonus barrage mixed in with the usual mortar and artillery fire: a twenty-minute torrential downpour of accurate machine-gun fire from No Name Hill. It started inexplicably and stopped just as quickly; we tended to our wounded and all was quiet.

The eleventh of November, my birthday, was a day like every other, only a bit colder. At dusk my patrols were ready and waiting for the shot of first dark to send them dashing off to the valley floor. This is how the war went after sitzkrieg set in. During the day both great armies lived underground, hoping not to get knocked off by the unrelenting bursts of artillery and mortar fire coming from across the way. At night the war moved into the valley, where small, lightly equipped patrols hunted each other down in no-man's land.

The key to the ambush patrols was to beat the Reds down to the choice ambush positions. Most sites, like the Pines—a favorite, just north of the Gap—were no bigger than a city parking lot, with only limited places to set up. The patrol would then set up a killing zone with all-round security in the hope, ideally, of taking a prisoner before dawn's first light.

Dark came, and out went the patrol; I'd stay in my CP, ready to pour in the supporting fires, until the men reached the ambush sites. I thought about Lieutenant Colonel William Locke, my battalion commander, who'd paid his daily visit that morning. Just two weeks before, I'd arrived at his CP, and in an instant I'd known that I'd soon be back on the line. Everyone had been moving briskly, packing up and getting ready to go. A rush of adrenaline had run through me, that familiar buzz that resonates in your gut all the time you're in combat. I'd liked the feeling.

Colonel Locke had been up front on a recon. I'd filled the time processing in and being briefed on battalion SOPs; at one point the battalion XO, a three-times-wounded WW II vet, had taken me aside to tell me that the Colonel was the meanest, worst-tempered hombre he'd ever worked for. Finally I'd been told the Old Man was back and would meet me in the battalion mess. I'd gone in, but the Colonel was nowhere to be seen. Then a small, thin captain wearing Medical Service Corps insignia and a Korean Military Assistance Group (KMAG) patch had walked in; as the mess was about to close, I'd decided not to wait any longer, and ate with him. We'd made the usual small talk, and then he'd started asking me what I thought of the 40th Division, what I'd heard about 2d Batt—really strange questions that started my sixth sense screaming. Why would an overage-in-grade MSC KMAG captain give a damn about this division or this battalion? Maybe he and the Colonel were pals; hell, the guy was so old, maybe his only friend in the world was the Colonel. So I'd answered his questions, but in a very guarded kind of way. About this time the battalion adjutant, Dick Weden, had come in. "Oh," he'd said, "I'm glad you found each other. Have you been introduced to the Colonel, Lieutenant Hackworth?"

Not only was this Colonel Locke mean, he was very, very sneaky.

Colonel Locke was Old Army through and through. The word was he'd risen to topkick before the war, then was battlefield-commissioned while with Merrill's Marauders in Burma. The man was mean as a snake and looked like one, too—a rattler about to strike. He was thin, almost bald, with a long face and thin, tight lips he mashed together like Humphrey Bogart. He chewed tobacco, had a stain from it on his cheek, and his teeth were ground down like an old horse's. To round out the picture, he also swore like a mule-skinner, and he ran his battalion on pure fear.

After we went on the line, he came to visit every day, thanks to the relatively safe road network that ran behind our position. Usually he walked the trenches before coming to my CP, casting his Old Army eyes over everyone and everything. Hearts throughout the company would freeze with fear. It took till the next morning to thaw them out, and by then he was on his way up the line again.

On my birthday morning, though, for some reason the troops had been spared. The Colonel had come directly to the CP and flopped down on my rack. How he was able to do this without wrinkling his starched, immaculate uniform I'd never know. We'd talked about the company, the battalion, and the other world "out there"; I'd been amazed at how cynical he was.

Then, as usual, we'd taken a walk down the long tunnel that led to my observation post, a first-class command center that allowed a good view of the entire company front plus a clear view of No Name. About halfway, there was a small step down and, as usual, I'd said, "Now watch your step, Colonel." He'd missed the step (which was also as usual), thumped his head on a supporting beam, and cut loose with the foulest tirade imaginable, in my direction: "You-goddamnmotherfuckingrottensonofabitchbastardofa-pissantlieutenant! Why don't you fix that fucking step?"

That had been just the start, and, as usual, Locke's assessment of Fighter's Old Man was broadcast for miles, to both friend and foe alike. I'd just "yes, sirred" and "no, sirred" until the barrage slowed down, only then reminding him (as usual) about the two-ton rock that lived under the step, and that to modify the tunnel fell into the category of building the Hoover Dam. Thinking about it that night, I had to laugh. Locke had skinned his head that morning. Pretty soon his skull would be as worn down as his teeth.

The patrol reported in from the first checkpoint. Negative. Nothing in the Pines—at least not yet—and no enemy in sight. Then, just as I was about to leave the CP, a huge wall of enemy fire crashed over the company sector from end to end. I ran to my observation post. It looked like the Fourth of July out there, with artillery, mortar, and direct-fire MGs blazing in the meanest barrage I'd ever seen. I called for artillery and mortars to lock our position in. If we were getting hit, the enemy attack force would be out in the open now; we'd smash them with our coun-terwall of fire.

The platoons had flipped on their radios. All re-ported heavy incoming but no ground attack, though

3d Platoon leader Joe Stokes had lost contact with his outpost. He said he'd send some people out to check on it as soon as the worst of the present barrage ceased. In the meantime our patrol at the Pines had seen no enemy movement. I told these men to sit tight and try to avoid making contact. I wanted only one ball game at a time.

Stokes reported contact—infantry force, size unknown, on his reverse slope. They weren't in his trench line; he'd had no penetration and didn't know where they'd come from. The other platoons still had no contact when I called Locke with a sitrep; he said E Company had been penetrated, which at least answered the question of where the North Koreans were coming from, but it had been a damn gutsy maneuver on the enemy's part. They had to have come up right through their supporting fires.

I had our FO lift the defensive fire everywhere along the company front except 3d Platoon, and I took off with my radio-telephone operator for Stokes's position. In their first real fight, my boys were cool, alert, and professional. Squad and platoon leaders moved back and forth checking their positions; troops challenged me right down the line.

We passed through 2d Platoon and entered 3d Platoon's trenches. It was a whole different scene at the top of the hill. Total panic. The boys had bunched up, leaving large areas of the trench abandoned. Mortar and artillery fire was still raining down; MG slugs were stitching the top layer of sandbags. The high-profile, shell-shattered bunkers we'd inherited (that had not yet been razed and rebuilt, an ongoing project) were taking fire right through the apertures; the guys inside were pinned down and couldn't return fire. I suddenly realized that was what the barrage the previous night had been all about. The North Koreans had been zeroing. Clever bastards.

I ran over to the E Company tie-in point. The penetration had come at Easy's first fighting bunker; enemy tracks in the wet ground ran right over the top of it. My guys got themselves together and sealed the penetration. We could hear a good firefight raging on the reverse slope near Stokes's CP—no one had a clue as to how many bad guys were down there, but at least now they had no way out.

I went inside the E Company bunker, only to find a certified front-line recreation center. A poncho was over the aperture. Candles were burning. Magazines and playing cards were strewn all over the place, and in the middle of it all were the bodies of two Americans who'd died having fun on the firing line.

Stokes appeared, steady and very much in control in his first big firefight. He was a good man, Joe Stokes. He'd graduated from Oklahoma A&M in agriculture; his father had destroyed his dreams of turning their panhandle plot into a prosperous farm by finding oil all over the joint. Stokes had actually been disappointed. Now he reported in, with his dry sense of humor, that gooks were still alive and well on the reverse slope, but being contained and "whittled down to size," with a dozen enemy dead already. He said there were no friendly KIA but at least ten wounded, and he'd still had no word from the OP.

I told him to clean up the reverse slope; I'd go down to the OP myself as soon as the incoming lightened up. Stokes moved out while I directed the weapons platoon leader to get tank, recoilless rifle, and .50-cal fire onto No Name to shut off the MG fire still ripping right into the position, and I organized a squad of Stokes's people under PFC Lindeman to check on the OP. I finally had a chance to check in with my CP; the patrol still had no contact. I told Adkins, my communications sergeant, to return these men to the main line and have platoon leader Joe Rice meet them at the patrol gate in front of his 1st Platoon. No doubt the boys below would be a little trigger-happy with so much action just up the ridge, but if Rice was out there, he'd make damn certain that weapons remained locked and the patrol not be chopped up by jittery friendlies.

We arrived at Stokes's outpost to find two men dead, bayoneted and their throats slit. The third man, Haley, was missing, and the enemy long gone. The OP had been taken by stealth and surprise; there were no spent cartridges to be seen, just long gray ashes from cigarettes that hadn't died as quickly as their smokers. A poncho lay crumpled at the bottom of the hole—a picture worth a thousand words. Haley and the two KIA had been sleepers—guys who'd habitually dozed off on the line, putting the rest of my soldiers at unnecessary risk. I'd ordered Stokes to make them permanent OP until they got their shit together (my reasoning had been that no one would dare screw off there); they must have thought school was out when they covered the foxhole with that poncho and lit up.

I spent the rest of the night with Lindeman and his squad, searching for the missing man in no-man's land. We went all the way down to the valley floor—which was still being pulverized by U.S. artillery fire—but Haley was nowhere to be seen. Fresh tracks gave us the first clue as to the size of the raiding enemy force: two, maybe three, platoons. Then it was getting light so we gave up the search, and with heavy hearts moved back to the OP to pick up the dead and take them to our lines.

By the time I got back to 3d Platoon, the enemy dead had been searched and neatly stacked, like sacks of potatoes. The North Koreans had put on a good show, even if they'd lost two dozen men. They'd knocked off the OP and taken a prisoner; they'd sneaked up the hill and slipped right through the weakest and most critical point in a defensive position —the tie-in point between two separate units—and swept undetected over the reverse slope. Only now did I find it was just the North Koreans' bad luck that ten of Stokes's men were leaving a sleeping bunker to relieve some buddies on line at the same time the enemy appeared on the scene, that I'd come up and closed the penetration behind them, and that the beautifully detailed map of our position (both fighting and rear), which undoubtedly had been made with inside information (probably one of the Korean laborers was a spy) and which we found on one of the dead, was a direct replica not of our position as we were rebuilding it, but as it was when we'd come onto the hill two weeks before.

The major lessons learned concerned sleepers, smokers, and sloppy procedures. Henceforth (following the lead of Red Smalling in the Easy Company days), sleepers would have the shit beat out of them by their leaders. Cigarettes, which could be seen for miles, were as good as an engraved invitation to the enemy to "come and get me," so from that moment forward, smoking was prohibited from sunset to sunrise anywhere on the hill. Transgressors would meet the same fate as the sleepers.

It had been sloppy not to inspect the Easy Company tie-in position every time we checked our line. If I'd been the 3d Platoon leader, I was sure I would have done so—at least I thought I would—but as company commander, I *definitely* should have. Henceforth, though, it would be the rule. We also placed tactical barbed wire, complete with mines and flares, along our reverse-slope boundary with E Company. This caused quite a row between me and the Easy CO, but I wouldn't bend. I was rarely burned more than once.

During the attack, the guys of 3d Platoon had bunched up, five and six guys in bunkers designed for two. It was a natural herd instinct I'd seen a million times, but it might have been prevented had a local counterattack force been appointed the moment we got on the hill and the guys trained accordingly. It should have been SOP; instead, more sloppiness on both Stokes's and my parts (and worse for me, because I should have known better).

After the wounded had been evacuated, I went back to my CP to record the action: the mistakes, the casualties, the lessons learned. My little book would be a valuable teaching aid; I'd go over it with the troops, and when we got into reserve, we'd go over it again, again, and again. But I did not write down my own mistakes. I didn't have to. My own lesson learned was indelibly etched in my brain: the image of two dead soldiers whom I'd known were irresponsible, yet whom I'd tasked with the safety of my unit. I'd violated security and sent them to their deaths. Haley, the third man, was the only soldier ever captured from my command; he was released some months later as part of Operation Little Switch. But the tragic, unnecessary losses—a direct result of the worst command decision I would ever make—were crosses I would bear for the rest of my life. *Happy birthday, Hack. How's it feel to be twenty-two?*

The first snow came on 17 November. Unlike the previous Korean winters, we were well-equipped from the start: warm as toast with cold-weather gear (including experimental pocket warmers) and lightweight, bulkless eight-pound armor vests that a .38 slug wouldn't penetrate. The latter reduced casualties and kept chests, backs, and guts warm; it was SOP to wear them on the hill twenty-four hours a day.

With the cold came more incoming and more enemy probes. It seemed as if the North Koreans were making one last effort before the real winter set in;

only then would they go to ground and more or less hibernate for the season. But my soldiers—who were getting better every day on the line—weathered it all, including some savage hand-to-hand combat against probes that made it through the barbed wire in front of the position.

Whenever I could get permission from Battalion, I'd have a turkey shoot. At Fort Benning they'd called it the Mad Minute—a demonstration designed to show students the Army's available combat power. On position, it served much the same purpose, but it also allowed us to test all weapons in a major shoot-out. On signal, after coordinating with units on our right and left so they wouldn't think the world was falling in, we'd fire every available weapon at the enemy's position: rifles, BARs, MGs, and recoilless rifles, as well as supporting artillery and whatever else was around, like tanks, mortars, and quad .50s. I set out in advance the number of rounds each weapon would fire, so the whole thing was controlled, but for those few deafening minutes it was the wildest fireworks display you could ever hope to see, with red tracers arching gracefully through majestic Willie Peter, and HE shells thundering down. You name it, we had it, and the troops loved it, especially at night. The turkey shoot also helped rotate ammo, thus ensuring good, fresh stuff when we needed it; on top of that, it must have had a pretty devastating psychological effect on the North Koreans across the valley (not to mention the damage it did to any enemy caught roaming around in no-man's land).

As confidence grew among the troops, so did improvisation. In the daylight hours, where any movement in the trenches brought mortar fire right onto your head, or a dalliance near an aperture of a fighting bunker was an odds-on bet you'd get one between the horns, the troops stayed underground, sleeping, writing letters, and inventing more savage ways of sticking it to the enemy. An old standard by now was the placing of 55-gallon drums of napalm (each with a white phosphorous grenade set in the top as a fuse) in front of each platoon. In an enemy attack, a wire running back to our lines would be pulled, and the whole jellied mess would go up in a fiery roar, lighting the battlefield like day and denying the enemy even a moment to hotfoot it out of there. Another was the old napalm-inside-the-suitcase trick: empty .50-cal ammo boxes filled with napalm, fitted out with a fuse and wrapped with barbed wire. This device could be thrown over the trench wall; the explosion scattered metal and barbed-wire fragments right, left, and center of the attacker. Unfortunately there was a lot of wastage with this one (troopers had a tendency to throw it at any and every noise), but at least we always roasted a couple of rats, and they were the enemy, too.

The morning of 18 December was cold and snow-covered. I'd stood the company down to ten percent (we stayed at ten percent during the day, fifty percent at night, and only when it hotted up did we "stand to" in the old British naval tradition, with 100 percent of the force locked and cocked behind their weapons and in their fighting positions), and because there wasn't anything urgent to attend to, I went out to my observation post to have a look at the battlefield before catching some shut-eye.

The OP was equipped with a battery commander's (BC) scope, a highly magnified binocular periscope with which at a thousand yards you could tell if a soldier had shaved that day. It was hard to put the thing to the test in the trenches though: our North Korean counterparts were masters of camouflage and deception, and during the day you could look into the enemy positions no more than 600 to 800 yards distant and not see a thing. Aerial photos for our area of operation showed their line to be entrenched in great depth—on the average, fourteen miles—with the mazelike, stacked positions having no tactical integrity, at least from a Western point of view. We'd heard that some of the Communists' underground chambers could shelter whole battalions; I believed it—they were great diggers—but to look across the valley, you'd never know.

As I'd expected when I peered through the scope, all was quiet. But when I turned my attention to the Pines, I saw white-on-white movement against the snow. I could barely believe my eyes. Bold as life, like animated snowmen, half a dozen North Koreans in overwhite camouflage gear were rolling up commo wire abandoned by U.S. patrols. At 1130 hours! Guess they thought, *It's daytime . . . Yanks sleep . . . no one will see,* and to the naked eye, it would have been true. Without the scope, there would have been no way to discern them against the landscape.

I called Joe Rice, a great patroller at any time but one who personally preferred daylight work. He immediately moved out with a five-man patrol. He packed his own radio so we had great commo; it meant I could watch Joe's movements and provide direction at the same time I kept my eye on the snowmen.

In the meantime I rang up Homer Smith to get cracking with a backup element, and gave my FO a warning order to be prepared to blow No Name sky-high. I brought the company to stand to, told the platoon leaders the situation, and ordered a good old-fashioned turkey shoot as accompaniment to Joe's action in the valley (firing on order, keeping the stuff high and only at the enemy trenches).

From my OP I watched Joe positioning his people. I saw the carefree North Koreans working through the Pines and disappearing into some old bunkers. I told

Joe exactly where they were. It was like watching a silent movie—an amazing thing to watch an entire action from beginning to end in such detail and in such safety. Joe moved like a stalking tiger, his men providing security from concealed positions. A North Korean stuck his head out of a bunker. Joe shot him. The guy fell back, and Joe threw a grenade. I told him another North Korean was crawling out the left side of the bunker. He moved over and shot that guy, too. The North Korean rolled down the hill as Platoon Sergeant Allison opened fire on him.

In the meantime the North Koreans in the trenches on No Name woke up. A machine gun opened fire. One of our patrol men fell. I pulled the chain and the turkey shoot began, like an erupting volcano. One enemy soldier got so excited that he jumped on top of the trench line, waving his arms wildly until he took a direct hit and was splattered across the hillside. I figured he was the company CO (who must have been even more shocked by what he saw in the valley than I'd been; imagine watching one of your patrols being scooped up in front of your own main line of resistance in broad daylight).

It was a magic morning. With only one casualty of our own, we'd netted two POWs and two enemy KIA, not to mention those killed during the company turkey shoot. Through my BC scope I watched Smitty's nine-man support group move swiftly forward to evacuate the POWs and our WIA. I told Joe's people to shift the enemy dead to a small clearing. That night we laid an ambush, using the dead as bait. An enemy patrol fell right into the trap: their comrades had frozen fast to the ground, and while a couple of white figures worked to break them loose, our ambush went into action and killed the whole enemy crew. All in all, it was not a bad day's work for Fighter.

Within a few hours of Joe's return, our position was inundated with visitors from Battalion, Regiment, Division, Corps, and Army. Our prisoners were the first to be captured in ages, and when the POWs admitted that they'd been tasked with getting intelligence for a regimental-sized attack—the North Korean recon patrol had moved into the Pines that morning to get a head start, but had been undone by their patrol leader, who couldn't resist picking up the rich man's wire—higher headquarters got so excited they could barely contain themselves. We got stacks of replacements and top priority on everything. Another element was brought in east of the Gap; G Company shifted over and took part of our line to give Rice's platoon (who would take the brunt of an enemy attack) a tighter, stronger position.

But Christmas came and went, and the attack never came at all, and after all the excitement, the general thought was that the North Koreans had called it off on the assumption that the POWs we took had compromised it, as indeed they had.

Guess those gooks weren't as dumb as we'd thought they were.

Chapter 10
Beating the Odds

★ ★ ★

With the New Year came the final good-bye to Colonel Locke. The meanest mother in the valley was going home. His visits had grown less frequent as he became a short-timer. On one of the last he'd been sitting on my sack, chewing tobacco and musing that he had only twenty-eight "goddamn days" to go. Without thinking, I'd replied, "Oh, no, sir, you only have twenty-seven," and he'd been surprised. How did I know? he asked. I was used to having to think quickly with Locke around: "In your battalion, sir, it's an officer's duty to know every important detail." I couldn't tell him we 2d Batt officers were counting down his DEROS (Date Eligible Return from Overseas) almost as eagerly as he.

Locke's last day in the battalion was related to me by Dick Weden, now HQ Company CO, who went to the rear CP that morning to make sure the Colonel got off all right. He told me Locke had gone into the mess about 0530 (old soldiers don't know how to sleep in), and when the mess sergeant served him his eggs, Locke had looked at them, put his hand under the plate, and slammed the eggs over onto the table. "You

goddamn people will never know how I like my eggs!"
he'd snarled. With that, he put on his hat, picked up
his gear (one tiny AWOL bag, when most senior
officers had two or three footlockers), got into his
jeep, and drove away—without looking back even
once.

At the end of February we were relieved and sent
back to Eighth Army reserve to train. As we slipped off
the hill, I saw my company together for the first time
in four months. It was one of the great shocks of my
life—suddenly I thought I'd been commanding a
company from the King's First African Regiment.
There'd been no natural light in the underground
bunkers; while we'd devised a great lighting system for
the CP (a truck battery hooked up to a sealed-beam
headlight), the troops had had to come up with a field
expedient. Some had had candles, but for most it was
mosquito repellent with a cloth wick. The latter sent
off pounds of black soot, and with water rarer than
good wine, no one had ever thought to wash the grime
off his face and hands. So it just sat there, getting
darker and thicker, until now, standing before me on
that cold, cold morning, wearing long, green field
coats and pile caps tied under their chins, were almost
200 black-faced hill people with straggly, long hair,
haunted eyes, and bedrolls under their arms.

Six weeks later Fighter Company and I (newly
promoted to captain) were back on the line, this time
east of the Gap. *Oh, for the days* . . . I'd sometimes
think about our last position. It hadn't been good, but
this place was horrific. We relieved a South Korean
unit that must have known as little about field sanitation as it did about fighting. The position on Hill 930
was basically a foul-smelling, open-air latrine; our
predecessors had crapped wherever the urge came.
The stench only got worse as the snow melted, reveal-

ing North Korean bodies hung on the protective wire in various states of decay. When our CP line went out and wireman Hansen left the trench to fix it, in the dark he found a Chinese tennis shoe near the wire. It was a great souvenir and he brought it back to show us. "Look what I found!" he shouted as he burst into the CP, only then noticing in the CP's dim light the greenish-black Communist foot that was still inside the shoe. He turned green, too, and immediately puked his guts out.

The sun never seemed to shine here. Cordite and smoke-generator fog kept the place gray and stinking. Nothing was growing; it had all been pounded away, making the hill like an elevated sand pit. Yet the incoming was still as regular as breathing, the noise so deafening, the barrage so intense sometimes that you were sure no one would survive. *It's always the one you can't hear that gets you,* you'd think, crawling inside your flak jacket while trying to figure the odds of one of those 120mm Soviet mortar shells bearing your name. Amazingly, we took few casualties. The troops just screwed themselves deeper and deeper into the ground.

Hill 930 was a steep, winding, thousand-yard climb from the nearest road. A sandbagged station at the base held prepackaged supplies; SOP was "both hands full," and a trooper's minimum load on the way up was two five-gallon cans of water—100 pounds' worth—or a case of C's, ammo, or radio batteries. This made for a bitch of a climb; it took a good hour considering the load you'd carry and your frequent dives into foxholes dug in along the way.

The relentless incoming notwithstanding, the position was easier to defend than the one we'd left six weeks before. It consisted of three ridgelines, each a steep, narrow company-sized avenue of approach that led directly into our battle positions. We'd inherited damn good wire and mine work (other than the sanitation conditions, the South Koreans we relieved had actually kept the position in fine shape) that channeled the enemy right into our defensive fires. The outpost line was excellent—well dug, good wire, with a formidable squad-sized bunker on the military crest of each ridge, with a deep, connecting trench back to the main line. A couple of hundred yards below we had nighttime floating listening posts (LPs), which would find the enemy and bop back to the nearest outpost, which, in turn, would call for help. Then we'd get artillery going—thousands of rounds' worth—and flares to light up the sky, while the OP took the attackers under fire and scooted back to the line. By then the rest of the company would be at 100 percent and ready to do battle, be it with grenades, bullets, or bayonets.

There were no trees left on the hill, yet looking into the nighttime darkness beyond which lay the enemy, it almost seemed like an impenetrable jungle out there. In silhouette you'd see metal stakes jutting up at weird angles, wrapped in barbed wire and haphazardly rooted in the earth; around these were big rolls of concertina wire. In a way it *was* a jungle—an awesome jungle of death—but by no means impenetrable. The North Koreans still had their gutsy little sappers—damn good soldiers, all of them—who'd crawl up to the line and silently clip through, or blow a hole in the wire with bangalore torpedoes. Their infantry would be right behind, to rush through the custom-made gap.

Our OP/LP system stymied most of the not-infrequent enemy attacks. Alert soldiers meant no Pearl Harbors, and our artillery defensive concentrations hammered down on the aggressors before they could breach the wire. One night we got more than fifty enemy KIA without one trooper's weapon being fired: the enemy walked right into a killing zone and got smashed.

The Americans really had the best, and best-supplied, artillery in the world. Historically it, and the eager outpouring of our assembly lines, had won every war since the North's heavy industrial base brought the South to its knees in the Civil War. Tactical skill, the abilities of generals—both came second to our capability to outequip and outshoot our opponents. I often remembered Italy in 1946, when I was detailed to guard German prisoners of war. One of the prisoners was a damn tough lieutenant captured at Salerno. He spoke English, so I whiled away my duty hours giving him a hard time. Once I asked him why, if he and all his kraut friends were such brilliant soldiers and such supermen, was fifteen-year-old me the one holding the weapon, and he was a prisoner of war. He answered me with a story. "I was an 88mm antitank battery commander," he said. "We were on a hill, and the Americans kept sending tanks down the road below. Every time they sent a tank, we knocked it out. They kept sending tanks, and we kept knocking them out, until we finally ran out of ammunition. The reason I'm here," he finished his story, "is that the Americans didn't run out of tanks."

Now the Air Force was doing a job on North Korea: 700 tons of bombs and thousands of gallons of napalm sometimes dropped on the capital, Pyongyang, in a day. It was a strategy of sorts: bomb them back to the Stone Age to keep them at the bargaining table at Panmunjom. The only thing that didn't track was my memory of things I'd read about Nazi Germany. We bombed them to kingdom come, too, but a month before the surrender, their wartime production levels were at an all-time high. Still, this doubt was easy to put aside when you were stuck in the trenches and the enemy was on the move: the more arty, the more air, the better.

One attack that did get through Fighter's barrier defenses was localized to 2d Platoon. When I saw that the rest of the company wasn't under attack, my RTO and I went racing down the trench to lend a little moral support. A mortar round came crashing in on top of the sandbag-lined trench right between us. Fortunately, it didn't knock me down. In fact, it kind of inspired me to pick up the pace on the downhill stretch. The RTO was packing a PR-10 and I had the handset; the radio cord between us went taut—he wasn't keeping up. After a few feet of this I turned around to tell him to stop dragging his ass, only to find it was about all he could do, and that was only because I was there pulling him along by the radio cord. The RTO no longer had a head. He must have walked right into that mortar round. Three feet ahead of him, I'd been untouched. It was the luck of the draw—and my first thought was I needed another RTO.

A few days later I had to brief four NCOs who were to lead a complicated patrol. We met at first light, the only time we could get away with it without being blown away by enemy sniper or mortar fire, and lay down in an open 75mm recoilless-rifle position. The sun was just rising as we poked our heads up, eyeballed the fog-enshrouded objective and rally points, and discussed the plan. When I was finished issuing my orders, I ducked and weaved my way back to my CP bunker, leaving the two patrol leaders and their FOs to tie down final details between themselves. Just as I was about to enter the bunker I heard a *whoosh* and an earth-shattering thump. Ugly, black 120mm mortar smoke rose from the position I'd just left. I ran back to find one leader dead, one guy with gaping chest wounds, and the other two minus legs—all from one round, out of the blue, right on target. I couldn't do anything for the chest wound, but I thrust my hands into the legless men's stumps to stop the wild rush of blood pumping out of their femoral arteries. I held on until the medics took over; before long, litter bearers had the KIA and wounded leaders on their way down the torturous windy trail, and I was left with the problem of who the hell I'd get to lead the raid. Of course, replacements were found, and the patrol crossed the LD on time.

One of the things about combat that remains unexplainable to those who've never experienced it is the apparent callousness in the face of death. I'd learned the first year in Korea that in war a soldier or a leader is about as indispensable as the hole left by a finger in a glass of water. Every good leader is missed—as an individual—and there are never enough real leaders, but there is always someone to pick up the chips and do the job. The fact is, generally there's no "time-out" for mourning on the battlefield. But it's really no different than the father of ten who comes home to find his house on fire with all his kids sleeping inside. He doesn't stop and cry over the first child he finds dead. To do so would be to sign a death warrant for the other nine. A CO is often in the same situation. To do anything but continue on would be complete dereliction of duty, and, in the larger picture, could possibly lead to even worse carnage among his troops. So you do what you have to do, and only later, when things settle down, do you allow yourself to grieve.

Life went on on Hill 930, and an interesting thing started to happen in Fighter Company. The boys doing all the fighting were doing it very well. They seldom got rattled, they handled incoming and probes in steady stride, like pros, and day by day ~~were~~ getting even better.* Yet at the same time, the quality of the chow was getting worse and worse. We had only one hot meal a day, and every night it was colder and more awful than the one we got the night before. An army travels on its belly, or so said Napoleon; food, mail, and thirty-six points—the magic number that meant you could rotate home†—were about the only damn things the troops had to look forward to, and the crap they were eating limited the horizons a bit too much.

I began a little investigation, only to find that the mess sergeant and cooks were completely burned out. Cajoling and threatening them didn't work, and when I realized nothing short of lining them up against a wall would, the only course of action was to fire everybody. I made rifle squad leader Sergeant Louis Bravo mess sergeant, and he went to the troops: "Any of you guys cook in civilian life?" He got about 200 volunteers, took the most promising off the line, and almost immediately started putting out truly incredible meals. Unlike the old crew, my gung-ho, newly ex-infantry cooks knew well how important food was to the guys on line; suddenly we were eating French and Italian, and Bravo's hailing from New Orleans guaranteed some wild Cajun delights. How the new cooks scrounged all the good things they did was something I was probably happier not knowing, but there was no doubt in my mind that Napoleon would

---

*In contrast to my first four-month line period with Fighter, when we'd taken an average of one casualty per day, in the second period (about three months) we had just two KIA and fifteen wounded, even as both incoming and enemy attacks were four or five times as intense.

†Three points per month in a noncombat role; four points per month that a soldier was on the line

have decorated Bravo's raiders on the basis of the first bite, every night of the week.

The mess experiment worked so well I decided to do it on the supply end, too. My supply sergeant was a nice guy, but his heart wasn't in it. He just didn't appreciate that extra pair of socks or that extra can of rations. So I replaced him with Sergeant Toohey, another fine rifle squad leader, who instantly became a master scrounger. There was nothing that boy couldn't get. "Here you are, sir," he'd say, flashing a great grin as he plunked his newest acquisition down before me. Sometimes I wondered if I should ask him for North Korean General Kim Il Sung's head on a platter. It might have brought the war to a speedy end.

After the food was squared away, Bravo got the idea of giving the troops a midnight snack of soup and coffee. Brinkley, one of the new ex-infantry cooks, thought this was a great idea and volunteered for the job. He organized a hill kitchen in a vacant bunker near the company CP, and soon every night we had hot soup (from those delicious dehydrated soup packets) and fresh, strong coffee just when we needed it most.

Then, in accordance with the Great American Dream, evolution occurred. Before I knew it, Brinkley had a big production bakery going on top of the hill. He carefully lined the hub of his booming enterprise with ammo containers to make it ratproof, and outfitted it with stoves and all kinds of kitchen paraphernalia. At midnight the warm aroma of cinnamon rolls and coffee cakes, hot soup and coffee, wafted through the position. Runners from each platoon shuttled mouth-watering treats from the bakery to their buddies. No doubt it pissed off the North Koreans, who didn't get a share; now and then they'd send a mortar round in Brinkley's direction, and our resident baker was probably the only cook in Eighth Army to get wounded four times. But the wounds were superficial, none of the cakes seemed to fall, and the bakery was always open for business the next night.

Lieutenant Colonel Herbert Mansfield, the commander of 2d Battalion at this time of my tour, came up to see us every week or so. I liked him. He was a WW II Airborne vet, and an old friend of the division commander, Major General Joe Cleland. Like General Cleland, who'd made me the youngest company commander in Korea when I was twenty-one and had since served as a mentor and fatherly friend, Colonel Mansfield took a keen interest in my development, offering regular and useful advice on all things military. He also wore his .45 along his spine under his web belt, a trick I loved and, from the moment I saw it, I adopted for my own.

Mansfield was always cheerful when he trooped the line, but as I got closer and closer to, and then passed, the thirty-six-point rotation mark, we got into a running argument about my going home. The bottom line was I just didn't want to go. For one thing, a three-year officer commitment had come along with my battlefield commission, and I hoped to see it out with Fighter Company; for another, it looked like the war would soon be entering its fourth year, and I couldn't see myself walking away. And then there was the issue of who I'd have to leave my company *with*, and as far as I was concerned, it couldn't be with anyone but the best. So the Colonel and I would fight. He would suggest people, and I would tell him they were wimps. I wanted Lieutenant Richard Alexander, a young officer from Boston who'd joined us in reserve and had since proved himself to be not only a stud, but the kind of guy who'd lead Fighter with the same spirit I had.

The thing was, when you're with a unit for a long time, it becomes a raging love affair. Fighter and I belonged together, and the hand-and-glove factor could be seen in the faces and manner of all the troops. They weren't exactly carbon copies of their Old Man, but they'd developed a certain style, I guess it could be called, from me. It was only natural; since I was a little kid, I'd always latched on to someone I respected, an Al Hewitt or a Steve Prazenka, and knocked off anything I liked about him to make my own. It was the same in the Army—my adopting Colonel Mansfield's pistol-packing procedure, for example. If a trooper likes his CO and the CO wears his hat at a bit of an angle, the trooper starts wearing his hat like that, too. If the CO acts cocky, confident, and sure of himself, so do the boys. It's kind of like tailor-making your own coat. You steal the best-designed sleeves, pockets, buttons, and lapels you see, and one by one put them on, until you've got the perfect coat, which, just by wearing it, you grow into until it fits and becomes uniquely yours.

I wanted Alex to replace me because we were cut from the same bolt of cloth. What I liked about him was he was a brave, no-nonsense man who was never exactly insubordinate, but close. Nothing was worth taking seriously, according to Alexander; as a result, he was a calm, cool platoon leader who looked after his troops (and they loved him for it), at the same time leaving lots of room for showmanship. I'd never forget the night an enemy force got itself behind Alex's patrol and I couldn't raise him on the radio to tell him. About the time I knew he'd be saddling up to come home, I got artillery and flares peppering in all over his planned return route (which was where the North Koreans were laid up). It was kind of dangerous, but I figured Alex would come up on the radio to tell us to shut it off and I could tell him about the enemy and an alternate return route. He didn't. In desperation, just when I knew he had only enough time to make it back to our lines before light, I stood on top of a front-line bunker and yelled at the top of my lungs into the dead-quiet valley below.

"Alex! This is Hack! Come back through the First Platoon. Don't go as planned. Come back through First Platoon!"

A moment later a voice bellowed up from no-man's land. "Okay, Hack! First Platoon!"

He told me when he got back that his radio had gone out; he'd assumed with all the friendly fire and all the light that something wasn't right, and had already decided to come back a different route. No sweat.

So I wanted Alexander. Mansfield refused. He didn't like Alex; he told me he was a "wise-ass." Which was true, but all my guys were wise-asses. Cocky wise-asses, in fact, because that's what I wanted them to be. You've got to be pretty confident to spend your days as a moving target. The next thing I knew, Mansfield decided to send one of his staff captains to take over Fighter. I hit the roof. I'd known the guy in Trieste. He was worthless as a troop commander, and I didn't want him having anything to do with my unit. Mansfield and I got into a very big argument, but in the end, naturally, I lost. The staff captain came up to take command of the company, and I went down to Battalion staff until I got my orders to go home.

Less than a week later I stood outside the battalion CP with Colonel Mansfield, watching my old company being savaged. The hilltop home of Fighter's CP and Brinkley's bakery had become an inferno. Staring up in the dark, it looked to us as though they'd been overrun, but there was no way to find out: Fighter was silent, with no one up there manning the radio or switchboard. I was getting more anxious by the second; the Colonel was worried, too, so when I sug-

Trieste United States Troops (TRUST) 351st Regimental Headquarters Company precedes the regiment in review, June 1950.

A soldier's soldier: Sergeant Steve Prazenka, Trieste, 1949.

Korea, April 1951. Third Platoon of George Company, 27th "Wolfhound" Regiment, crapped out on the side of the road. In the foreground, platoon leader Walt Schroeder (standing) and platoon sergeant Hackworth.

Captain Jack Michaely. As skipper of G Company/27th Wolfhounds, in the first year of the Korean War Michaely was the longest-serving rifle company commander in the 25th Division.

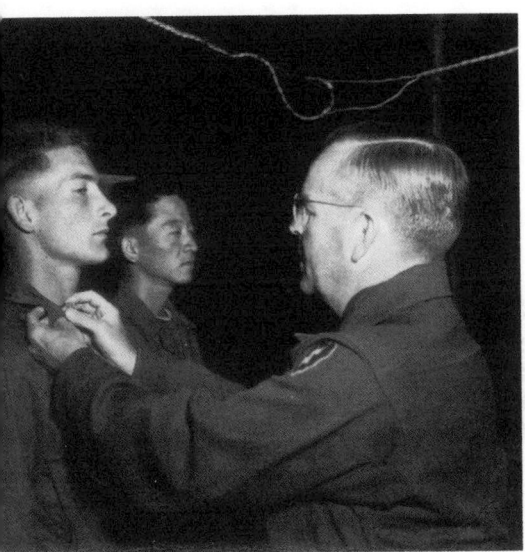

The battlefield commissioning of Sergeant Hackworth by Brigadier General J. Sladin Bradley. Twenty-fifth Division Headquarters, Korea, 5 May 1951.

Great fighter Federico "Chris" Crispino. Korea, September 1951.

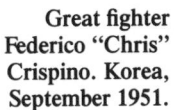

Hell-raising Raider Jack Speed and his Thompson submachine gun. Korea, October 1951.

The 27th Wolfhound Raiders. Front rank from left: Salazar, Evans, Mayamura, Lipka, Sovereign, McLain. Middle distance: platoon sergeant Crispino. Foreground: Lieutenant Hackworth.

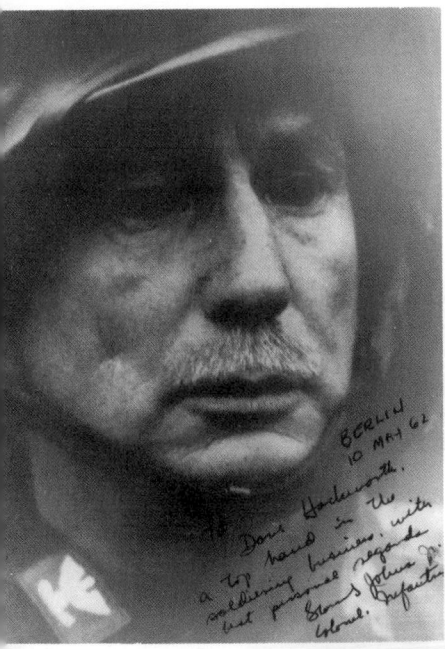

Colonel Glover S. Johns, great leader of men. In August 1961, Johns' 1/18th Infantry "Vanguards" reinforced the American garrison in West Berlin when Khrushchev built the Berlin Wall. Thanks to Johns, this show of force was a near-perfect military operation.

With the 1st Brigade, 101st Airborne ("Screaming Eagles") Division at My Canh, Republic of Vietnam, February 1966. The previous day the 1/327 Tigers had run into an NVA buzzsaw in this rice paddy. The enemy had deployed along the hedgerow to the rear.

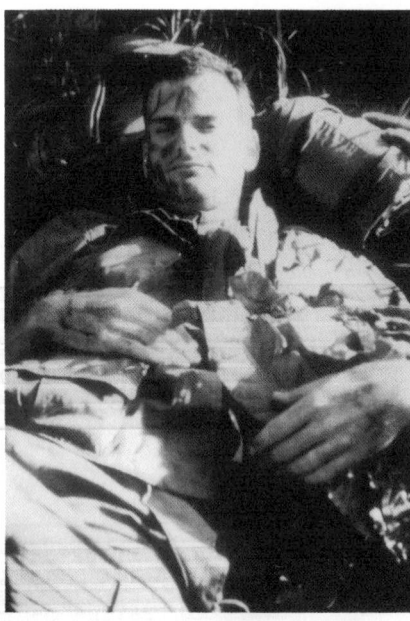

The bravest of the brave: battalion surgeon "Doc" Raphiel Benjamin, before an air mobile assault.

The day after the My Canh fight. From left: Hack, Johnny Howard, Don Chapman.

June 1966. After the 1/327 "Above the Rest" Battalion's triumphant return from the Dak To battlefield. Foreground: PFC James Deardorff. Background: Hack and 1/101st Brigade commander General Willard Pearson.

The 1/327 Airborne Infantry Battalion marches proudly into the Screaming Eagles' base camp after their victory at Dak To, June 1966.

Brigade commander Hank "the Gunfighter" Emerson confers with battalion CO Don Schroeder. Mekong Delta, 1968.

A memorial service for the men of D Company, 4/39 Infantry, who died when their position was overrun. Fire Support Base Danger, Mekong Delta, March 1969.

gested I go up and find out what was going on, he gave me the green light and I was off, radio operator in tow. We ran straight up the hill, through Easy's trenches. It was a quick trip, mainly because hardly anyone bothered to challenge us. When I hit Fighter, the first thing I heard was "Halt!" Just one of the guys doing as he'd been taught.

"Hackworth!" I yelled, and kept running.

"Halt!"

"Hackworth!"

"Halt!"

"Hackworth!"

"Shit, sir, it's great to hear you," I heard again and again as I moved through the trench. All I wanted to know was what the hell was happening. No one had any idea. All they knew was they got hit bad, no artillery went out, no one could raise the CP on the phone, and it looked as if the penetration had been right up the center of the company sector. I bumped into Alex, who'd taken command by default. He'd sealed the penetration and was now cleaning up the gooks on the reverse slope. When everything was under control, I ran down to the company CP. Inside, all was quiet. The commo sergeant was dead, blown up by a grenade. The inner door, between the commo shack and the CO bunker, was closed. I kicked it open. There, sitting on the little chair that used to be mine, was the new captain, head down between his legs, crying. I walked up to him and belted him in the mouth.

I got on the horn to Battalion. I told Mansfield the situation, and that I'd assumed command from this babbling son of a bitch. And I told him he damn well better give Fighter to Alex, whose platoon had just saved the whole unit moments before. *Now* he agreed.

I went out to the OP in front of 2d Platoon. It was just getting light, and in about fifteen minutes it would be a very uncool place to be. But I wanted to have a last look. I wanted to figure out for myself how it had happened, how—after all the months of combat, all the love and the hard, hard work all of us had put into it—I had come to receive as my farewell present the vision of my company being overrun.

Fighter's men were cleaning up the battlefield, evacuating our dead and wounded. But as I watched the sights, and listened to the sounds, of death all around me, I suddenly felt, somehow, removed. As if I were watching, from a great distance, a surreal dumb show not intended for an audience.

For almost three years I'd seen, heard, and smelled death among my friends and among my men. But in that moment I knew that never before had I *felt* death so strongly. It was a dull horror that spread from my gut to my heart, to my limbs and to my head. And I knew that the fate of Fighter was no longer in my hands, any more than George or Easy or the Raiders would ever be again.

It was time to go home.

Chapter 11
Between Wars

★ ★ ★

The Korean War ended about six weeks after I returned to the United States, leaving me with a postcombat hangover for which no "hair of the dog" cure existed. Almost immediately I left active duty to pursue my long-neglected education—the only hope I had, warned my Army mentors, of surviving the inevitable postwar troop-strength cuts. I did join the Reserves, however, so I wouldn't completely lose touch with my first love; still, when I returned to active duty in 1955 with two years of college behind me, it was to an Army world entirely different from the one I'd left.

This was one in which the mettle of men counted for little and "push-button warfare" was the perceived wave of the future. In this New Army, I was assigned to an air defense outfit and spent the next few years staring up at the sky, waiting for the Soviet air force to strike. As an air defense commander, my finger was ever on the button, ready to let loose with any number of projectiles from America's rapidly growing missile arsenal against whatever the Soviets threw at us from theirs.

A three-year tour in Germany followed, during which I was both promoted to major and happily returned to the ways of the Old Army I'd grown up in, thanks to a stint with the 1/18th Infantry "Vanguards" under the command of the best commander I'd ever known, Colonel Glover S. Johns. And for all the talk of push-button war, when the Cold War talk of the fifties exploded into a near shoot-out in August of 1961 with the Communists' building of the Berlin Wall, it was not missiles, but men of the thin red line who provided America's show of strength, when the Vanguards traveled 435 miles in a 491-vehicle convoy through twenty Soviet divisions and 110,000 East German soldiers to reinforce the U.S. garrison in the beleaguered city of Berlin.

Meanwhile, American muscle was beginning to be flexed in Southeast Asia, and I wanted to be part of the action. In 1962 I volunteered to go to Vietnam as part of the American training mission whose purpose was to advise and train the South Vietnamese Army (ARVN) in its ongoing struggle against Ho Chi Minh's Communist guerrillas. My application was rejected on the grounds that I had "too much combat experience," or so said the guys at Personnel; it seemed that the Army's priority was less in training the South Vietnamese than in providing a taste of battle to green American lieutenants who, sharp and dedicated as they might have been, knew next to nothing about infantry combat and had little to offer the Viets they advised.

So I did not get to go to Vietnam in 1962, but I did get the next best thing: an assignment to the 101st Airborne Division at Fort Campbell, Kentucky. For me, at the age of thirty-two, to be a paratrooper in the crack "Screaming Eagles" was a lifelong dream come true, and it kept the warrior in me happy for two and a half years, until after the Cuban Missile Crisis, after

South Vietnamese President Diem's and then U.S. President Kennedy's assassinations, after the Tonkin Gulf episode and the escalating tit-for-tat engagements between Viet Cong guerrillas and American air power which culminated in the VC bombing of the U.S. Embassy and made the insurgent war in Vietnam boil over. Then, finally, I deployed with my Airborne brothers to "the only war we've got."

Chapter 12
Shadows, Boredom, and Victor Charlie

★ ★ ★

The 101st Airborne Division was rated as one of the U.S. Army's top units. Like its sister division, the 82d, it had captured the American imagination from its earliest days, with jumps at Normandy and Holland during the Second World War. Its role in the Ardennes offensive of World War II produced a rich supply of battlefield lore, immortal words such as McAuliffe's reply of "Nuts" to German demands for surrender, and an unknown paratrooper's "They've got us surrounded, the poor bastards," in response to the division's plight.

Few would disagree that paratroopers were an unusual breed of men. Some might even say they were a little nuts. ("Why would anyone jump out of an airplane?" went the rhetorical old saying. "The thing is flying along perfectly well, and there's a guy up front who can put it down on the ground for you. So why jump?") But despite this "leg"—non-Airborne—sentiment, few could honestly argue that the paratroopers weren't the elite of the Army, or that paratroop units were not filled with a cross section of the best studs around. General James "Slim Jim" Gavin was right when he said that if you want to find out if a guy will fight in battle, find out if he'll jump out of an airplane; the average paratrooper was motivated, aggressive, tough-fibered, hard-living, sometimes reckless and even wild.

Airborne was unique. There was the adrenaline rush of the jump itself—the butterflies in your stomach beforehand, the cold wind lashing your face as you stood in the door waiting for the green light, the merciless prop blast as you took the plunge, and then the falling, falling, confident your chute would open but never sure until (thank God) the sudden jerk that told you it had. Then you simply sailed, feeling pretty invincible, with your main concern a rendezvous with the drop zone (DZ) and not with trees or poles or other hard, immovable objects on the ground. And then you landed, and when it was over, everyone was smiling, laughing, happy. Airborne provided a unique sense of oneness among its ranks. From the lowliest private to a two-star general, the shared danger of jumping out of a plane—onto a hot *or* cold DZ—had a leveling effect.

The bonding effect of shared danger meant, too, that no one was unaffected when another man's exhilaration turned to terror, as in the story of the aircraft that ran into engine problems after it had dropped all its troopers in a training jump, leaving the two static (administrative, nonjumping) jumpmasters to decide whether to bail out over the DZ or limp back with the plane to its base in Ohio and go through the hassles of getting home. The jumpmasters chose to bail out with the aircraft's emergency chutes, and on the way down one of them had a malfunction. When the man's body was recovered, it revealed that he'd clawed the whole way through his field jacket, his fatigue jacket, his T-shirt, *and* his own stomach, frantically searching for the D handle on the reserve chute. It was an ingrained thing—main chute malfunctions, pull the D ring on your reserve over your belly. The problem was that the two jumpmasters had used Air Force chutes, which had no reserves. *But for the grace of God, there go I,* thought paratroopers all over the land.

Though inactivated after the Second World War, in the late fifties the 101st "Screaming Eagles" dusted off their parachutes to meet another "rendezvous with destiny" (as the unit motto proclaimed) when they were the Army's first division to be equipped with tactical nuclear weapons. In 1965, some two and a half years after I joined the newly designated 1st Brigade of the 101st (1/101), we took off again, this time as the first U.S.-based unit to be deployed to Vietnam. As the brigade's Operations officer (S-3), I planned and coordinated the move.

I arrived in Vietnam with a brigade advance party about ten days before the troops. Our mission, to prepare for the rest of the unit's arrival, proved difficult, in that the staff of the Military Assistance Command, Vietnam (MACV), didn't seem to know what to do with us. Finally they decided that we would deploy to Cam Ranh Bay, to secure the large-scale construction activities under way along the bay's nineteen-mile peninsula (eventually to result in a first-class harbor, an air base, and other huge logistic facilities). And it was at this time, when I went to recon the huge area for the first time and to work out how to defend it, that the war really began for me in Vietnam.

Grady Jones (S-3 sergeant major), Hank Lunde (S-3 Operations), and I borrowed a jeep from the Special Forces team we were staying with at nearby Dong Ba

Thien, and we tooled down the road toward Cam Ranh Bay. The Green Beret intelligence sergeant had said Dong Ba Thien was a "safe area," so we took our time. The weather was absolutely beautiful, and there was much to be admired in the peaceful, lush green countryside. But as we drove along admiring it, the sultry afternoon air was punctured—*ba dit dit dit*—as a hidden automatic weapon suddenly sent a dozen slugs over our heads. We unassed the jeep in a big hurry and went prone. All was quiet. We searched the area, but there was nothing to see. No sniper, no weapon, no tracks. It was almost as if we'd imagined it. Except that we hadn't, and I'd learned the first of many valuable lessons in the new war: there were no safe areas in Vietnam.

The arrival of the Screaming Eagles' 1st Brigade (which included manuever battalions 1/327, 2/327, and 2/502) in July 1965 brought the total number of American personnel in Vietnam to 79,000. Though the first few weeks after the troops' long boat journey were scheduled for everyone to regain land legs, adjust to the heat, and square away gear, within three days of the brigade's welcome at Cam Ranh Bay by General William Westmoreland—ex–101 commander, now COMUSMACV*—our units were conducting squad- and platoon-size local patrols throughout our area of operation.

At night, on position along the perimeter, skittish green troopers saw a VC behind every bush. Exploding grenades, tracers, and the *bang-thump* of M-79s (a superb 40mm direct-fire infantry weapon) kept everyone awake and on edge as many of the soldiers created a mini-war among themselves. Fortunately, no one

---

*Commander, U.S. Military Assistance Command, Vietnam

was killed. After a few nights' worth of Custer's Last Stand, the brigade commander, Colonel James S. Timothy, issued an order that no rounds would be chambered, a move that significantly reduced the troopers' panic.

The brigade began to settle down as the soldiers got used to the jungle, its shadows and its noises. The only problem was that then they got bored. The men wanted to mix it up with "Victor Charlie," the Viet Cong, and basically Charlie didn't want to cooperate. In fact, despite Province intelligence claims that there were *"beaucoup* VC" in some parts of our AO, we saw very few during the five major operations the 1st Brigade conducted in its first month in Vietnam. Instead, our guerrilla enemy was like an audience at a play in which we, the counterguerrillas, were the unwitting actors: the VC sat in their darkened redoubts and watched and learned, while we played out our roles, warts and all, on a well-lit stage.

The 1st Brigade left Cam Ranh Bay in the last week of August, in what would prove to be only the first of many moves. Over the next six months "Tim's Traveling Trouble" (as we were called in honor of our commander, Colonel Timothy) would travel hundreds of miles by air, water, and road to hot spots in South Vietnam. There was much to be learned as we went along; sometimes those hundreds of miles could have been a million, so different were the terrains from one another and the ways that Charlie fought.

In the Central Highlands there were vast jungles complete with tigers and monkeys and an enemy who, until our arrival, was systematically strangling the countryside, totally disrupting the economy by mining and cutting deep, impassable trenches in the roads, thereby preventing the rural community from getting its products to market on the coast. At Qui Nhon, on the South China Sea, vast expanses of rice paddies (whose harvest we were tasked to protect) offered little cover and concealment to us, but somehow plenty to our cunning opponent, who whittled away at our ranks with snipers and booby traps and the overwhelming support of the people. Lai Khe-Ben Cat was different yet again, with vicious mines and booby traps planted deep within virtually impenetrable double- and triple-canopied rubber-tree jungle.

Our first Highlands mission, to secure the deployment of the 20,000-man-strong 1st Air Cavalry Division and their 420-odd choppers to their base camp at An Khe, was probably the hardest for everyone. Though the brigade successfully opened up and secured Route 19 for the 1st Air Cav's deployment, it was not a fear-free walk in the sun. The road, which linked Qui Nhon on the coast with An Khe and Pleiku in the Central Highlands, was the one on which Mobile Group 100 (*Groupement Mobile 100,* or GM 100), France's finest, had been annihilated eleven years before at the end of the Indochina war. The burned-out hulls of French vehicles, still dotting both sides of the road, provided a sobering image for even the most gung-ho "let's go get 'em!" guys in the brigade.

Still, when a subsequent contact on Route 19 yielded one enemy dead carrying documents identifying him as a member of the 95th Battalion, 2d VC Regiment, it was a day worth celebrating. We'd known all along that the 95th was operating somewhere around An Khe, and the Intelligence shop at Brigade had been working overtime to find them. Now that one of them had been killed along Route 19, we doubled our efforts to get a fix: the 95th was a force to be reckoned with, the fight the troopers needed to get over their boredom, to have their shot at the VC and feel as though they were really in a war.

As intelligence came in and began to form a pattern, the brigade continued to beat the bush. A Hawaiian cook in the 2/502 brought us our first substantial clue: a People's Army, Vietnam (PAVN)* troop he'd captured while scrounging for souvenirs during a patrol he'd joined for the fun of it. The POW was a talkative guy who assured us his comrades were in the vicinity. Brigade Intelligence officer (S-2) Joe Hicks had him flown over the area to see if we could get an exact fix on where. Unfortunately, the POW was scared stiff on his first airplane ride, and couldn't recognize his own belly button at 100 miles per hour, much less the battlefield on the ground below. Fortunately, at just about the same time, a USAF Forward Air Control (FAC) aircraft took fire from a .50-cal machine gun in the vicinity of what we believed through radio intercept was our opponent's battalion command post. After that we thought we had all the pieces of the puzzle, and moved quickly to prevent the 95th from moving first.

Operation Gibraltar, the 1/101's first major confrontation with Charlie, kicked off as scheduled early on the morning of 18 September. Two A1E Skyraider airplanes prepared the single landing zone (LZ) with bombs, and the 2/502 Battalion, under the command of Lieutenant Colonel Wilfrid Smith, conducted an airmobile assault into a clearing in the village of An Ninh. Insufficient troop-lift helicopters meant the 2/502 had to go in piecemeal, three platoons at a time. Insufficient planning time meant no one at brigade or battalion level had had a chance to scrutinize the aerial photographs we'd received late the night before,

*Soon to be known as the North Vietnamese Army (NVA)

which would have clearly shown that An Ninh was not the wisest place to conduct an airmobile assault: the area around the LZ there was nothing less than an armed camp. "Many comrades said they wished the Americans jumped down from helicopters right in this area so they could deal them a long-remembered blow," claimed the author of a VC after-action report on Gibraltar captured months later. ". . . Their landing from helicopters in this area will be a golden opportunity for our unit to achieve merit because we do not have to move, nor minutely investigate, or to spend sleepless nights and exert any effort. Their landing here means certain death for them."

The anonymous scribe was not far wrong. The 2/502 landed dead in the middle of the 95th Battalion's training base. Their LZ was the very same dry rice paddy the VCC troops used to train for defense against airmobile assaults. Though the first lift came in more or less unopposed, when the second lift arrived fifteen minutes later, the LZ was an inferno. Two helicopters were downed right there on the LZ. The commander of B Company was hit while still inside his chopper and was evacuated immediately. The seven U.S. Marine choppers provided to augment elements of the combat-seasoned 52d Aviation Battalion (who'd provided our initial lift) refused to land at all, and instead just turned around and took the troopers they were carrying back to the loading zone.

A third lift, onto an alternate LZ 800 meters away, met with equally heavy ground fire. Alpha Company's CO was hit as soon as he landed (and was immediately evacuated), and in total, the third lift managed to discharge only thirty-six men in two isolated units, totally cut off from each other and the elements of the other two lifts. Meanwhile, C Company's Captain Rawls, who'd come in on the first lift, was killed by machine-gun fire while rallying his troops to attack,* and battalion commander Smith, who was pinned down behind a paddy wall, found himself with no company commanders and fragments of companies fighting independently all over the battle area against a well-entrenched, well-equipped enemy who had rehearsed just such a contingency dozens of times. The VC had gotten their wish.

Smith himself had come in on the second lift. "What's your situation?" Colonel Timothy asked some minutes later, from the command and control (C&C) chopper in which he, Joe Hicks, and I were hovering above the battlefield, as soon as the ground commander established contact with us from the hot LZ.

"We've got a hundred and thirteen dead!" Smith cried.

Timothy looked at me, incredulous. "He's panicking," I said. "There's no way he could take that many casualties in five minutes." And even if he could have, it would have been impossible for him to make any sort of accurate assessment in the time he had been on the ground. Under fire like that, everything becomes exaggerated; my biggest fear in the C&C was that the colonel was going to lose complete control of himself as well as the battle. But as one of the 2/502 officers opined later, "Colonel Smith was never *in* control to lose it," and I believed it was true. From the moment the first elements of the 2/502 hit the ground at An Ninh, it seemed that anything that could possibly go wrong with the operation went wrong, and with a vengeance.

The landing zone Smith had chosen was outside the

---

*When Rawls's body was recovered, his arm was outstretched, his hand pointing directly toward the machine gun that cut him down.

range of our artillery. The task force the arty was moving with was being held up on the wrong side of a mountain range, due to roads turned into bogs by heavy rain or cut by the Viet Cong. Smith had knowingly taken this risk of being beyond the artillery fan: "I don't need artillery," he'd declared in response to Lieutenant Colonel William Braun's concern that Braun's 2/320 Airborne Artillery would not be able to support Smith's assault. "I've got my tac air." The only problem was, come the morning of the operation, Smith did *not* have his tac air. After the first two A1E Skyraiders prepped the LZ and flew away, there was no tac air at An Ninh for a full hour and a half after the 2/502 landed there. Back at Qui Nhon it had been discovered that the fuel for the A1Es had somehow been contaminated, and the planes were grounded. Until MACV scrambled jets out of Bien Hoa to pick up the tac-air slack, the 2/502, except for helicopter gunships, was on its own.

Meanwhile, up in our C&C bird, we received word that not one of the twenty-six troop-carrying choppers designated for this mission was still operational. All had taken multiple hits and could not fly. One of the fainthearted suggested we tell the 2/502 to E&E— escape and evade—forgetting completely that this situation was, in fact, tailor-made for Airborne. The Airborne's very purpose was to drop behind enemy lines. Its men were *trained* to be surrounded and to fight in isolated pockets of resistance. So I called Operations sergeant major Grady Jones, who'd been traveling with the waylaid task force in a jeep outfitted with all our maps and S-2/S-3 gear; he parked on the side of the road, popped a smoke, and soon Timothy, Hicks, and I joined him on the ground to decide what to do next.

Colonel Timothy organized another task force composed of elements of the 2/327, the remnants of the two 2/502 companies that never made it to the battlefield, and elements of the 23d ARVN Ranger Battalion. Captain Duane Messer, the Rangers' fine senior adviser, was authorized to send only two of his companies, but when he heard what a mess we were in, he brought the whole battalion anyway and said he'd worry about the legalities later. We had to tap the 1st Air Cav for lift; with every troop-carrying chopper attached to us out of commission, theirs were the only immediate air assets in the vicinity. But when Bob Miller, my S-3 Air, called over to the Air Cav to request some helicopters, the Cav's chief of staff said, "No way."

"What do you mean, 'No way'?" I yelled through the radio when Miller reported back to me.

"That's what I said," he replied. "I told him we had a battalion getting the shit kicked out of it to protect the 1st Cav's ass and it'd be a nice idea if they'd give us a little support. He said they didn't have flak jackets, and flying without them would violate all their SOPs." (Later I heard the Cav's real bitch was that our action would cheat them out of a few of the thirty precious combat-free days they'd been promised in-country to get themselves set up at An Khe.)

Word traveled fast that we were getting zapped. Before long Lieutenant General John L. Throckmorton, Westmoreland's deputy, flew up from Saigon to find out who was responsible for this disaster and what the hell we planned to do about it. By then we were locked and cocked except for the Air Cav's assets; Timothy explained the situation to the General, Throckmorton made a few calls, and the next thing we knew, the "Flying Horsemen" 1st Air Cav came galloping to the rescue.

Sort of. For reasons unknown, the Cav dropped the

second task force (Task Force Collins, named for the 2/327's CO) at an LZ not two kilometers from An Ninh, as Colonel Timothy had chosen, but five. This destroyed any hope of their linking up with and taking the heat off the 2/502 at all that day. Two daring Air Cav pilots did get much-needed ammo resupply and an 81mm mortar into the battle zone, though, and were able to evacuate five wounded before they had to break off because of heavy enemy fire. ("The choppers weren't even landing," said one participant after the fight. "We were just throwing bodies in.")

On the ground the battle was fought by the NCOs, who'd become the commanders by default as the officers were, one by one, killed or seriously wounded and Colonel Smith remained pinned down behind his paddy wall. But the biggest sting of the fight was word that Major Herb Dexter was also killed. A 7th Div Korea vet with three Special Forces tours to Vietnam under his belt, in this, his fourth tour, Dexter, too, had taken on the role of platoon leader in the effort to turn the battle around. He was hit five times as he led a small band of courageous paratroopers up a heavily fortified, enemy-held hill that dominated the landing zone. "Don't pull back. Don't pull back," he said as he died, and his men heeded him, taking the objective a short time later in hand-to-hand combat, with one brave trooper even storming an enemy mortar and ripping its sights off with his bare hands.

The guys probably best off were the thirty-six who'd come in on the third lift. Though under constant attack, cut off from one another (in groups of eight and twenty-eight men) until noon, and then cut off together from the main body of the battalion for the rest of the day, throughout the battle these men were in the good hands of platoon sergeants Robert Jack and Robert Wightman, two old soldiers with years of combat between them. Wightman had actually found himself in, and fought himself out of, a virtually identical cutoff situation a dozen years before in Korea.

The 2/502 troopers performed magnificently throughout the battle, but never more so than in the early, crucial hours, in the absence of air support, artillery, *and* the commanders all had assumed would be there to lead them. They survived their baptism of fire with sheer guts. At one stage late in the day, a recon man named Freeman even took five prisoners with his disassembled M-16. (The weapon had jammed and he was cleaning it when he saw a VC patrol approaching him. He jumped up and pointed the barrel assembly at them; they threw up their hands and he marched them into his unit's nighttime perimeter.)

Fortunately for all concerned, by midafternoon tac air was in abundance, almost all that was available in-country. Bob Miller had so many planes stacked up, he had to provide alternate targets throughout the battlefield just to unload the ordnance. The first day's forty-seven air strikes punished Charlie royally, suppressed a lot of his fire, and let our troops come up for air, but close-in requests within 100 meters of friendly positions during the belly-to-belly fighting accounted for two B Company deaths and a number of injuries throughout the day. By nightfall the Air Cav had lifted the 2/320 Artillery into range of An Ninh. At our request, they also set up one of their own batteries nearby to support Task Force Collins (which was beyond the 2/320's fan), and mistakenly proceeded to blast the shit out of Collins's CP. It wasn't the Cav's fault. In the hurry and the heat of the battle, no one had thought to make sure they used the same artillery deflection as the 2/320. Obviously they did not, and it was just luck that among the eleven friendly casualties that resulted from the accident, no one was killed.

That night, flare ships circled overhead, keeping the area lit up like day. By morning the VC had gone to ground, and though Operation Gibraltar continued for two more days, with the 2/502 being extracted and Task Force Collins mopping up the area, the worst was over. The net result of the fighting was friendly casualties of thirteen KIA and forty WIA (twelve of which were from friendly fire), for an enemy body count reported to be 257 KIA, most the victims of our tac air. Only twenty-one enemy weapons were recovered, but twelve prisoners were taken, a number of whom were unquestionably hardcore NVA regulars, "fillers" infiltrated down to join VC Main Force (regular) units and buck up their southern counterparts.

General Westmoreland, along with some twenty reporters, was at Brigade headquarters at An Khe when the 2/502 was extracted. Colonel Smith was immediately flown there to meet him, to give his report and quash early press accounts that the 2/502 had been badly mauled at An Ninh. The following day he was flown to Saigon to do it again for the press there. Though Smith had been pinned down throughout the first bloody day, and destroyed most of his documents in anticipation of being overrun, he would receive a Silver Star for gallantry in action during the operation. His battalion was awarded a well-deserved Presidential Unit Citation, though less for their tactical brilliance than for their guts and absolute refusal to give in.

How lucky the unit actually was, in the earliest moments of the battle, to survive what ended up being the buzz saw of a well-trained, well-armed Main Force VC unit would not be known until the 1st Air Cav captured that VC after-action report on Gibraltar some six months later. According to that document, the VC knew we were coming as soon as we started planning. The minute we'd informed the "friendly" Viets in the district that we were going into the area, the word was passed along to the VC. The 95th also had a pretty good idea where we would be landing, and for two days before the battle, they trained on position there. But since nothing ever goes exactly according to plan, as prepared as the VC at An Ninh had been to receive us, when the 2/502 made its initial airmobile assault, Charlie ended up being as surprised as we were. While huge pots of still-boiling rice, ammo, and other gear found by our troops in hastily abandoned enemy campsites told the tale on the ground, the VC after-action report filled in a noteworthy blank: as the initial A1E air strikes and the first 2/502 lift went in, all the VC leaders, from squad level on up, were at their battalion CP, chalk-talking a sand-table exercise of the expected battle.

The air strikes cut the phone wires between the battalion commander and his companies, and throughout the subsequent fighting the VC troops fought as isolated bands with no guidance from the main boss. And at the outset of the battle, until the squad, platoon, and company leaders got back to their units from the battalion CP, the VC troops fought with no guidance at all. Just one irony of this could be seen in a story related after the battle by 2/502 recon man John Reed, in which, soon after they landed as part of the first lift, a number of 2/502 recon guys saw a dozen Viet Cong in black pajamas tearing across the river just beyond a treeline north of the LZ. The recon group opened fire, only to be stopped by their sergeant because the enemy did not appear to be armed (firing upon unarmed Viets was prohibited under General Westmoreland's strict rules of engagement), and these

VC got away. But they were never identified, and the question would always remain: what if they'd been among the unit's platoon and company commanders? And if they were, how different would the battle have been had our recon guys killed them and the enemy lost all its key leaders, as the 2/502 lost theirs?

* * *

Chapter 13

A Different Kind of War

★ ★ ★

By the time the 1st Brigade left An Khe for Qui Nhon, the men were well on their way to becoming seasoned vets. Gibraltar had bloodied us and taught us to respect our foe. Overall confidence had steadily risen, both through the countless patrols and operations, and from observing the predominantly nonparatrooper 1st Air Cav guys going through *their* opening-night jitters. How quickly our men had forgotten their own. Comments like "What were ya'all shootin' at last night, Leg?" (which had been heard from the moment the Air Cav arrived), now, on the eve of our departure, had given way to "Hey, Leg, what're you gonna do when we're not here to protect your ass?"

About the same time that we moved out of An Khe, Colonel Timothy sent me down from Brigade Operations to the 1/327 "Above the Rest" Battalion as executive officer. I was thrilled; first, I was nothing if not a warrior (and brigade staff was no place for a warrior, *especially* during a war), and second, the 1/327 was my favorite of the three battalions, a close-knit, spirited unit that well-reflected a long history of strong leadership.

For the troops, the forty days the 1st Brigade spent in the Qui Nhon area were characterized by snipers and booby traps, mines and monsoons, and one rice paddy after another. The paddies all looked alike, and as such made navigation hell. On one occasion, a company landed on two separate rice-paddy LZs, only to find both were wrong. Booby traps were responsible for many, many casualties in the 1/327 during this period. The enemy had an incredible array of the things, which they attached to the doorways of vacant houses and shrines, on gates, and especially along the tops of paddy walls. There were hand-grenade booby traps with one or multiple trip wires secured to trees and rocks. There were more grenades, pins removed, held tight by a bag of rice, a rock, or a potential souvenir (a VC flag, for example), that were activated simply by picking up the item under which the primed grenade lay.

Some of the best VC booby traps were made in the U.S.A.: Air Force "dud" cluster bomblets, modified with a pressure device and buried just below ground level to blow when a trooper stepped on them, or 81mm and 60mm dud mortar rounds, buried "nose up" and similarly pressure detonated. The VC used anything careless American soldiers left behind (C-ration cans, for example, formed the basis of many lethal enemy devices); deadlier still were the items the VC gave *back* from time to time, like U.S. grenades they policed up on the battlefield. A less-than-savvy American trooper might pick up one of these seemingly abandoned grenades and add it to his kit; during a fight days or weeks later he might use it and find himself dead the second he pulled the pin: the VC who'd found it first had replaced it on the battlefield only after removing the delay.

This sort of thing really played with the troopers' minds. It was hell never knowing if you were going to have a foot after your next step. It also gave rise to enormous frustration and anger among them. They seldom saw Charlie at Qui Nhon (though he was actually much more plentiful there than he'd been at An Khe), yet every day Charlie was bleeding them. They'd go into villages almost completely bereft of males, and after the women and old men had explained that all their husbands and sons were in the army or dead and "No, no VC here," our soldiers would move on a few hundred meters only to have one of their number killed or wounded by a sniper holed up in the village they'd just left.

The coastal monsoons made things even more grim. With the onset of the rainy season, the flat, open rice paddies, already sniper-, booby-trap-, and punji-stake–infested, became like rivers. At one stage the brigade CP was actually washed away when it was set up on ground a speck too low. While C Company, 1/327, used captured sampans to improve their mobility through the flooded paddies, most of the troops just sloshed through the chest-deep water with weapons held over their heads, simultaneously trying to fight an unseen enemy who could see them for miles.

I was not involved in many combat activities while my new battalion was at Qui Nhon. Most of my run-ins were with higher-ups, who somehow hadn't figured out that our stateside fatigues and leather jump boots were absolutely wrong for the jungle (the fatigues were too hot, the jump boots cracked from the dampness and the soles fell off within two weeks), and that three months is too long for men to be eating canned C rations three meals a day. Finally I summoned the 1/327's Logistics officer, Captain

Tom Hancock,* and explained his saw it. "Hancock," I said, "I don't care how you get what we need or where you get it, just get it."

And he did. Hancock was the best scrounger I ever met in the U.S. Army, a Robin Hood in fatigues who, at my direction, scrounged from the rear-echelon commandos at absurdly well-supplied Army service and support units for the troopers of our destitute battalion. (Survival was the only law of the land, as far as I was concerned; the combat units had the right to whatever we needed to ensure that the troops' welfare was looked after.) When I told Hancock, for example, that I wanted the battalion to have a decent hot meal when the companies returned from one of their Qui Nhon operations ("They've been on C rations forever, for Christ's sake . . ."), Hancock, who'd once been a general's aide, put on his aide-de-camp insignia, commandeered a small boat, and motored out to a ship in the Qui Nhon harbor. He told the captain he represented "the General" and that he needed some steaks, etc., for a VIP show for some Vietnamese. Whether the ship's captain was more impressed with Hancock or with the souvenir gifts of captured weapons the S-4 presented was hard to judge, but he gave Hancock everything he wanted, times three.

When the troops next got back from the paddies, the wonderful smell of grilled steaks and barbecued chicken was wafting through the camp to greet them. Hancock had scrounged an extra load of beer, too, and before long one slightly mellow, very happy battalion was moving through the chow line, courtesy of Tom Hancock. Unfortunately, one of the cooks had received a "Dear John" letter that morning, and elected the middle of the party as the moment to blow

---

*A pseudonym

his brains out. He lay down on the ground, stuck an M-16 in his mouth, and let loose on full automatic. Though I wasn't there at the time, word had it that his hungry fellow troopers, deprived of decent food for so long, didn't miss a lick.

By the time the brigade left Qui Nhon, it had been on continuous missions for 100 days. Phan Rang, home of the 1st Brigade, 101's new, permanent base camp, afforded the troopers a well-deserved rest, and it also gave my battalion the opportunity to reorganize according to proven operational needs. By now it was obvious, for example, that we didn't need an antitank platoon in this jungle war. But we certainly did need a fourth maneuver element, so we inactivated the antitank platoon, incorporated the battalion's recon platoon, and created an eighty-man, all-volunteer light company, the "Tiger Force," to act, in the main, as the battalion's long-range reconnaissance and ambush element, and as a fourth maneuver force as required.

Phan Rang also gave me the opportunity to get to know the young officers of the 1/327 and find out what they were made of. Cards being just about the only nightlife Phan Rang had to offer, this "getting to know you" generally took place around a poker table. I cleaned out most of the guys on a regular basis, but as testimony to their mettle, they always came back for more. Lieutenant George Perry from Abu Company, for example, was one of the worst card players I'd ever met. It finally reached the point where I'd tell him to stay home and get a good night's sleep, that I'd be happy to prorate his losses against his track record and bill him in the morning. Whatever I said, though, Perry was always at the table that night.

Sparkling entertainment at the officer card parties was provided by battalion assistant S-3 John Dalton Howard, a.k.a. "Gentleman John," a West Point lieutenant, a great practical joker, and one of the funniest guys I'd ever met. Johnny came to every game, but when asked to play, he'd usually sit back, beer in hand, and say, "No, my job here is to enhance the conversation." And enhance it he did, with jokes and complete recitals of Rudyard Kipling and other military poems.

Also at the poker table in Phan Rang, though I hated to admit it, I finally met my match. Captain Benjamin L. Willis was the best poker player I'd met since Dell Evans in Korea. My longtime belief that great warriors were (or should be) great poker players was certainly borne out by Ben; his incredible common sense and street fighter's cunning made him, in my view, among the best American guerrilla fighters in the Republic of Vietnam.

From time to time, on nights when poker got old and/or a fair amount of boozing had gone down, we'd conduct a raid on downtown Phan Rang, specifically on Madame Nhu's House of Pleasure. It hadn't taken long to find out who shared my view of combat soldiers and sex (those of "rampant libido," as Johnny Howard so succinctly would observe); on the nights themselves I'd send word down to the company CPs that "Major Hackworth requests your presence at Madame Nhu's," and when all interested officers were assembled (normally a wild, drunken mob), we'd pile into jeeps and head into town. Usually the subsequent events were pretty straightforward, although one notable exception was the night everyone wanted a second round and no one had enough money to pay for it. The Vietnamese madam happily accepted a transistor radio as compensation for her girls' double rations rendered (the radio belonged to one of the lieutenants, though God only knew why he'd brought it along); from that point we had it made in the shade until the MPs started banging on the whorehouse door, presumably because of all the Airborne jeeps outside. My guys were all on the second floor. As the situation hotted up, we scrambled to make our getaway, and I found myself scaling down the side of the building with another battalion officer, employing tactics neither of us had used since our rappelling training days. Fortunately, the whole group got out intact and we soon roared off into the night, beyond the clutches of the law.

We spent Thanksgiving at Phan Rang, and the holiday had no sooner passed when the 7th ARVN Regiment was decimated in a battle with Main Force VC units at the Michelin rubber plantation near Ben Cat, just forty-five kilometers from Saigon. In a combined operation with other American units and the 1st Battalion, Royal Australian Regiment,* two battalions of the Screaming Eagles' 1st Brigade were tasked to secure the plantation and get the VC.

The initial role of the 1/101 units was to take over the defense of Bien Hoa Airfield. Relieved of this wait-around mission some days later, we moved overland to Lai Khe and the Michelin plantation to commence Operation Checkerboard, a mission that began with a massive airmobile assault—the first lift alone was composed of forty UH1D troop-carrying choppers (also known as "Hueys" or "slicks"), able to carry two complete rifle companies into the battle area simultaneously.

Airmobile assaults were both exciting and frightening. Each one was a gut-churning event not dissimilar to the moment before you unassed an airplane with a parachute on your back. The chill down your spine

---

*Australia was just one of a number of countries represented in the "Free World Forces" fighting for South Vietnam, with whose units we periodically conducted joint operations.

and the tightening in your stomach started the moment you loaded into the chopper. You sat down on your steel pot—few trusted the Huey's thin underbelly to keep them in full possession of their most vital organs—and soon you were bolting skyward, as if ascending in a high-speed elevator.

The slicks moved in a line, like giant locusts; approaching the LZ, they swung into a big orbit, staying out of the way of the tac air preparing the ground below—you could see the napalm and cluster bomblets crunching down and the big geysers created by heavier bombs. Then the tac-air aircraft pulled away with a flourish, and artillery rained down as the slicks were joined midair by gunships, which would, when the artillery was lifted, hose down the treelines with machine guns, rockets, and fast-firing M-79 guns while the slicks sat down and discharged their troops. Only when they'd landed did the slicks' door gunners open up, while troopers (eight per bird, four per door) hit the ground running with hearts in mouths—bent double to avoid the whirling *thump, thump, thump* of the chopper blades, through the noise and confusion —to secure the treeline for subsequent lifts to go in without covering fire.

It was a concerto of awesome firepower coordinated with split-second timing, an intricate ballet of man and machine. Everybody had to have his act together —troopers, crews, artillery, and Air Force supporters —because on top of everything else, it all happened at more than 100 miles an hour.

I was on the ground with the troops during Checkerboard, sent (with no need for a second invitation) by the 1/327's CO, Lieutenant Colonel Joseph Rogers, to see how the companies were doing since their reorganization at Phan Rang. No major contacts with the VC occurred during the operation; while the Lai

Khe-Ben Cat area proved to be a major logistic base for the Viet Cong, complete with a hospital complex, training facilities, and large-unit base camps and mess halls, judging from the lack of booby traps among these installations and the freshly prepared, still-warm food we found in cooking pots, the VC units who lived there had decided to run away rather than take us on.

Still, they'd left calling cards throughout the rubber plantation and double-canopied jungle, making the battlefield particularly grim. Like Qui Nhon, wherever a trooper walked there seemed to be a mine or an explosive booby trap. We had a number of casualties, and countless near misses. Other primitive but highly effective devices we encountered included tiger traps with their razor-sharp bamboo spears at the bottom, but much worse were the huge logs the enemy had rigged up and hidden in trees. The unlucky infantryman who sprang the concealed trip wire of one of these would find 200 pounds of teak, usually studded with spikes, catapulting down on him at fifty miles per hour.

The jungle held the routine unpleasantries of red ants and leeches as well, but more dangerous to the soldiers was their own behavior within the bush. Just one example was the several friendly casualties that occurred when a grenade was tossed, hit the trees, and bounced back on the troops. It was a common accident; the men still had not come to terms with jungle fighting. Before Vietnam, the Screaming Eagles' long orientation had been for desert warfare; the overall lack of training for the jungle had troopers sounding and acting like a herd of elephants crashing through the forest.

Nowhere was this more clear to me than when Operation Checkerboard drew to a close and I accompanied Lieutenant Pat Graves's B Company platoon on the way out of the jungle. It was an experience that made me well respect the enormous difficulties the ground-pounder in Vietnam faced: machetes wielded against the dense, uncompromising bush that rose into double and triple canopy (making the day like night), point men changed again and again as the exhausting job of hacking through it overtook them. Then, suddenly, the dark, dank, impenetrable jungle opened up. But it did not reveal daylight; instead, the presence, five feet in front of us, of another unit. Fortunately, they were 2/502 guys, doing the exact same thing we were. Due to Graves's unerring navigation, we'd hacked our way right into our link-up point with the 2/502. But what was most amazing was that neither group had heard or seen the other until that very moment, both so busily and loudly hacking away. It was just good luck all around that neither was VC.

But where *were* the VC? While Checkerboard proved successful in terms of disrupting the enemy's logistic system—VC tunnels were blown up; half-built VC villages were burned down; enormous quantities of rice, ammunition, and items such as VC black pajamas were uncovered and destroyed—the major purpose of the five-day mission, to find and destroy the VC unit that had mauled the 7th ARVN Regiment, was not met. In the biggest U.S. operation to date, with probably 15,000 troops beating the bushes, we failed to even find the enemy (that is, in large formations or numbers), much less destroy him. But where had he gone? He had to go somewhere. No doubt to his sanctuaries in Cambodia, or somewhere within the densely forested War Zone D, adjacent to the Cambodian border, or War Zone C, which led virtually to the gates of Saigon, or perhaps even under our very feet, in his vast tunnel complexes. So early in the

war, the failure of Operation Checkerboard to find
the enemy was ample illustration of the limitation of
the Americans' large-scale, incredibly expensive multi-
battalion operations. They were simply no match for a
cunning foe who lived by Mao's conviction, "Give me
a path wide enough to move a mule and I will move an
army."

Chapter 14
Task Force Hackworth

★ ★ ★

Although the 1st Brigade, 101st Airborne Division, would continue to play fire brigade the rest of its first year in Vietnam, the days of Tim's Traveling Trouble came to an end in early January 1966, when Colonel Timothy led the 2/327 "No Slack" and 2/502 "Strike Force" battalions on an operation 100 miles to the north, to the city of Tuy Hoa and its rice paddies by the sea. From there, while the 1/327 stayed behind to secure (and conduct patrols from) the brigade's base camp at Phan Rang, Timothy turned the 1/101's command over to Brigadier General Willard Pearson, and went on to his next assignment as the Vietnamese II Corps senior adviser at Pleiku. Other than that, the month of January passed pretty uneventfully, at least for the 1/327; considering what the month of February would bring, this was absolutely all for the best.

On 7 February the 2/502 and the 2/327 were heavily committed up at Tuy Hoa. Under the command of Lieutenant Colonel Hank Emerson, the 2/502 was operating in a brigade-size AO; "the Gunfighter," as the Strike Force commander had been dubbed, had fights going all over the battlefield. He'd already committed his reserve when the morning of 7 February brought that one fight too many: elements of Emerson's C Company, commanded by Captain Robert Murphy, were pinned down and in danger of being flanked and destroyed by an NVA force of unknown size. The 1/327 had been called up from Phan Rang a couple of days before for just such a contingency; now new brigade commander Pearson said he wanted me to take a task force to relieve and reinforce Murphy. "You have the Tigers and Bravo Company," he said. "Now go get 'em."

I assembled a light CP group, which included the assistant battalion S-3, Don Chapman, our 2/320th Artillery liaison officer (LNO), Don Korman, me, and all relevant RTOs, and hopped into a waiting chopper. We made contact with Murphy (who was mighty cheerful for a guy whose company was up against a force with what he estimated were at least a dozen machine guns), and after having a good look at the battle area, we selected LZs, coordinated fire support, and returned to Tuy Hoa, where I briefed Bravo's CO, Al Hiser, and Tiger commander Jim Gardner on the plan.

Murphy's company was stuck in the northwest corner of the bombed-out ruins of a village called My Canh 2. My idea was to have the Tigers come up on the surrounded unit's southern flank, while B Company swung around by chopper to set up a blocking position deep behind the enemy. After tac air and artillery preparation, the Tigers would hit the enemy and roll up their flank; I figured at that point the enemy would break contact and run, only to get caught in the trap I'd set behind them with Bravo Company.

The Tigers led the way out and I went with them. We landed at an LZ quite close to the battle area. The men spread out and moved like old pros through waist-high grass. I, on the other hand, was walking on air. Ever since I'd arrived in Vietnam—now some eight months ago—I'd lived for the prospect of another combat command. Hell, I'd been dreaming of another combat command since I left Korea in 1953. And then to get one with the Tigers (whom I'd secretly considered "my boys" since the creation of the elite force) was the greatest break I could have asked for.

We guided on the sound of Murphy's firefight. C Company's commander was also putting max tac air and artillery on the enemy surrounding him, but it wasn't doing much good—the enemy soldiers were belly-to-belly with Murphy's men, and to close them down effectively would have resulted in a hell of a lot of friendly casualties as well. We moved forward continuously, killing as we went about ten enemy stragglers who'd been dumb enough to take potshots at the Tigers. These men were inveterate NVA troops complete with khaki uniforms and armed with AK47s —upon examination, members of the elite 95th NVA Regiment, the unit known to be operating in this area, whose activities during the Indochina war had given the bloody Street Without Joy its name. They were probably the most formidable enemy fighters in South Vietnam. "Do I get the CIB now?" Don Chapman, who was hiking along behind me, asked only half jokingly each time an enemy shot rang out. "No, Chapman, not yet," I'd reply, having a quiet chuckle, remembering what that Combat Infantryman's Badge meant to me when I went through my much-longed-for baptism of fire.*

---

*By regulation, the CIB was awarded to an infantryman after he'd participated in thirty days of ground combat. In the 1/101 we were all getting combat pay from our first day in Vietnam, so generally speaking, our rule was that a guy got the CIB only when he'd actually been shot at.

We reached a small knob by a river, across which we could see Murphy's people lying on the ground around the foundations of blown-away houses. I wasn't satisfied with the update Murphy now gave me by radio, so I took advantage of a bamboo bridge that crossed the river very close to our little knob and went over to the village to see what was happening myself. Unfortunately, a wide-open field about fifty meters long lay between the far side of the bridge and Murphy's position, so when Darryl Nunnelly, my longtime RTO (who had to accompany me lugging his bulky PRC-25 radio), and I dashed across the bridge, we became shooting-gallery ducks for some very professional marksmen armed with automatic weapons who were holed up in a hedgerow beyond the field.

After crawling around the battle area a little bit, talking to Murphy, and eyeballing the situation as he saw it on his side of the river, Darryl and I ran back across the bridge, unscathed despite the enemy machine guns that fired as enthusiastically at our backs as they had at our chests, arms, legs, and heads on the way over. My original plan still held. After telling Gardner what I knew about the location of enemy positions in the hedgerow that faced the open field, I ordered the Tigers to strike the enemy's flank and roll it up, in order to unpin Murphy and send the NVA scurrying into Bravo's waiting ambush. It was a neat, clean "hammer and anvil," right out of Fort Benning. With that I gathered Korman, Chapman, Nunnelly, and the rest of the CP group, and with the Tigers behind us providing effective covering fire, we hightailed across the bridge. Korman, who was the best artilleryman I'd seen since Allan Bell in Korea, neutralized the fire-swept open field on the far side with smoke and HE arty shot, and though the run was a little hairy, the shortcut saved us valuable time.

"Do I get the CIB now?" Chapman panted when the CP group arrived intact at Murphy's position.

"No, Chapman, not yet," I said, and directed my guys to dig in fast and deep: automatic weapons were stitching all over the area. We set up in the rubble of a bombed-out building, and while Korman put together his artillery fire plan and Darryl and the other RTOs started digging a foxhole large enough to hold the entire CP group, I took Chapman with me on a little mosey around the battle area. We crawled through the rubble of a couple of buildings, then crawled on through a ditch along a paddy dike. Suddenly an NVA soldier popped up in front of us, out of a hole he'd burrowed into the side of the dike. He was a little above us as the three of us started shooting, but we hit him first and all his slugs went high, right over our heads. "Do I get the CIB now?" Chapman asked dryly.

"You got it, man." I laughed.

The first thing I saw when we got back to our command post was Darryl setting up his 292 (two-niner-two) antenna, a heavy, unwieldy son of a bitch to carry around but worth every pound and more in terms of the best possible commo. Then I saw Korman talking on the radio. Then I saw the Tigers on the attack—and I couldn't believe my eyes. Gardner and his people were walking across the open field between the bridge and Murphy's position. Rather than taking the well-concealed approach to My Canh along a dry streambed on their flank, the Tigers had forded the river (many of them were soaked to the neck), and now they were marching straight across that field in a perfect skirmish line, like Pickett's division at Gettysburg. I was stunned. But it was too late for him to turn around, and there was no way to stop him; all the 2/502 guys in the village could do was start putting as much suppressive fire as they could on the face of the hedgerow to Gardner's front, to keep the enemy down. Incredibly, the Tigers were taking no casualties as they advanced toward My Canh. In fact, it seemed as though they weren't even being fired on. But then, about twenty meters from our position, with one step they walked into a wall of lead.

Our opponent was indeed a force to be reckoned with. The discipline of this element of the 95th NVA, so skillfully dug in and camouflaged along their hedgerow wall, was iron-tight. Not one shot had been fired prematurely, and when they did open up, they mowed my Tigers down from end to end across that open field. Those who survived immediately charged the treeline through the fire (an act that took courage beyond words), and from that moment on, for both Tigers and members of C2/502, it was bloody hand-to-hand with the enemy all the way.

I watched from my tac CP forty yards away. It was like a 3-D movie—a collage of khaki, green, and scarlet red—and wholly outside my experience. I'd never seen our Viet enemy voluntarily intermingle with American troops. I'd never seen him stand and fight. It quickly became clear that he wasn't going to fall into the trap I'd set for him with Bravo Company, so I called Hiser and told him to punch through the enemy's rear.

The dug-in NVA had numerous heavily reinforced machine-gun positions at My Canh, but one in particular, about 100 meters from our CP, was causing problems. That machine gun had one of my elements stopped. As I talked to the tac-air forward air controller about closing it down, an Australian voice came through the radio: "I've got a Canberra light bomber here with 250-pound delays on board. Can you use them?"

"Are you real accurate?" I asked.

"I reckon," the Aussie pilot said.

I told him the situation and where the bunker was, popping a smoke for reference. When he did a dry run to have a look at the bunker himself, his twin-engine bomber flew in so low I almost could have reached up from my hole and touched it.

"I see it," the pilot's voice came through the radio as he pulled his plane up. "This'll be a live run, so tell your chaps to get their heads down."

I watched the first bomb being released. It came in on an angle, and as it zoomed over our hole, it looked as if it was no more than a few feet away. On delay, it sank into the ground not far from the targeted bunker and exploded with an earthshaking *bwoom*. After examining the damage, I asked the pilot if he could shift the next run three meters to the right.

One by one all the Canberra's bombs were dropped onto this single target. The pilot's accuracy was incredible; he was able to carry out every adjustment I made precisely, no matter how small. We never did get a direct hit on the bunker, but close enough that even the most gung-ho NVA inside would have been battle-rattled into submission, if not unconsciousness.

"How was that, mate?" the pilot asked when the last of his ordnance was expended.

"Great, man, you saved our ass. Thanks a lot."

"Good hunting and good luck," he said, and flew away.

"Okay, let's see if we can clean up that position now," I said to my held-up element. The men started toward the position, but—*rat-tat-tat-tat*—the minute they stuck their heads up, they felt the fury of the exact same machine gun from the exact same bunker. This enemy was hardcore.

By now the afternoon sun was waning. I was damned anxious; we had no semblance of a perimeter, and having had no luck in knocking out the most lethal of the NVA positions, with dark on its way I was really worried about medevac and resupply. Throughout the day, through trial and error, we'd discovered a way to bring helicopters in without subjecting them to direct enemy fire. What concerned me now was that dark would prevent the critical accuracy required on the pilots' parts in maneuvers like "Go back one klick [kilometer] and get on the deck, come in on the deck at 182 degrees, and when you see a smoke in front of your nose, flare back and land right on top of it." (And the final warning: "Don't go beyond that smoke, or you're gonna find two antiaircraft machine guns firing right down your throat.")

I was also terribly worried about getting the men set up for the night. While B Company had run into some heavy fighting and broken off their attack, the Tigers and Murphy's men were still in the thick of it, with the Tigers being held up in a trench south of the village by four machine guns. As daylight grew shorter, so did my patience with my boys. "Goddamn it, Jim," I yelled at Gardner on the radio, "get those positions cleaned out right now. No more fucking around, do you understand? It's getting dark. Knock out those guns, and I mean now!"

I was not in a position to see what happened next, but as the story was related to me by Dennis Foley, Gardner's XO, Jim made my words his personal mission. He took as many grenades as he could carry in his shirt and started running up the trench by himself. Slugs were snapping all around him as he ran to the first machine-gun bunker; he threw himself against it below the hole, pulled the pin on one of his grenades, and threw it in. As the grenade went off and the machine gun in the bunker went limp, Gardner moved on to the next position. He repeated the drill, only this time someone inside the bunker threw the grenade out of the hole, in front of him. Jim was hit as it went off, but he just took another grenade, threw it into the hole, and permanently closed down the gun inside.

To the astonishment of his men, he pushed on to the third bunker, an antiaircraft position that contained a machine gun mounted on a tripod. The Tiger CO destroyed that gun, too, with another grenade, and then burned an X across the aperture of the bunker with his rifle to make sure there was no one left alive inside. But this moment proved his downfall: simultaneously, an enemy machine gun in yet another position took him under fire and hit him four times across the chest. Jim reportedly turned around and said, "It's the best I can do," and then he dropped, KIA.*

Gardner's courageous bunker-busting did not unpin the Tigers, and I needed them to break contact and link up with Murphy's people. It was the only way we could set up a defensive perimeter before dark. I moved as close to them as I could (which still left us separated by a fairly open space in the village), and got Dennis Foley on the horn. "You're in charge," I said. "I want you to collect your guys and get out of there. I'm right across from you. We'll lay down covering fire and a lot of arty. When it comes in, haul ass over here to my position."

The brave Tigers dodged and weaved their way across that open space under heavy fire, and arrived, miraculously, 100 percent intact. When Dennis joined us, Darryl and I were lying behind a blown-down coconut tree, on the other side of which a whole bunch of pigs were frantically running around. While we remained sheltered from the steel cyclone going on just over our heads, from time to time we'd hear a loud squeal as one of the pigs got caught in the cross

---

*James Gardner received the Medal of Honor posthumously for this action.

fire. One pig had the good sense to hide on our side, but then, when we suddenly got an intense amount of small-arms fire, the pig stuck its head up and got blown away. Insufficient training. Meanwhile Foley took a slug through his helmet; it came out the front, not touching him but knocking one of the arms off his glasses. It was the second time he'd been hit like that since the battle began. The first had been during the Tigers' initial attack, when he'd taken a slug in the back that actually went right through his jacket and equipment, missing his body entirely. The boy had luck.

I'd been talking down choppers all afternoon with great success. One of the most recent lifts had carried a magazine reporter who jumped out of the bird in a yellow short-sleeved shirt and baseball cap and dashed over to our fallen coconut tree. "Hi!" he chirped. "Where's all the action?"

I pointed straight up and went back to fighting the battle. A short time later I noticed the reporter was poking his head over the log, taking a few photographs and coming back down. "Hey, Mr. Reporter," I said, "that's not a very cool thing to do. Stick your camera up and take pictures, but not your head, or it'll be good-bye, Clark Kent." Not five minutes later I looked over again, only to see one very dead reporter—he'd taken a slug between the eyes.

I'd just finished telling a couple of Tigers to stack the reporter's body with the rest of our dead when the voice of an unknown chopper pilot came up on the radio. "Savvy Volley 5," he said (addressing me by my call sign), "this is Outlaw 5-3. Inbound. Resupply and PAX [passengers]. Mark LZ. Over."

"Outlaw 5-3, this is Savvy Volley 5. Look, it's really hot down here, so I'm going to tell you how to get in."

I started giving the pilot my detailed instructions, but almost immediately he interrupted me. "Savvy

Volley 5, just tell me where you want me. Don't tell me how to do it, okay? I think I'm a little more qualified than you in this job."

"Look, buddy," I snapped, "this is a bad, bad LZ here. Come in a certain way or you'll be blown out of the sky."

"I say again: if you want these supplies, just mark your LZ."

"Roger on that," I said, and popped a smoke.

It was like watching a movie in slow motion. First the ship was coming in. Then the ship was being stitched, as greenish-blue NVA tracers burst out of enemy positions. Then the ship was losing control. It was quietly beautiful and, in a way, exceptionally funny to see it spin out and crash on the deck. I sent an element over to retrieve the supplies and the freshly wounded. No one was badly hurt, though Doug Holtz, who was kicking out the supplies as the battalion's support platoon leader, got an easy Purple Heart when a bullet zinged across his ass. Holtz was another lucky guy: this was his fourth Purple Heart, and he'd never received more than a scratch. The worst casualty in the incident was the chopper itself: $300,000 worth of lift destroyed with a couple of nine-cent bullets and the help of a smart-ass pilot who knew it all.

As night fell, we buttoned up. I had Bravo Company set up a perimeter on the outskirts of the village, and the Tigers and C2/502 set up the best perimeter they could in the village itself. We brought in mortars and dug in deep, concentrating our efforts on blocking the enemy's withdrawal routes, mostly with artillery. Enemy dead were strewn all over the area; while I was sick in my heart over the Tiger casualties, at least we, not the enemy, held the village of My Canh.

Then Al Hiser called me with his casualty figures. Nineteen KIA, he said. A score of wounded. I felt as if

I'd been slugged in the gut with a sledgehammer. "What?" I asked—I didn't believe him. He repeated the figures, and tears sprang to my eyes as Hiser went on to explain how he'd launched his attack just as the Tigers had: across a wide-open field. His 2d Platoon had been mowed down.

All told, the battle had claimed the lives of twenty-six of my men and wounded twenty-eight, losses far too heavy to claim "victory," although that was how the newspeople and higher headquarters would describe the battle, with the price in U.S. lives only "moderate." It was a terrible price, in no way justified by the sixty-six NVA bodies and twenty-odd Chinese-made crew-served and individual weapons we found the next morning, or the fact that we were the proud possessors of this demolished village, which we'd soon pull out of anyway. The fact was, we had attacked machine guns as the British and French had in WW I. The fact was we'd been sucked in and eaten alive. I was heartsick at the result.

Task Force Hackworth was disbanded when 1/327 battalion CO Rogers and his staff flew into My Canh the next afternoon. (After a first-light artillery and tac-air strike, the remnants of Bravo Company had entered My Canh unopposed that morning, the NVA having run away throughout the night to fight another day.) I couldn't have been happier to see Doc Raphiel Benjamin, the battalion surgeon, hop out of that chopper. He was the one person I knew I could talk to about the tragic events of the day before.

Raphiel was my friend. The Baton Rouge–born doctor had volunteered for the 1/101 to get out of a boring job with the 70th Engineer Battalion, and we'd hit it off from the first day he joined the 1/327. We'd started out sharing meals; before long I'd started sacking out on one of the stretchers in his aid station, and at night when there were blackout conditions and we couldn't read, we'd just bullshit across the tent until we fell asleep.

And now he would be my sounding board for the disheartening events that had taken place at My Canh the day before. But that night, just as we started talking, a firefight broke out on the east side of the perimeter, complete with flares, grenades, and blazing rifles. We ran over there. "Hold your fire," I shouted over the din. "Hold that fire!" The leaders along the perimeter heard me and took up the call. Before long the weapons were silent. "All right, what's happening here?"

"There was a lot of firing at our outpost, sir," Johnny Adams, the 4.2-mortar platoon leader, reported. "Then there was firing into our perimeter, so we fired back."

I called out to the two men on the outpost, but there was no reply. Raphiel and I headed into the night.

We snaked our way out of the perimeter until we came upon the OP. It had been overrun, and a still-lit cigarette glowing in the darkness beside two very still bodies explained how. For me, it was 11 November 1952 all over again.

The two men were still alive, if only barely. After spraying the area and flipping a couple of grenades, I took one of the guys by the legs while Raphiel tried to grab the same one under his arms to take him back to our position. But the doc's hand kept slipping away— one of the guy's arms had been blown off at the shoulder. Raphiel got hold of him somehow, and we rushed back to the perimeter, yelling our names to prevent being knocked off by our own people. We put the first guy into Doc Benjamin's tiny hex-tent foxhole/surgery and the good doctor went right to work. But it proved to be a losing battle. Just as one of the medics got back from the OP with the second casualty, Raphiel shook his head. "No," he said, "I've

lost this motherfucker. Pass me the other one." We
put the second body down, but it was too late. He was
already dead. "Shit," said Raphiel. "Shit, shit, shit."

My eyes stung. Raphiel, unlike me, was not prone to
using profanity. He probably wouldn't have called a
dead patient a "motherfucker" back home in Louisiana.* But back home in Louisiana he wouldn't have
been living the no-time-for-bullshit soldier's life, either, or trying to save lives by flashlight in a muddy
hole in the dark of night.

"Gentleman John" Howard, battalion poet and
fearless fighter, took an M-79 and, alone, started out
into the darkness to see if he could find anything. He
fired at some movement but couldn't see the result;
though we didn't find a body in the morning, some
bloodied gear on the ground nearby was evidence at
least that Johnny had hit home. Meanwhile, I let the
word go forth that at first light every leader was to take
his men out to that OP to have a firsthand look at that
cigarette and the blood of those two dead men in that
foxhole. Furthermore, I said that anyone who smoked
between seven in the evening and seven in the
morning—on the line, in the base camp, even on
R&R in Hong Kong—might as well get his ass out of
the battalion, because if I caught him, he'd spend the
rest of his tour with a split lip and two black eyes,
courtesy of my fists.

Operations in the Tuy Hoa area continued. Task
Force Hackworth was reestablished for one independent mission when Colonel Rogers wanted a little
extra experience on the team, and with Abu Company, a platoon of Tigers, and a little CP group, I eagerly
moved out into the unknown.

---

*On the other hand, in the Airborne, the term "motherfucker,"
unless spoken harshly, was among the highest terms of endearment.

We infiltrated into our AO by stealth, moving out of the battalion's temporary fire base on foot and at night. Choppers would have gotten us there a hell of a lot faster, but they made enough noise to virtually guarantee there'd be nothing to get when we got there: any enemy within five miles would say, "Yanks come, we run away," and be gone before we even set down.

The operation was five days in length. At the outset I made a rule that for the duration there'd be no resupply aircraft buzzing around dropping in hot food or ice cream or beer, and no commo with higher HQ either, except a daily report via Darryl's radio and two-niner-two antenna. The kids weren't shook by the new ground rules at all. They sneaked through the forest like a silent pack of Daniel Boones, all of them so much into the spirit of things that even the wounded didn't bitch; they just hobbled along on their sprained ankles, knowing the pain could be lived with and there was something more important going on. ("Look, man," I'd explained, "we're here sneaking up on the enemy and we're not giving our position away. Sure you've got a little scratch. You don't see any helicopters evacuating the NVA out, do you? What do they do? They stick with their outfit and walk and heal up. They're hardcore. But *you're* hardcore, too.") Why the troops took so easily to the on-the-job-training guerrilla game was probably partly because it was different, partly because it was fun, and partly because they knew we really were right on the NVA's tail. Signs were everywhere—recent camps, recently used trails, broken branches.

As my task force crept on, I could feel we were on the edge of a great fight. The adrenaline was pumping; with each more careful step I knew we were getting closer. Then, after so many of my troops had braved their minor wounds without even a whimper (or at least one I heard), my own operations sergeant got sick. Sick-sick, like he was going to die, according to the doc, who was the senior aid man and a top medic.

Thanks to Raphiel Benjamin, I thought I knew quite a bit about diagnostics and field medicine. I felt particularly savvy about hepatitis and gonorrhea; these, along with malaria, were the most common complaints voiced by the scores of battalion members who wandered through the doc's tent in the middle of the night while I tried to sleep on the other stretcher. For suspected hepatitis cases, Raphiel always stuck his hand under the trooper's rib cage to see if his liver was hard. For gonorrhea he'd just say, "Reel it out and let me have a look," and then if things looked drippy, he'd tell the guy to come back in the morning for a shot of penicillin.

It seemed pretty straightforward, and I was sure a little of Doc Benjamin had to have rubbed off on me by now, so I got the operations sergeant to lie on the ground and, having ruled out clap from the outset, put my hand under his rib cage as I'd seen Raphiel do a million times. Though I had nothing to compare it with, the patient's liver felt pretty hard, and since he was moaning, I concluded he had hepatitis. It broke my heart to blow our cover and call in a medevac (our prey would undoubtedly fly the coop the minute the chopper blades whirred), but I wasn't going to let the guy die out there. While some of the men started cutting out an LZ, I took a piece of cardboard from a C-ration box and wrote a note to Raphiel. "To Doc Benjamin, Battalion Surgeon. I'm referring this patient to you because, in my opinion, he suffers from acute hepatitis. Please have a look at him. I will be interested to know what your conclusion is. Sincerely, David Hackworth, Forward Doctor." I gave the tag to the sick sergeant and he was flown out.

Sure enough, our elusive enemy disappeared entirely, and we came back to the fire base the next day empty-handed. That disappointment, however, was nothing compared to the news I got when I went to Raphiel to check on my patient. "About that diagnosis," he said. "He had pneumonia. Good try."

Chapter 15
About the Horse

★ ★ ★

The people of Tuy Hoa successfully completed their rice harvest, and the 1/101 turned its attention to the jungles and mountains in the surrounding area. The next ten days or so were singularly uneventful, until the morning of 4 March, when I saw an old Viet gentleman walking toward the 1/327's battalion perimeter. I told our S-2, Lieutenant Jerry Nakashima, to go talk to the guy and see if he knew anything.

The old man told Jerry he'd just seen "men from the North" wearing khaki and carrying "long stove-pipes" moving toward the village of Thanh Phu. The only reasonable interpretation of this was that a North Vietnamese unit carrying large mortars was setting up in a village to our southwest, but the question then was whether the old Viet was for real or a setup—a VC supporter, or perhaps just an innocent old man whose family was being held hostage by the NVA—to lead us into a trap. In either case, this kind of "volunteered" information was a typical enemy ploy, and in assessing it, the only thing I had going for me was my instinct and the quaint way the Viet described what he'd seen to make me feel he was telling the truth.

I gave Colonel Rogers the intelligence and the circumstances in which we got it. He swung A and B companies, which were just returning home from another operation, toward Thanh Phu on separate axes, and by the time we'd organized our tac CPs (the Colonel decided to tag along with the Abus while I went with B Company), Bravo had already made contact just outside the village hamlet of My Phu.

The subsequent fighting in and around My Phu was vicious. What seemed at first to be light fire from a squad-size enemy element within a short time became heavy automatic-weapons fire from an enemy force of two or three companies. For a moment it seemed we'd been lured in: the enemy was fighting from well-dug and fortified positions, just as they had at My Canh. But all was not as it appeared. When I landed in the middle of B Company's fight, one of the first things I saw was an NVA company frantically running in all directions. We'd caught them on the move, a fact confirmed later in the day by a POW, who added that the NVA unit's intention had been to set up mortar positions to blast our fire base while hitting us with a three-company ground attack. The old Viet man had been right.

B Company was fully engaged, kicking ass but also taking casualties. Even though they'd been surprised, the NVA's SOP when on the move, to always have pre-dug defensive positions for just such a contingency, diminished our initial advantage. One of Bravo's medics took a slug in the back of his head. Raphiel, who was on the ground treating the wounded the whole time, didn't think he'd make it but felt it was worth a try, and together we dragged the medic along the ground in a poncho to a safer spot. ("Safer" in this fight was relative: across the battle area you couldn't lift your head without drawing fire.) I called for a medevac and instantly a chopper was on the scene, its pilot asking for landing instructions. "Look, it's really hot down here," I told him. "You're going to have to volunteer for this one 'cause you may not make it out."

"Just tell me how to do it," he replied.

I told him what I thought the best route would be, and the pilot followed my instructions to the letter. As the chopper landed, Raphiel and I rushed the wounded medic to the open door. The chopper crew chief grabbed him and pulled him inside. Slugs were buzzing and snapping around the chopper like flies in a slaughterhouse as I turned to thank the pilot. Only then did I find this was no ordinary airplane driver, but Major Dave George, a dear friend of mine from the interwar, peacetime days.

We shook hands and started catching up on old times over the din of his helicopter, completely forgetting we were on the battlefield. It was probably the only reason neither of us got hit. "You've won me for life, stud," I told him as he prepared to carry the wounded away; it was the first of many medevac runs that good man and his brave crew would make to My Phu.

Enemy dead were strewn all over the hamlet. Hiser and the men of Bravo had learned well at My Canh: at My Phu they did not assault fixed positions. Instead, they hunkered down and let firepower dig the enemy out. Still, in the wake of their casualties and in the fog of battle, I wasn't sure who had the upper hand. All that changed when I saw one young black trooper firing like fury down a wide ditch with an M-79. I raced over there to see that he'd killed some thirty NVA soldiers single-handedly. Such carnage on so small a section of the battlefield was a picture that said everything to me—suddenly I knew we had a solid victory on our hands.

Meanwhile A Company had taken seven casualties in an attempt to come to our assistance and encircle the enemy forces. Over the radio Colonel Rogers (who had gone airborne in his C&C to have a look at the whole fight) told me he thought we should break off. "No, sir," I said. "We've got to capitalize on this. We've got the enemy on the ropes. We're winning this one."

"I agree with Hack," said General Pearson, who was monitoring our net from his bird above the battlefield. The two commanders then decided that because I was on the ground, I should take command of the engaged troops. It was another lucky break, but it was almost (and permanently) lost when, a short time later, Raphiel, Darryl, and I were leaning against the blown-out wall of a house and an enemy machine gun opened up right at us. How the gunner managed to stitch the wall *between* Darryl and me, and move on to stitch *between* me and Raphiel, and not hit any of us was a miracle or a fluke beyond belief, but that was exactly what happened. Of course, we immediately shagged ass out of there—it wasn't a very cool place to be.

The battle began to settle down to a slow, methodical, inch-by-inch finding of the enemy's dug-in positions and one by one destroying them. Just as dark was coming on, Abu's company commander, Hal Eaton, staggered into our position. It was very strange. He came out of nowhere, and he had to have walked from A Company straight through the NVA positions to get there. But we quickly found out how he'd done it: he was in shock, having taken grenade fragments in his throat.

Only then did I get the full story on Abu's casualties. They were staggering. Not one officer of the three rifle platoons remained. All had been killed or wounded, with the greatest shock of all being word that platoon leader Harry "The Horse" Godwin, a top combat leader and soldier revered by his men, was dead. Harry had made his name at Qui Nhon, where his favorite trick had been to deploy his best sharpshooters and then get on top of rice-paddy walls and run. The purpose of the exercise had been to get a concealed VC sniper to take a shot at him; then, as this six-foot-three ex-Marine and top college athlete kept on running, his sharpshooters would nail the sniper. The scheme had worked very well, but as cat-and-mouse games go, it had been altogether too dangerous, and I'd quietly told the Abus' skipper, George Shevlin, to put a good harness on "The Horse" and rein him in. Now it looked as though I'd only postponed the inevitable.

At dark the Abu weapons platoon (which was fighting as a rifle platoon, and had been held as such in battalion reserve throughout the day) infiltrated the battle area and linked up with the remnants of its company. While Bob Press, Abu's first sergeant, took command of the company, I radioed Harry the Horse's platoon. I spoke with Staff Sergeant Travis Martin, the only NCO left, and asked him if he thought he could run Harry's platoon for the night. "You bet, sir," the squad leader replied, "I've been training for a situation like this for ten years."

I directed A Company to get themselves squared away along the enemy's escape route to the south. Bravo, meanwhile, consolidated its positions along the escape route to the west. As both companies evacuated their casualties, I knew we desperately needed more men on the ground; with C Company off on a brigade mission, all I had as reserves were the Tigers, who'd spent the fight so far securing our fire base (a stupid damn job for them anyway). I decided to bring them in.

"What about my security?" the artillery battery CO screamed through the radio when I gave him the word. "I need the infantry to secure me!"

"Well, you're not going to have them tonight," I replied.

Denying the artillery its security was far less a concern to me than eliminating my reserve (especially since the arty battery was well-organized to be able to defend itself). But I was convinced we were soundly trouncing the enemy. What I wanted now was to get as many escape routes blocked as we could, then blow the hell out of the center of the NVA positions and catch the enemy troops with infantry ambushes as they scurried for safety. More and more, through my own experience and as it meshed with what I'd read of the French experience, as well as the views of the old Indochina hands and what Hank Emerson was doing in the 2/502, I was concluding that this was the way to fight the NVA and the VC. The ammo was free—only the taxpayer paid for that—and it made a lot more sense than trying to close with our hardcore opponent as we had at My Canh and suffer excessive casualties.

The Tigers were inserted at 2100 hours, in the brigade's first nighttime airmobile assault. They moved into their multiple ambush positions without casualties, despite being under fire from the moment they stepped out of the choppers at their one-bird LZ. Of the score of NVA stragglers killed throughout the night, the Tigers were responsible for about a dozen. Unfortunately (though predictably) many NVA escaped, too, through our far-too-open net, and bugged back to the hills.

Come the early dawn, Darryl Nunnelly and I left B Company, where we'd spent the night, and moved out to the Abus' position. With us, as well, was the redoubtable Tom Hancock, who would replace the wounded Hal Eaton as A Company's commander.

To appreciate how the tragic events of 4 March affected the men of Abu Company, it is necessary to understand the Abu spirit and the Abu history. The Abus had actually evolved from another unit, the Ibus, a.k.a. Item Company, 187th Regimental Combat Team. As the story went, in 1952 the companies of the 187th decided that rather than use standard military phonetics (i.e., Alpha, Bravo, Charlie) to identify themselves, they would give themselves names. Animals seemed to be the order of the day (L Company became Lion, M Company became Mighty Moose, and so on), but poor Item found the only animal that began with an *I* was a wading bird called an ibis, which just wouldn't do. It was Item Company's commander, Captain Robert Channon, who came up with the mythical Ibu (in fact, an acronym for *I* is the *B*est *U*nit). All that was needed then was to decide what this never-before-seen creature looked like. Remarkably, the task was accomplished in a very short time: the Ibu had a gorilla's body, a lion's head, a moose's horns, and an alligator's tail, and wore (for all eternity) a parachute and jump boots, and clutched a pistol in its right hand and a knife (dripping blood) in its left.

The Ibu proliferated quickly, finding its way onto guidons, company signs, swagger sticks (an ivory Ibu on one end, an ivory jump boot on the other), and the legs of many an Ibu NCO, in the form of a tattoo that stretched virtually from ankle to knee. When, in 1956, the 101st was reactivated and the 3d Battalion, 187th RCT (of which Ibu was a part) was incorporated into the 1/327 Battlegroup, instead of gracefully bowing out, the Ibu, fierce figure of yesteryear, just

changed its name: Abu, to accommodate its new company designation (A Company, 1/327).*

For old-timers and newcomers alike, the legend of the Ibu/Abu was the glue that cemented the men of A Company together. At Fort Campbell a good number of Abu's NCOs had been with the company since its early Ibu days; even with rotation and normal attrition in Vietnam, on 4 March many original Abus, like First Sergeant Bob Press (who'd started out as a squad leader in 1956), remained. Unlike Bravo Company, which had had its baptism of fire in February, the fine, cocky troopers of Abu had not seen a major battle in Vietnam before My Phu. Their losses, thirteen KIA and almost forty WIA, knocked the remaining members for one serious loop. The shock was only compounded by the death of indestructible Harry the Horse—if Harry died, the company's collective thought seemed to be, how could any of the poor mortals among them survive? The unit's morale had not just been damaged, it had been destroyed, or so it appeared when we arrived at their position—a rice paddy in the center of which were Abu's dead, neatly stacked row on row, and covered with ponchos—on the outskirts of My Phu.

I was quietly briefed on the events of the previous day. On Hal Eaton's order, Abu's 3d Platoon had assaulted across a dry rice paddy and taken eleven WIA in less than fifty yards, with six more lost when they'd attempted to advance over a dike on My Phu's perimeter. Harry Godwin's 2d Platoon had attacked

---

*The history of the Ibus was provided by Sergeant Major Leo B. Smith (Ret.), with additional information from Colonel Robert Channon (Ret.), and Master Sergeant Lyland "Ole" Baumann's 1963 "Origin of the Abu," published in the Fort Campbell newspaper and reprinted in the Abu/Ibu newsletter No. 1, 25 March 1986.

across another open paddy, this one 75 yards long with absolutely no cover or concealment; the strength of the platoon had gone from thirty-five to eight men before they were halfway across, with the weapons squad suffering 100 percent casualties. Among the KIA were Harry the Horse (who'd led the attack) and his RTO, Reuben "Sweet Daddy Grace" Garnett. The story went that Harry fell first, and when Sweet Daddy automatically went to his aid, he was dropped by the same gun that had killed his friend. Sweet Daddy was holding Harry's hand when he died; so far from home, the bond of love and friendship these two men shared in life and death transcended the separate worlds they'd known in America—Harry Godwin was an old-line southerner, and Reuben Garnett a black man born and raised in the ghettos of Philadelphia.

The Abu survivors sat dazed and defeated, hunkered down behind rice-paddy walls. I knew I had to get them back on their horses immediately or they'd never ride again. "So you guys have taken your lumps," I began, and proceeded to remind them of who they were ("The Abus, the best!"), and what Abu, the 1/327, and the U.S. Army paratrooper was all about. Then I tore their collective ass for violating the basics, which had led to all their problems in the first place.

I must have begun my speech squatted down near the troopers and then stood up and started walking around, because suddenly a sergeant called out, "Get down, sir! There's a machine gun in that house" (referring to a substantial stone structure in the village behind us).

"Fuck a lot of machine guns," I replied, and marched over to the paddy wall beyond which stood the house. I turned to the men. "Who's going with

me?" I asked, and hopped over the wall. I started moving toward the house, using paddy walls as a concealed and covered approach. I was damn scared—I didn't want to go like Jim Gardner—but since I'd gone through the village with Darryl and Hancock on my way to Abu's position and hadn't seen a single live enemy, I figured the odds had to be on my side. Besides, the exercise was worth it if only to set an example, and make the Abus grab hold of their bootstraps and pull themselves up. Some, mostly NCOs, were already doing so—about a dozen had followed me over that first paddy wall.

When I got to the side of the house, I threw a grenade through the window, then jumped up and hosed down the dead crew inside. Then I formed a skirmish line of the troopers who'd joined me for a sweep through the village. I was end man, moving along a paddy wall. We hadn't gone very far when I saw sudden movement on my right. Out of a spider hole popped an NVA soldier holding a rifle in one hand, a grenade in the other. The guy was about to throw the grenade in front of the skirmish line. I could see there was no way I'd be able to spin my rifle around fast enough to stop him, so I just dropped my weapon and tackled the guy. I threw his grenade away and dragged him out of his hole. He was wounded, probably in the previous day's fight, and I turned him over to Press with instructions to get a chopper to evacuate him to Brigade HQ, and make damn sure no one killed him in the meantime. The Abu boys weren't butchers, but after what they'd been through, the passion for revenge would naturally be high.

Hancock and I personally counted 118 dead NVA troops on the ground at My Phu before I left him to his new command. He was a good choice as skipper, as competent an officer as he was a scrounger, and the ideal guy to charge up the Abus, having been A Company's XO both at Fort Campbell and in the early Vietnam days. Unfortunately for all concerned, however, Hancock was not so lucky on the battlefield. Less than twenty-four hours after he took command of the Abus, he was evacuated to the States, his hand badly wounded in the mortar attack on our fire base that the 95th NVA, our opponents at My Phu (as they'd been at My Canh), went ahead with, just as one of the POWs had outlined, despite the beating we'd given them the day before. So Hancock was gone. Captain Wayne Dill, a replacement from the 82d, and a brave, solid soldier who was not afraid to tell the boss what he thought, became the Abus' new Old Man.

The 1st Brigade received a well-earned Valorous Unit Citation for the Tuy Hoa operations, and the 1/327 got a separate one for My Phu. VUCs weren't easy to come by, so both brigade and battalion were damn proud. For my guys in the 1/327, though, the experience at Tuy Hoa had meant a lot more. The soldiers had begun to get hard there, not just physically, but upstairs, where it really counted. After eight months in Vietnam they'd dealt death and seen death in numbers none could have imagined. They'd endured leeches and jungle rot, constant, heavy rains and clammy clothes that chilled them in their sleep, and the "wait-a-minute" bushes that could hold a trooper as tenaciously as a strand of barbed wire. Many fought malaria and hepatitis; all fought fear, not just of the enemy, but of the snakes, the tigers of the Central Highlands that reportedly pounced on troopers, the monkeys that dropped out of trees at night like stealthy Viet Cong (at least one of these was hacked to death by a trooper with a machete in the dark), and of course the night itself. But through it all they'd learned, and little by little exchanged bravado for real confidence.

Everyone did, if they stayed long enough—even the pilots like Outlaw 5–3, who'd insisted on having his chopper blasted out of the sky at My Canh. I met him again four months later, at a big party we threw in celebration of the battalion's brilliantly fought, end-of-tour graduation exercise, the battle of Dak To. When Outlaw 5–3 heard one of my guys call me Savvy Volley 5, he came over to introduce himself and tell me that as a result of our last encounter, he'd left his know-it-all, God's-gift-to-aviation days behind. That same evening a lot of other pilots came up and introduced themselves as White Eagle 4 or Splendid Horse 2 or whatever their call signs were, and mentioned the operations where we'd served together.

It wasn't too often that guys on the ground met the men who supported them, and vice versa—we were all generally just voices on the radio—so there was an immediate camaraderie among us. And there was a lot of mutual respect, too. We looked in awe at the pilots for some of the amazing risks they took in our support, particularly to evacuate wounded soldiers on the ground; the pilots treated us infantry guys as if we were Wyatt Earp gunfighters in the old Tombstone bar, the ones who dished it out and had to take it the hard way.

In a high-tech world, the pilots somehow made their helicopters a romantic symbol of a bygone era. They rode those choppers as they would have done their horses in the old Cav or cowboy days, coming in guns ablazing, swooping down over the battlefield "to save the day" with their tremendous mobility and firepower. Unfortunately, the feeling of power most chopper drivers felt could work both for the infantry and against us: overenthusiastic pilots sometimes got a little carried away, firing first and only then ascertaining whether the target was friend or foe. This developed in the infantry a definite ambivalence toward the fliers and their gallant steeds, but like a lot of relationships, love-hate or other, if it were all weighed up, we wouldn't have dreamed of letting them go.

Chapter 16
The Battle of Dak To

★ ★ ★

When Walt Meinzen, Colonel Rogers's successor as CO of the 1/327, was evacuated the night before the 1st Brigade's next big mission, I had already been in Vietnam for thirteen months (the last of which had been up at Brigade again, as General Pearson's executive officer), and was soon due to rotate home. So I was incredibly surprised when, the morning of the operation, General Pearson called me to his command tent at the Central Highlands Special Forces camp at Dak To to tell me that I was to take Meinzen's place as commander of the 1/327. "Major, you were down there seven months and you know it better than anyone," he said. "We're going to have some tough opposition this time, so get read into the plan. Any questions, come back to me."

I arrived at the battalion and it was old home week. All the old-timers rushed up with a chorus of "Great to have you back"; it was as if I'd been away at Brigade a year rather than a month. I had a look at the battle plan. The 1/327's mission was to relieve a nearby Special Forces camp at Tou Morong, atop a high mountain reportedly surrounded by a large NVA force and under the constant harassment of mortar fire. A year before, the June monsoons had provided the backdrop for the enemy to successfully overrun eight such outposts (including our present base at Dak To) near the Laos-Cambodia–South Vietnam border; with the monsoon season of '66 about to start any day, the powers that be felt it better to relieve and abandon Tou Morong rather than take the risk of a replay of the events of the previous year.

No two commanders see a tactical problem the same way. Just two hours before the airmobile assault that would begin the operation, as I examined Meinzen's attack plan for the first time, I knew I'd alter it the moment we hit the LZs behind the Tou Morong objective. My reasoning was simply that I didn't think the NVA gave two hoots in hell about destroying the Special Forces camp at Tou Morong. What they wanted was to destroy the relieving force. I was sure we were being enticed into a very conventional (by guerrilla standards) Viet Cong insurgent trap, that of luring the counterinsurgent force into a situation by making it believe that one of its camps was threatened, and that a quick victory could be achieved in the process of saving the day. The fact that two NVA "ralliers" (so-called for their apparent rallying to our side) had just given themselves up at Dak To and reported that the SF camp would soon be hit only added to my conviction that Tou Morong was a trap.

Meinzen's plan called for a rifle company to attack parallel with each of two roads that led to the camp (one from the north, one from the east), with the third company remaining at the LZ, north of Tou Morong, with our command post and mortar platoon. I felt sure this was exactly what the enemy expected, and they would be waiting along the two roads in ambush. So I decided after the airmobile phase we'd go cross-country instead, despite the hellish navigation and difficult terrain. We'd take our time—Tou Morong had been "under siege" since the middle of May (it was now 3 June) and another day or so wouldn't hurt them.

The Tigers had secured our LZ on D-1 (the day before I joined the battalion), and now our airmobile assault was made unopposed. We made our way overland, two companies moving abreast, their scout sections deployed well in front of the main force. With our big fists locked together, the enemy realized he wasn't going to get his pound of flesh for free, and in the two days it took to get to our objective, we had less than a handful of contacts.

We reached the Tou Morong camp and prepared for the movement of its 150 inhabitants down the hill to Dak To. The North Vietnamese had broken off their mortar attacks on the outpost, no doubt damn disappointed we hadn't stumbled into their trap. Still, their plans had not been completely foiled: according to Don Korman, who'd heard about it over the artillery net, while we were traveling cross-country the day before, the 1/42 ARVN Regiment had made *their* approach to Tou Morong along one of the roads, been ambushed just as we would have been, and taken four dead and nineteen wounded.

Two/502 CO Hank Emerson and General Pearson and his staff flew into Tou Morong for a "what to do next" conference: should we continue to look around here or give up and move elsewhere? Between the ARVN ambush and my gut feeling, I knew that regardless of his present silence our foe was still in the area. But before I joined the powwow, I wandered over to one of the inhabitants of Tou Morong, a

Montagnard corporal,* who confirmed it. I pulled out a map. "Where are the NVA?" I asked him.

"Down there," he replied, indicating a valley below the outpost.

"Are there many NVA there?"

"Many, many. Maybe a regiment. Maybe more."

"Do you know that for a fact?"

"Oh, yes," the Montagnard said, "I patrol there, but I never go there now. None of my men will go there."

"Thanks a lot," I told him, and joined General Pearson and his staff, the latter of whom were firmly of the opinion that the 24th NVA Regiment, our reported opponent, had vacated the battlefield and therefore so should we. Of course, Pearson's staff didn't know what the Montagnard corporal had told me, but as I listened to their argument, it quickly became clear that through some very serious breakdown in communication they also didn't know about the previous day's ambush of the ARVN unit on the road to Tou Morong. As such, their arguments for leaving were totally logical, even if they were totally wrong. Meanwhile I was smelling an incredible firefight that would put the 1/327 well in front of Emerson's 2/502 in terms of the friendly (but no less serious) "we're the best unit" rivalry we shared in the brigade, so when Pearson asked for my opinion, without going into details I said I thought I might stick around Tou Morong for a while and have a look in the valley.

"It's all yours," the General said.

I deployed my units in a recon screen, little fingers to wind carefully down the valley, each platoon no more than an hour's reinforcement time from anoth-

---

*The Montagnards are the indigenous mountain people of Vietnam.

er. Ben Willis's Abus* made three sharp contacts with an estimated reinforced platoon of NVA; tragically, during the fight a friendly artillery barrage landed right in the center of one of Ben's platoons, killing five troopers and wounding five more. Everything stopped while we sorted out the debacle and evacuated the casualties. It wasn't exactly the greatest way to start the operation.

As darkness fell I had everyone hold up and dig in, planning to continue the hunt come first light. All was quiet until 0200 hours. Then Captain Don Whalen's B Battery, 2/320 Arty, which was in direct support of us—and under the 1/327's operational control (OPCON)—came under attack from an estimated battalion-size enemy force. Heavy mortar fire preceded the assault; then, with bugles blowing, the NVA came at the position in waves, as the Chinese had in Korea, and as the Viet Minh had against France's elite Mobile Group 100 on this very same Central Highlands ground a dozen years before. The gunners quickly found they were virtually on their own: only one platoon of all of A Company, 2/502, which had been tasked with securing Whalen's battery, actually got into position to help them. (A2/502, which was also OPCON of the 1/327, had been too spread out from the first. When the enemy hit, the unit was basically overwhelmed, many of its number being pinned, the outpost squad closest to the enemy's ingress route nearly being trampled by racing hordes of enemy soldiers intent only on Whalen's position.) Meanwhile, with a "Smokey the Bear" flare ship hovering over the battlefield, dropping flares and lighting the ground like day, Whalen's artillerymen

---

*Willis had taken over the Abus some six weeks before, when Wayne Dill came down with malaria. Since his recovery, Dill had commanded C Company.

fought like lions for their lives and their positions, even reclaiming overrun guns and firing them point-blank into their attackers' ranks.

Dawn was fast approaching. I called the Tiger commander, Sterling Fairchild,* whose unit was near the action, and ordered him to set up an ambush on the trail I was sure the enemy would use to withdraw before first light. The Tiger CO started to bitch over the very busy battalion command net that he didn't want to do it. He was close to rotation and didn't want to get knocked off. I had more things on my mind than Fairchild's DEROS. "Just do it," I snapped.

Next, I got Ben Willis's Abus moving toward Whalen's battery (while supporting the defending gunners with 81mm mortar fire), and B and C companies poised for a first-light airmobile assault deep behind the enemy's escape route. Between these units and the A2/502, I had five strong forces to chop up the NVA withdrawal and pick off their stragglers. I was confident because I felt I'd been down this road before. The situation was not that much different than what the Wolfhounds had experienced in April of '51, at the outset of the Chinese Spring Offensive. Then, the Chinese had penetrated G Company and had us all on the run, but by the morning the penetration had been sealed and the Chinese could not withdraw. They were caught in a sack not unlike what I was trying to draw now, and we had destroyed them in detail.

I don't know how or when I got word that Fairchild had disobeyed my order. All I know was that the ambush was not set, no sack was drawn, and come the dawn many an enemy soldier slipped away down that very trail. Fortunately the plan was not totally blown

---

*A pseudonym

despite what I considered Fairchild's act of cowardice. Between my other elements and our tremendous supporting fire (including "Puff the Magic Dragon," an aircraft whose mounted Gatling guns spat 450 rounds per second, enough to cover the area of a football field in three seconds, a slug hitting every square foot along the way), a first-light sweep of the area revealed eighty-six enemy dead from the 24th NVA Regiment. Our own casualties for the night were four American KIA and ten wounded.

Still, I was furious, and after moving B and C companies out by chopper to sweep down from Whalen's position toward the valley of the Montagnard corporal's "many, many" NVA, I brought the Tigers in and relieved Fairchild on the spot. I didn't give a damn if he was a short-timer. Almost everyone was, and some were well past their rotation dates. And in Fairchild's case, while it was bad enough that he, a Regular officer *(and commander of the Tiger Force!)*, bitched out loud on the battalion command fact that he clearly disobeyed an order that might have changed the course of the battle soon to follow was inexcusable. So I relieved him, and brought in another young captain, Neville Bumstead,* to take his place. I wanted to get the Tigers out into the field again right away, just in case any of them had soaked up their erstwhile commander's cold feet.

In the middle of all this a reporter came up to me, introduced himself as Ward Just from the *Washington Post,* and said he wanted to go along on one of our patrols. I gave him to Bumstead and the Tigers and hoped he'd keep his head down. Fortunately the initiative was all ours as the Above the Rest com-

---

*A pseudonym

panies—each broken into platoon-size formations (giving me nine maneuver units plus the Tigers)—combed the dense Highlands bush killing stragglers, two here and four there.

It was the beginning of six days of continual contact for the battalion, trying days, but ones in which the men, after a year of growing on the battlefield, remained strong, resolute, and courageous. Besides an enemy who "hugged our belts"—intermingled with our forces—to neutralize our incredible firepower, the men fought lung-busting hills and virtually impassable jungles—terrain as bad as, if not worse than, the worst in Korea, more like the Huertgen Forest along the Siegfried Line.

On the second full day of combat, 7 June, Bumstead's Tigers wandered right into the middle of an enemy base camp. By mid-afternoon they were under a tremendous amount of fire, and the new skipper was beginning to crack under the strain. Charlie Company, under the command of Wayne Dill, moved to reinforce and got into a wild fight of its own; Willis, who'd been in a tough fight since his Abus jumped off the day before, also went to the rescue, while we kept the Tigers alive with 155 and 105 artillery fire blasting with pinpoint precision around their position.

Meanwhile, word came that the Tigers had taken terrible casualties, among them the reporter, Ward Just. A wounded civilian was a drama I didn't need at this moment, and the only thing worse was the news that Dill's unit, having extricated itself from one fight, had again locked horns with the enemy just 100 meters from the Tigers. As night fell, Willis's Abus formed a perimeter around the Tigers *and* the beleaguered members of Charlie Company, giving all within a chance to breathe while continuing to slug it out with the enemy themselves.

From the Tigers came word that eight of the wounded were critical: without medevac they wouldn't last until morning. But medevac seemed like an impossible dream. No way could a chopper land at the Tiger position, heavily wooded and ringed as it was by determined, well-entrenched enemy troops, and in the dark yet. Still, an all-volunteer chopper crew dared to try it. They used a USAF HH44 "Husky" rather than a slick or other medevac aircraft. The bird hovered over the Tigers, and one by one the brave crew winched the eight critically wounded on board, as the enemy fired enthusiastically at them from below.

All eight cases made it off the battlefield alive. But later, when Ed Abood, my XO, brought me the casualty list from the brigade collecting station, the flawless operation suddenly displayed a worrisome hitch. The civilian reporter's name was not among those reported to be evacuated from the Tigers. Civilians had priority in this kind of situation, so I was pretty concerned; when I called Bumstead, he explained that Just had refused evacuation because there were men far more seriously wounded who deserved priority. It was an exceptional gesture on the reporter's part, and one that won me for life.

When the balance of the Tigers had been sprung and had come home the next morning, they totaled just sixteen effectives, nine of whom were wounded, and a single NCO. We filled up the unit with new volunteers, but whatever plans I may have had for them or my companies went on hold in the afternoon, when Hank Emerson called me and said his C Company was in a big jam and about to be overrun. Battered Willis and the Abus, who had already been in constant, tough contact with the stubborn NVA for more than two full days, were in the best position to go to the rescue; I turned them around and on they went. I gave Emerson operational control of Willis' A Company, but mother hen that I was, I set one of my radios on the 2/502 battalion frequency to make sure my men were okay.

What happened next, on 9 June 1966, was one of the great tragedies of the entire two-week battle. The 1/327 had so far borne the brunt of the fighting at Dak To, and we would continue to do so for ten more hard-slugging days. But the newspapers did not report that Ben Willis and the Abus got into the fight of their lives that day, taking twenty-six wounded and six dead on the way to rescue the C2/502, or that one of Ben's platoon leaders, Lieutenant Ken Collins, had his eye blown out during the battle but continued directing his platoon, holding his eyeball in his hand, or that, when the whole thing was over, Ben's men, wounded and all, refused to be lifted out, determined as they were to go out under their own steam. Instead, the headlines blared that West Point football hero Captain William S. Carpenter, Jr., onetime all-American "lonesome end," now commander of C2/502, courageously dropped napalm on his own troops.

The reason for this drastic course of action, so the story went, was that Carpenter was surrounded, had taken heavy, heavy losses, and believed his unit was on the verge of being overrun, with the enemy already swarming among his people. When the incident was over, while it turned out that his unit had suffered some six KIA and twenty-five seriously wounded, enemy dead on C Company's hill were as scarce as hen's teeth.

The publicity that ensued was not Carpenter's fault, nor were the John Wayne–like embellishments of the story each time it was reported. Still, in terms of unit pride and unit rivalry between the 2/502 and the 327 (units that, at Bastogne twenty-some years before, had stood back-to-back, taken the best the enemy could dish out, and stopped them cold), the effect of the affair was devastating. And when it was all over, ironically, about the only one among the men of the 1/327 who had a good word to say about the tragic incident was Ben Willis, whose Abus had taken the brunt of it in the effort to relieve Carpenter's company. "I can't in my heart blame Carpenter for anything he did," he said. "Unless you're there, on the ground, in that damn jungle, under that triple canopy, nose to nose with the other guy, you don't know. And if you don't know, you shouldn't pass judgment." Ben was right, of course. But for me as the battalion commander of one damn heroic battalion, it didn't make the heavy Abu casualties, or all the Carpenter headlines, any easier to swallow.

The next day the refitted Tigers were on their way out again to join Dill's Charlie Company in the attempt to relieve Willis, who was still engaged. Dill found himself in continual contact throughout the day, however, and Willis was left on his own to conduct a nighttime withdrawal from his position. By that time Pearson had told me a B-52 "arc-light" strike was on the way; I left Charlie Company (which remained in contact much of the next day) and the Tigers in the area until the very last moment, fixing the NVA in place with dummy radio traffic so the enemy wouldn't realize we were pulling out in preparation for it. The arc-light strike dropped silently from 30,000 feet, cracking like a thousand thunderbolts on impact, leaving the ground pockmarked with deep craters, like the dark side of the moon. Both the 2/502 and the 1/327 went in right afterward with little resistance. It was estimated the million-dollar strike was responsible for some 200 enemy casualties.

Like most of the men in the battalion, I went from the sixth to the twelfth of June with virtually no sleep. I was a walking zombie by the time we pulled back for the B-52 strike; as soon as Willis got out and we got him refitted, I hit the sack for twelve straight hours, and I doubt if I ever slept better in my life. Fortunately, the first couple of post–arc-light days were quiet, giving everyone a chance to catch up on much-needed rest. Only then did the monsoons come. Luck alone had brought them late, but their absence had been decisive.

The NVA's plan had been to lure a major U.S. unit into this area of Vietnam at a time when the terrain and weather favored them. If the NVA had had their way, the monsoonal rains, mists, and low cloud cover would have rendered our air power impotent, and only two forces, theirs and our infantry, would have squared off against each other at Dak To. In that scenario, they thought, the Americans would have been chewed up, just as we'd been in the past. But while the good weather did foil the NVA plan, I felt sure they would have had a harder time with the 1st Brigade than they'd expected, even if the weather had gone their way. We'd learned quite a bit over the last year, and air power notwithstanding, this time around we had generally refused to attack the enemy's buzz saw. The only time we really played into their hand was during the relief of Carpenter, and had that not all happened so quickly, I might have recognized in the situation a typical NVA ruse: most likely, the 2/502 company, like Tou Morong, was just the lure, and the relief element—the Abus—was really the juicy morsel the NVA were after.

It would have been good had Operation Hawthorne, the name given to the relief of the Tou Morong outpost and the subsequent events, ended after the B-52 strike. As it was, the search-and-destroy missions in the area continued, and on 17 June the weary Abus, low in NCOs and platoon leaders, high in new replacements and guys just days from rotation, made contact with a small NVA force.

There was no point in taking a lot of casualties. Willis played it safe and called for fire support. But the 1st Air Cav gunships that came to his aid made a terrible error: instead of shooting up the enemy, they shot up the Abus, wounding twenty-one (including Willis and the rest of the officers, most of the NCOs, and, worst of all, every single medic) and killing XO George Perry, our not-so-good-at-poker but very good buddy, with a tiny piece of shrapnel through the heart. It was a tragedy only compounded by the fact that Perry, two weeks over his DEROS, hadn't even had to be there. He'd just wanted to help Ben and his beloved Abus, and the plan had been for him to take the first resupply chopper out, get his gear, and go home the next day. It was a damn shame.

Word of the fiasco quickly got to my tac CP. I immediately grabbed Darryl and called Raphiel at his aid station at Dak To. The doc in turn grabbed Milton Turner, the medical platoon leader, and a medic named Nichols, and together with a couple of engineers with chain saws, they made their way by chopper to the battle area.

There was no landing zone near A Company's position (hence the chain saws to cut one out), just steep hills and thick forest no different from most of the Highlands. In my C&C I told the pilot to get as low as he could. We churned through the underbrush, the chopper blades cracking like gunfire against the bamboo and treetops as we cut a hole inching us toward the jungle floor. About fifteen feet above what might have been the LZ, Darryl and I jumped out, and radioed Raphiel that that would be the only way in for him and his people, too.

The doc was none too enthusiastic about the idea of jumping in. But when he got to the site, the longer his chopper hovered with him sitting inside it (so he told me later), the more he started thinking he'd be a lot safer on the ground than up in the air, because in his mind's eye he could vividly see an enemy trooper taking aim at him at that very moment. After a very long few seconds, it just became too much for him, and he jumped out of the bird, picked up his aid bags, and headed into the bush. Turner and Nichols were delayed in joining Raphiel in patching up Ben and his troops when the engineers jumped out of their chopper and each promptly broke an ankle, but soon things started getting squared away. Luckily, Willis wasn't hurt too badly and could stay with the company.

When there was nothing more to be done, Raphiel and Turner hopped onto the last medevac chopper out without even a good-bye, leaving young Nichols, Darryl, and me out there without ponchos, without anything to protect us from the torrential rains that followed that night. Having assumed the good doctor would want to suffer right along with me, I was a little aggravated that Raphiel hadn't stuck around, but I couldn't really blame him. After all, he'd been there when we needed him, to care for the wounded and set an example for the medics in his charge, and he hadn't even had to do that. No one forced Raphiel Benjamin, the battalion surgeon, to tag along on operations, or to jump, figuratively *or* literally, into the fray, though that was exactly what he did throughout some of the worst of the 1/327's fighting at Tuy Hoa and Dak To. The adventure part had died quickly for this civilian doctor whom I considered among the bravest of the brave, but still he was always there, because he knew we needed him. And in just the same way, the gutsy forty-man medical platoon Raphiel oversaw knew we needed them. Consequently they flinched at nothing, paid the price in blood, and as a unit completely turned over three times in one year.

I didn't know what it was about medics. I used to think they joined the Medical Corps because they had a double load of courage, but maybe it was just the title itself that transformed them into the most valiant band of men I ever knew. Medics didn't wait for a miracle to pull the wounded to a safe shelter—they *were* the miracle that pulled, slid, dragged, and packed shattered bodies out of danger. And they performed miracles: stopping bleeding, stopping shock, relieving pain with morphine, and getting IVs going to pump life into broken fighters. Many packed M-16s along with their forty-pound medical kits, but their job was to save lives, not take them, and they risked their own, again and again, answering calls that took them right into the line of fire—machine gun, mortar, sniper, mines—without hesitation.

Their most powerful medicine was their encouragement ("You got it made . . . just a scratch . . . you'll see that girl again"), a never-ending patter to keep minds occupied while deft hands administered aid or tried to sort out a stomach or a chest ripped open by shot. Grievously wounded soldiers were further assisted by the brave pilots who performed medevac missions, but it was the medics who made the difference on the ground, until the choppers could get in.

Selfless and serving beyond good sense, hundreds if not thousands of medics died in the line of duty, to save not just their buddies but the life of every man who fell on the battlefield. From my experience in two wars, it is these men, the medics—the "docs"—who hold the most special place of respect and trust in my infantryman's heart, and I'm sure there are a couple of million other men in the United States alone who feel the exact same way.

On the eighteenth of June, a resupply aircraft arrived at Willis's position with the bum's roll (complete with poncho) I'd neglected to take along with me in my haste to get to the Abus the day before. The first thing I did was brush my teeth—in the jungles of the Central Highlands it was about the only thing you could do to remember you were a civilized human being. You couldn't wash up there (during the monsoons you were always wet anyway), you couldn't shave (the slightest nick, like the inevitable cuts, rashes, or jungle sores, turned septic). The damp, dark jungle was not particular: *everything* rotted there—your boots, your clothes, your skin. It was a hell of a way to have to fight.

We spent the day beating around in the woods, but no contact was made. The enemy force had pretty well vacated the area; after the severe beating we'd given them, we figured they'd slipped back into Cambodia to regroup. With that, word finally came we'd be heading back to the brigade's Dak To base, where it had all begun some seventeen days before. General Pearson popped into my forward CP to tell me about the move: "Hack, I've given Emerson the aircraft. They're going to pick him up first, and then come back and get you."

I quietly imploded. The 1/327 had done the bulk of the fighting; the 2/502 ended up getting all the press *and* all the glory as a result of the Carpenter incident, and now, to top it off, Emerson's people were getting the aircraft and going home before mine.

"Never mind, sir," I told the General. "I don't want any choppers. I'll walk my battalion out of here."

"What do you mean?" asked Pearson.

"We'll just sweep back," I said. "I got over a hundred replacements in the last two weeks. Almost all the platoon leaders and NCOs are new. It'll give them a good shakeout, and we'll screen the battle area right back to the Dak To airfield."

The ten-mile walk took a night and a morning, and it *was* a good training exercise, not just for the new men, but for the guys who'd been there all along, if only to shake out their hangover from the big fight. We made no contact, but almost lost a man when a viper crawled into his fart sack and bit him. A night medevac saved his life, and the rest of the journey was without incident. Just shy of Dak To proper, I sent a radio message to battalion Administration officer S-1 Glynn Mallory to bring out the battalion colors and company guidons. I assembled the company commanders and told them we were going to march home walking tall, and show the 2/502 and the rest of the brigade who the *real* soldiers were in this outfit. Soon my well-proven battalion had lined up at proper intervals in a column on each side of the road, and we began to hike home.

I was leading, followed by the colors, my command group, and the Tiger commander, and then the rest of the battalion, each company led by their individual commanders and company guidons. And as we got closer to the base camp, the little "entrance" Glynn Mallory and I had set up just started to build. It was as if someone had said, "Hey, there's a parade!" and everyone wanted to get into the act. All the support people rushed to the side of the road to cheer us on—even an ad hoc band that started playing "Stars and Stripes Forever"—and with every cheer my boys stood taller and their stride grew that much jauntier. As we passed the 2/502 assembly area, about twenty feet from the road stood Hank Emerson, by his CP. He was fresh out of the shower, and he was shaving. He looked toward the road for a moment, his mouth agape, and then he just shook his head. "Hackworth, you son of a bitch!" he called with a smile.

"Above the Rest, sir," I shouted, and gave him a snappy salute. It was a rare thrill to outgun the Gunfighter.

In a totally uncoordinated effort, people were coming from everywhere to look at the warriors. General

Pearson had even fallen out with his staff in front of the brigade HQ to salute the battalion as we marched by, and just before I peeled off to join them, a group of aviators did an impromptu five-airplane flyover of the columns in our honor.

I, too, saluted my fine companies as they strutted past, filthy and unshaven, jungle boots rubbed white with wear, still with camouflage in their helmets, some bandaged up and limping like little drummer boys. It was, then and forever, the proudest moment of my life. We'd taken twenty-seven dead and 129 wounded, but we'd killed 276 NVA for the price. The men had fought bravely and well against terrific odds and in bitching conditions—they'd been in Vietnam for a year and *they'd learned.*

Chapter 17
Hardcore

★ ★ ★

The soldiers of the 1st Brigade, 101st Airborne, did learn plenty during that first year in Vietnam. Unfortunately, then they went home, taking all their lessons with them and leaving the men who replaced them to learn the same lessons for themselves. This pattern was repeated throughout Army units for the duration of the war (as it had been throughout the Korean conflict as well), leading Vietnam expert John Paul Vann to remark that the United States was not in Vietnam for ten years, but for one year ten times.

As the conflict continued, the basic experience of the soldier who served in Vietnam only decreased, as the regulars from units forged over years in peacetime finished their stints and were replaced by draftees processed through basic and advanced individual training mills in four to five months. And, as the years passed and antiwar sentiment ballooned on the home front, the draftees themselves became more surly and less receptive to knowledge that would keep them alive. Even those who brought some spark with them into the training usually had it snuffed out by their mostly draftee instructors, who had already spent their year in Vietnam and were now marking time in the training centers until their two-year hitch was up.

It was in this climate of wholesale unpreparedness and angry resentment that after two and a half years in noncombat assignments—first at the Pentagon, then studying the war with Army historian and apologist S.L.A. Marshall, then commanding a training battalion at Fort Lewis, Washington—I returned to Vietnam in January 1969 as a lieutenant colonel, to command the 9th Division's mostly draftee 4th Battalion, 39th Infantry.

There was no sense in showing this sorry outfit I was in a state of shock. It wasn't just that the CP group slept on cots inside tents, that they had folding chairs and stateside footlockers, portable radios, and plastic coolers filled with beer and Coke at their fire-support base out in the field. More than that, it was that they had portable toilets, too, and apparently were blissfully unaware that just nearby their troops were crapping on the ground and not even covering it up.

And then there were the soldiers themselves. Throughout the fire base (the purpose of which, as designed by the French during the Indochina war, was to protect the artillery battery deployed at its center), amid the shit and the toilet paper and the machine-gun ammo lying in the mud, were troops who wore love beads and peace symbols and looked more like something out of Haight-Ashbury than soldiers in the U.S. Army. All were low on spirit and a few were high, openly, on marijuana. There was minimum security. Few men carried or cared for their weapons—most had let them go red with rust as they strolled around without them. Grenades weren't taped, and when a unit moved out, most of the gunners wore their ammo

Pancho Villa–style, the ideal way to guarantee a weapon jam sometime down the track, when dirty, dented cartridges were inserted into their M-60s.

I realized that to make this unit an effective military force I'd have to implement about a thousand changes. So I figured we'd start with five a day—little things, *basic* things, like "wear your steel pot," and "clean and carry your rifle at all times," and "ammunition will not be worn Pancho Villa–style." My first order upon taking over the battalion was that come darkness the fire-support base perimeter would pull back 300 meters. The previously unchallenged troops instantly began to grumble at this, but the truly mutinous feeling did not begin until my next order, which was that anything the men couldn't carry twenty-four hours a day was to be gone on the next chopper. Good-bye tents and cots and rucksacks and footlockers. The bitching and moaning began in earnest as piles and piles of junk mounted at the LZ to be whisked away by Chinook. But I didn't care. I wasn't there to have them like me.

By midnight, as per my instructions, the battalion was dug in in new positions, with security out. A short time later we were hit with a barrage of rocket and recoilless-rifle fire, but most of it fell on the *old* positions. The following morning Bob Press, the Abus' first sergeant in our shared 1/101 days, whom I'd nabbed for my sergeant major in the 4/39, reported a big decrease in the bitching as he toured the perimeter. It hadn't gone unnoticed by the troops that there'd been no casualties the night before, where in Press's estimation "at least twenty would have been headed for hospitals or zipped up in body bags" had they been sleeping on cots or even just above ground (much less in the old positions). So I won a few hearts and minds the first night.

But none too many. For the first month I was with the unit, I refused to crack a smile. And by constantly demanding professionalism from everyone, just about everything I did pissed somebody off. Bravo Company even put a bounty on my head; I called their bluff on an early operation when I found myself part of their skirmish line approaching a small enemy force in a clump of nipa palm, a type of vegetation ubiquitous to the Mekong Delta, the immense alluvial plain in which the 9th Div operated near the southeastern coast of South Vietnam.

A fight seemed imminent, and since my experience told me that soldiers in a firefight are generally too busy, too scared, and place far too much faith in their leader's ability to get them out safely to knock him off, I felt it was a perfectly unperilous (for me) opportunity to make Bravo shit or get off the pot. So I moved up well in front of the advancing skirmish line, with my back an easy target for even the sorriest rifleman in Vietnam. And I was right. Thoughts of wasting the battalion commander were forgotten as the little fight heated up; working together with a common purpose, we killed a few VC in exchange for not a single B Company casualty, and I don't think I heard much about a price on my head ever again.

The men of the 4/39 had no unit identity, and no pride in themselves. As a first step toward rectifying this, I decided to call my hard-luck battalion "the Hardcore," and the troops "Recondos" (the latter being the nickname of the 1st Brigade, 9th Div, of which the 4/39 was a part). When a soldier saluted an officer, I insisted he say, "Hardcore Recondo, sir!" and when the officer responded, it had to be with a heartfelt, "No fucking slack!" At first my cynical hippie troops sniggered over what they considered "GI Joe bullshit," but it didn't matter—I knew the time would come when it would mean one hell of a lot to each and every one of them.

Simultaneously, I started establishing SOPs that would not only keep the troops alive, but also give them, for the first time, the feeling that they were in charge of their situation, not at the mercy of the VC or their insidious booby traps. (In the six months before I took over the battalion, the 4/39, without meeting the enemy at all, had taken casualties in the equivalent of 100 percent of its unit strength, from rockets, mortars, booby traps, and friendly fire.) The SOPs included such things as every officer having to read Mao's *Little Red Book* (how could we beat an enemy if we made no attempt to know what made him tick?) and 100 percent stand-to's prior to dawn, dusk, and sometimes in the middle of the night, any of which might occasionally be augmented with a Mad Minute.

The 4/39 quickly began to shape up. Just days after I arrived, Brigade CO John P. Geraci gave us an invaluable push when he made the Hardcore the base of an independent task force and assigned us to the Plain of Reeds, a sprawling AO that in WW II would have been assigned to an entire field army. Our mission was to deny Viet Cong infiltration from nearby Cambodia through the Delta by picking off the VC at (and between) their many way stations in the area.

With few exceptions, we didn't make much contact in the three weeks we were there, but the Plain of Reeds mission gave me a unique opportunity to shake down the battalion and mold it into a fighting force with no interference from above. We moved our fire-support base every three days, each time digging in, filling sandbags, the complete drill. Each morning we were joined by an Air Cav troop from the "Black Hawk" Squadron (7/1 Cav), and with these pros, we methodically searched the wide expanses of tall elephant grass that particularly characterized the Plain of Reeds. While the rifle companies generally worked over large areas in a loose recon screen (saturating the AO in the hope of stirring up a contact), based on intelligence, we also "jitterbugged" (a series of predesignated helicopter insertions made one by one until a contact was made) and conducted "eagle flights" (helicopter raids in which we went right to a suspected target).

Both jitterbugging and eagle flights were ideal techniques for the Delta, terrain so flat it was just one big landing zone. While employing them, my fledgling battalion was hunting Charlie, but perhaps more important for the moment, the troops were getting damn good training along the way. And the Black Hawks, without whom it would not have been possible, were the best Air Cav I could have asked for. Theirs was a unit filled with bold and gutsy crews who knew their jobs and had little fear. They were a colorful bunch who wore blue Civil War campaign hats, had yellow crossed Cav swords painted on the noses of their choppers, and actively employed a bugler. They were characters—the real stuff of Hollywood, as *Apocalypse Now* would show a decade later.

The best way I knew to shape up the 4/39 was by day-to-day personal example, by slowly but constantly tightening the screw. I had a lot of fun playing squad and platoon leader again for those few weeks in the Plain of Reeds, checking out the leaders and getting to know all the troops as I taught them how to soldier. I soon discovered that all the 4/39 had really needed was a good kick in the ass, which included creating or bringing in leaders who cared for their men, and giving the men some sense of real purpose. Just prior to my arrival, the battalion's assignment had been the morale-busting exercise of division base-camp security at Dong Tam; now, as early as two weeks into my tenure, the troops were getting into the spirit of the hunt, rising to the challenges that daily confronted them, and even beginning to see themselves as warriors.

Throughout this period we got max support and encouragement from Colonel Geraci (or "Mal Hombre," as he was known by his radio call sign), our rough, profane, grizzly bear of a brigade commander, who ate staff officers uncooked for breakfast, but whom the troops idolized and who loved them in return. Geraci was completely decentralized in his approach, allowing me a free hand to shape up my unit as I saw fit; his noninterfering ways gave the Hardcore a chance to experiment and grow, opportunities we were all grateful for, especially when the day came that Geraci was no longer with us, and an unexpected enemy—the Beast of Delta Tango*—suddenly reared his perfumed head.

This is how it happened. One day, a strange voice using Mal Hombre's call sign started issuing orders directly to my engaged companies on my battalion command net. This was something that just wasn't done. "I don't know who you are, but you sure as hell ain't Mal Hombre," I said, "so I advise you to get off my net. It's seriously obstructing my command and control."

The voice immediately informed me that I was, in fact, speaking to the new commander of the 1st Brigade, Ira Augustus Hunt, Jr. Hunt also happened to be the division chief of staff. "All right, Mal Hombre," I said, "but if you have instructions for me,

---

*Delta Tango was the military phonetic code name for the 9th Div's base camp at Dong Tam.

give them to me on your brigade command net, which I am monitoring, and get off my internal net so I can fight my units."

"Pop a smoke. I'm coming to see you," he responded on the brigade net. I did, and before long a spit-polished chopper landed and out stepped my new CO. Ira Hunt was a tall man, handsome, but turning to fat. He looked very much a soldier, all fitted out with a rappeling rope, trench knife, and grenades (like John Wayne in *The Green Berets*), with the only perfumed-prince touches being the starch in his perfectly faded fatigues, his spit-shined shoes, and the sleeves of his shirt, each rolled up exactly five times and ending in a precise, two-and-a-half-inch roll. "Hackworth," he said, "Colonel Geraci's gone back to the States on emergency leave. I'm the interim brigade commander until a replacement comes in. Meanwhile you will do what I say and when I say it."

"Just stay off my battalion command net," I replied. "I will not allow you or anyone else to deal directly with my companies."

As one of my units was still in contact, I turned my attention to them. Hunt snapped that we'd talk "later," and ran back to his chopper with a horde of followers/assistants close behind.

The interim brigade commander—who wasn't even an infantryman, but a West Point engineer—promptly forgot my warning about speaking directly to my companies on my battalion net. Finally I just told my boys to "skip rope," which was the battalion's informal code for "go to another frequency," and we got on with the fight while Hunt presumably was kept busy playing with the dials on his radio.

A few days later the battalion was sent into the east side of Dinh Tuong Province, which was notorious booby-trap country and a hell of a place to fight. As we went into the field, I reminded my commanders not to allow their units to be lured into a wood line by a fleeing Viet Cong only to find themselves knee deep in mines. The 4/39 had the chopper assets that day (the assets were shared among the brigade's four battalions, so we generally had them every fourth day), and we began methodically searching the AO. Throughout, Hunt was up above in his chopper, overflying, oversupervising, in general playing what we called "Great Squad Leader in the Sky," without any apparent appreciation of the circumstances on the ground.

The whole morning passed with no contact, and Hunt met me on the ground where my chopper was refueling. "You're not making enough inserts," he said. To Hunt, the whole thing was only a numbers game (in this case, the more inserts, the more contacts), and he actually went on to warn me to get with the program or else. I was insulted. "I don't tell you how to build bridges," I replied, "so you don't tell me how to fight my battalion."

In the afternoon, elements of D Company were inserted into both ends of a canal. With the help of gunships, they flushed out and killed a dozen VC and captured one prisoner. It was a good start for the new D Company commander, ex-1/327 Tiger Dennis Foley, whom I'd recruited for the Hardcore team and who'd taken over his command just a few days before. Now Dennis reported numerous mines and booby traps in the contact area. I told him to break off and head for a pickup zone while Captain Emile "Chum" Robert, my magnificent artillery LNO, peppered the trees with artillery and organized the Air Force to put in a napalm strike. But then Hunt piped up on the radio. "I want the area swept," he ordered.

At this time I had only just begun to make progress getting my superiors to recognize that a field full of VC mines and booby traps, however primitive the devices, was just as deadly to life and limb as the mine fields of WW II and Korea. In wars past, you didn't go romping and stomping around in mine fields if you valued your life, or order your men to if you valued theirs. So there was no way I was going to send my infantry into this mine field now. But I couldn't tell Hunt that—my intuition was he'd use my refusal as an excuse to relieve me. *(He refused to fight the enemy, General. Killed twelve, captured one, and ran. No fighting spirit, sir . . . no fighting spirit.)* So instead I just said, "Roger, on that. I'll go down and brief the commander myself while I pick up the prisoner."

I told Foley to squat right where he was, but to dummy radio traffic as though he were moving, because I knew Hunt would be monitoring our net. With that I took the POW back to my forward CP. All too soon Hunt landed as well, lumbered over and launched into an incredible tongue-lashing. "Pursuit! Pursuit!" he screamed at me. "That's what war is all about! You don't win by bugging out!"

"Colonel Hunt," I said, as pleasantly as I knew how, "I'd like you to look at this prisoner D Company picked up. You know, sir, I think he's top brass. Just look. He's got smooth hands and feet. Look at his neck muscles. He probably hasn't carried a thing for the last ten years. And look at those intelligent eyes. You know, sir, I wouldn't be surprised if this bastard were a general!"

In an instant Hunt forgot about inserts. He forgot about monitoring my radio. He forgot about sweeps. There, before his eyes, was ninety-eight pounds of instant glory. Imagine, the first Viet Cong general captured in the war, captured in the command of Ira Augustus Hunt, Jr., West Point engineer. "You know, you might have something there, Hack," Hunt said warmly, newly friendly, like a used-car salesman about to close a deal, and he eagerly disappeared with his spoil of war. Interrogation would prove that the "general" was in fact a lieutenant with no intelligence or career-enhancing value for Hunt at all, but the ruse at least let my men keep their legs, and it got the Great Squad Leader off my back for the rest of the day.

By day's end D Company had killed some thirty VC and captured one almost-general. Before releasing the assets, I put the battalion in three company-size ambush positions, which, over the next three days (while the choppers were rotated to the other battalions and we were foot mobile), would serve as the nuclei for small recon, combat, and ambush patrols. Bone-tired, I got back into my chopper and headed off to Fire Support Base (FSB) Moore, where the 4/39 had colocated with the brigade HQ since the end of our Plain of Reeds mission.

As soon as I landed, ex-1/327 Tiger commander Nev Bumstead, now the 4/39's Operations officer, ran onto the helipad. "Thought you should know, boss, Colonel Hunt ordered me to dispatch some ambush patrols along the MSR.* He thinks the VC will be hot and heavy tonight." It was Tet of '69, and Hunt had already told me he expected a replay of the previous year.

The rage started building. "Did you do it?" I asked.

"Had to," Nev replied. "You weren't there and he wasn't going to wait around."

I was livid. Hunt probably thought since I'd obediently eaten shit all day, he could now start issuing orders to my squads—and through my S-3, a *staff officer* yet. In the Army I came from, senior officers did not break the chain of command, and staff officers never issued an order unless it was first

---

*Main supply route

approved by their immediate CO. These were cardinal rules in a unit, ones that preserved its command and control.

I stormed past Nev into the tactical operations center (TOC). I canceled the patrols. Within minutes a raging bull in the form of Colonel Hunt came barreling in. "Hackworth—" he bellowed.

I interrupted. "Colonel, I think we should step outside." I wasn't going to talk to him in front of my men, particularly not if I ended up punching him out.

We stood by the heavily sandbagged entrance of the TOC. "Colonel," I began, "you've been on my ass all day, just generally fucking me around and fucking things up. You don't issue orders directly to my subordinates, and I'll be damned if you think I'm going to take your shit."

"Let me remind you, Hackworth, that I am your brigade commander and you are being insubordinate."

"You can pull rank all you want, Colonel, because no matter what you are, you're not a soldier, even if you do stick your nose into everything as if you know what you're doing."

"I could relieve you, Hackworth!"

"Yeah? Well, go ahead. But if I leave this battalion, I promise I'll take you with me, Colonel. I'll only be pushed and bullied so far!"

I was so angry I could have killed Hunt then without a moment's regret. He must have read my thoughts, because he soon retreated to more secure territory. Only after he'd gone did I discover a more concrete reason for his withdrawal: throughout my tirade, I'd unconsciously been pounding my fist again and again into a rock-hard sandbag on the edge of the TOC, until the rugged nylon cover had ripped and the bag caved in.

Dusk came and time passed. Little by little my rage began to settle. Then I was informed I was wanted at Brigade. I felt an inner stab. I knew Hunt was going to relieve me.

With heavy heart I walked over to the brigade CP. Most unexpectedly, the first thing I saw was Hunt pacing back and forth in front of a bank of radios. From the sounds of the radio transmissions, I knew someone was in a hell of a fight, and from the worried look on Hunt's face, I knew who was getting the raw end of the deal. "Colonel," he said to me as he pointed to a map, with what seemed barely controlled hysteria, "we put a LRRP* team in here. They're in real trouble. One of their insert choppers has been shot down, they're on the ground, surrounded, and they've taken heavy casualties—sixteen WIA out of eighteen men. I want you to take my loach† and go up and see what we can do."

"What do you mean, 'we'?" I asked. It seemed to me. the reason those LRRPs (pronounced "lurps") were in trouble was that Hunt hadn't followed proper deployment procedures. Normally a division LRRP team was attached to the battalion in whose AO it was to be employed. Then the battalion commander controlled its insertions, and took care of the team with, say, a backup reaction force ready to launch if the LRRPs ran into the slightest difficulty. At the very least, Hunt's LRRPs should have had a pair of supporting gunships from the beginning, which might have taken a little heat off while the soldiers were sorting themselves out. But no. And no surprise the result. "Get me all the choppers you can spring loose," I said. "Get all the gunships to report over the

---

*Long Range Reconnaissance Patrol
†Light observation helicopter (LOH)

contact area, and all the slicks here to pick up my C Company. Tell them we'll operate on my battalion command freq." I turned and started for the bunker door. Hunt followed me.

"Colonel, do everything you can to extract them."

"Colonel Hunt," I replied, "if I get those people out, I never want you to fuck with my battalion again. You just tell me what you want done and when you want it done, but keep off my ass while I'm doing it. Do you understand?" Hunt gravely nodded his head. He knew as well as I did that if that LRRP team was eaten up by the Viet Cong, his chances of becoming boy general wouldn't be red-hot.

While Nev alerted Gordie DeRoos's C Company to prepare to move to a pickup zone to conduct a night air assault, I met Chum Robert at the helipad. A loach was waiting. Once airborne and over the contact area, I switched the helicopter's radio to the LRRP patrol frequency. "Mayday! Mayday! Mayday!" was all I could hear amidst the background chatter of automatic weapons and exploding grenades, whose fires I could see on the ground below, silhouetting the downed chopper in the middle of a mangrove swamp. I figured the LRRP RTO was so rattled he had a death grip on his "push to talk" button (although later I would discover this was not the case; the handset had actually been broken or shot in half and could not receive). "Work up a wall of steel around those cats," I yelled to Chum. "Start way out and walk it in till it's right around the chopper. Then keep it up until I tell you to lift it." The shells would keep Charlie from doing anything too provocative for a while and buy us a little time. Because that's what I needed: just then Nev called to say that the choppers had not shown up yet at the pickup zone.

Chum was putting in his artillery fire six rounds at a

time in a precise circle around the downed chopper. It was a technique we'd used many times in the Highlands with the 101; not exactly the safest procedure in the world, but it was better to run the risk of stray shrapnel skipping into the position than to allow the VC to overrun the outnumbered, crippled force. I tried to contact the LRRP RTO again. "Mayday! Mayday! Christ, someone help us! Mayday!" was all I could hear.

"Hardcore 6, this is Blue Jay 6," the 9th Div aviation battalion commander radioed from his C&C bird. "I'm twenty minutes out with your insert. Got eight gunships with me. Request sitrep."

"Not good," I replied. And it wasn't good, if for no other reason than I didn't know what the situation really *was*. If I could only talk to someone on the ground. As it was, I couldn't send Gordie's men in there. To send troops in without knowing the situation on the ground would be cold-blooded murder.

"Red light, sir," said my pilot. "I'm running out of fuel. I'd like to break off."

"How much have you got?"

"Twenty minutes, sir."

"Stay on station. There's a 55-gallon drum stashed five minutes from here." We had drums hidden all over the battlefield for such contingencies, but in this case I didn't know what good it would do. Maybe it would keep us airborne, but what I needed was someone on the ground to run the show. I didn't know what to do. DeRoos's people would be on station in no time. *You've got an excuse to break off,* I told myself. *You're running out of fuel. They're not your LRRPs anyway* . . . By this time my pilot was squirming and moaning about having only minutes left of flying time and here we were out in the middle of the Delta with bandits all around us. I appreciated the problem. "Look, I'll tell you what," I said. "It'll solve all your problems. Land."

"No way, sir! I'm not gonna land. I *refuse* to land."

"Chum, get your shit together, 'cause we're going down there," I yelled. "Just get us as close as you can to that downed chopper and drop us off," I said to the pilot.

"I'm not going to land," he replied.

I took my .38 out and thumped it up against his head. "Land or you're dead."

He decided to land.

We got a lot of fire as we came in, straight down like an elevator beside the crippled chopper. Some of the LRRP people saw us coming and raced through the waist-high water to grab the loach's skids, trying, as the pilot hovered some six feet over the scene, to claw their way into our bird. They were going to pull us right out of the sky. Chum and I had to kick them off just to be able to get out ourselves.

As my pilot (the soon-to-be recipient of the Distinguished Flying Cross for his part in the mission) flew away, Chum and I waded through the mangrove swamp. The LRRPs and the downed chopper crew were bunched up and in a state of panic near the broken bird. As Chum got artillery erupting all around us, I just started grabbing people and throwing them into the fight. "Get your ass over here and fire in that direction!" I said again and again until we'd formed a loose perimeter and word came that DeRoos's C Company was overhead and ready to come in. Then it was just a question of getting those men on the ground, a drill complicated both by the downed bird splayed across the two-chopper LZ and the fact that the VC must have decided they'd better do whatever they planned to do while they still had a chance to do it, and mounted an attack from one quarter. Chum turned off his artillery as I directed Blue Jay 6 to make a couple of runs over the bad guys; the gunships hosed the area down well with rockets blazing, and the VC attack ceased.

DeRoos was still hovering overhead. With a strobe light in a steel pot (so it couldn't be seen except from above), I stood near the downed helicopter and directed the first slick in. Having fought in the Highlands where LZs were usually even smaller than this one, the procedure was old hat to me but hard on these 9th Div pilots who were more accustomed to the wide, pool-table-flat expanses of the Delta plains. Soon Chum took over the job of bringing in the slicks. One by one each discharged its troops, and while I put the new arrivals in position on the ground, Chum backloaded the wounded LRRP troops and chopper crew and got them out of the contact area. Finally, when C Company was all in and the LRRPs were all out, Chum and I jumped into the last outgoing chopper (leaving DeRoos's very competent force to knock off the VC and secure the downed bird until it could be pulled out the next morning) and returned to the brigade fire base.

The LRRP extraction was without a doubt the biggest risk I took in my life, and probably in Chum Robert's life as well. Never before or after that night did I go into a situation totally blind, without even one clue to help me calculate the odds of success, or even survival. And though I liked to think it was dedication to duty that forced my hand, it might just as well have been ego—the ego of a guy who (everybody knew) always made touchdowns and just refused to fumble now—and to prove to Ira Hunt that I was a thousand times the soldier he could ever dream of being. And despite the fact that he probably would have had to kiss his stars good-bye if I had failed, I never got over the feeling that a big part of him would have been very pleased if I had. As it was, he didn't utter a peep throughout the affair, and afterward generally left me alone, tactically speaking, for the rest of his twenty-day tenure as brigade CO.

Chapter 18
The Whole Bag of Tricks

★ ★ ★

An established sniper capability in Vietnam was the brainchild of Hank Emerson, my friend and competitor from our days as battalion commanders in the 1/101st. Emerson had envisioned a program of division snipers who would be farmed out to units in the field as required; I wanted to take it a step further and develop a strong sniper capability on the battalion level.

So when I brought my guys back after their training at the 9th Division's excellent sniper school, I outfitted them with sniper rifles and starlight scopes, and put them up in the four observation towers of our fire base.* A good sniper could drill your teeth with one of those scopes if you were unfortunate enough to be

---

*Fire Support Base Danger, as our fire base was called, was a mini-fort designed to protect our six 105mm artillery pieces. At each corner of the base was a manned observation post on which personnel radars were mounted, and fighting bunkers were cut into the berm walls all the way around. Cyclone wire covered the apertures of every bunker, to detonate incoming rocket-propelled grenade (RPG) rounds before they hit their mark. Concertina wire

picked up walking along on a night patrol, and in conjunction with the small personnel radar system brigade CO Geraci had introduced (which could locate by "blip" any and all personnel approaching the base still outside the starlight scope's range), we began to get good numbers of enemy dead. The only problem was that once Charlie realized we'd learned to pierce the night somehow, he didn't come around anymore.

It was the way he was with everything. Whatever magic formula for winning the Americans came up with, the minute Charlie figured out that whatever we were up to was bad for his health, he just stopped playing the game, at least until he came up with a countermeasure. For example, when, before long, the 4/39 started doing tremendous damage to the Viet Cong outfits in our AO, and no matter how they tried to outfox us, we were too organized and too alert to fall for it, they simply rethought their situation and returned to a very old practice. They packed about 300 pounds of explosives into a box, put it on a catapult not unlike the ones used in medieval times to crash into an opponent's fortress, and in the middle of the night flung the damn thing over our berm. If it had not been for a two-and-a-half-ton water tanker that was fortuitously parked between my CP complex and the outer berm, and that took the brunt of the blast, the CP would have been leveled, killing me as well as a number of the snipers (who were wounded as they slept in a bunker nearby). But I had to hand it to the Viet Cong. They were like little ants struggling with a crust of bread. They never gave up, and nothing wore them out.

So meanwhile, they stopped playing ball with our

---

laced with booby traps and flares ran out 500 yards from the base and ringed the entire position.

snipers in the observation towers. We needed a new gimmick. I called in Larry Tahler, a draftee, Officer Candidate School (OCS) lieutenant and nice Jewish boy from New York who'd found his niche as the snipers' boss. I told him my problem and asked him to have a think about this idea I had, to put snipers on choppers. In short order, "Night Hunter" was born.

Two snipers and three helicopters—a slick and two gunships—made up each Night Hunter team. The choppers flew in blackout, the slick just a couple hundred meters off the deck, its sniper passengers lying prone in the back, checking out the crisscrossing Delta canals and trails with starlight scopes. The gunships, meanwhile, hovered maybe 500 meters overhead. If through their scopes the snipers saw enemy below, they and the slick's door gunners would take them under fire, with weapons loaded with tracer rounds. This showed the gunships exactly where in the pitch-black night the target was, and in turn the gunships would hose the area down. The slick could also drop Air Force flares to light up the contact area, and a reaction force was always ready and waiting at the fire base if a target justified "piling on."

From the outset, Night Hunter was incredibly successful, with scores of dead VC and no friendly casualties at all. Geraci, who was still in command when the program began, loved the idea and loved the result, and made sure Tahler (who as "Night Hunter 6" was in charge) got the assets every night. After one particularly fruitful nighttime outing, Geraci even ordered everyone who'd participated to his office at 0700, to give each one an award.

Then, from Night Hunter evolved another role for the snipers, this one in daylight. In the early hours of the morning, two-man sniper teams, armed with sniper rifles with silencers and smokeless ammo, an

M-79, and a radio, would be inserted around the battle area by unescorted slicks. Under a hessian camouflage cloth, positioned feet to feet on their bellies, these guys would just lie on the ground in the middle of bandit country waiting for something to happen. If they saw a half-dozen VC coming toward their ambush, they'd start with the last guy and pop them all off one by one. If the enemy were spotted nearby but going in the wrong direction, that is, away from the ambush, the snipers would just call for artillery or air strikes to drive them into range.

As with Night Hunter, the daytime sniper program was tremendously successful. The result of it all was that the snipers, like the Tigers before them in the 1/327, became my pets. I called them "my little babies," and showered them with attention and recognition for their contribution to the battalion's effort. I even gave them their own uniforms (camouflage, à la Tigers) with the added touch of black berets with a red Recondo patch sewed on. In many respects the snipers' job was "easier" than the average trooper's sorry lot in a line company (the snipers didn't have to slog through the chest-deep mud of the paddies for days on end, or constantly be on the lookout for killer booby traps), but what they did, especially on the daylight operations, took an incredible amount of balls, and I admired them for it.

The psychological element of the job couldn't be dismissed, either. The high-powered sniper scopes brought the enemy (visually) within arm's reach, a connection between the hunter and the hunted that most infantrymen were spared. A certain constitution was thus required in a sniper, especially when among your targets could well be women or young girls. This was the case for Larry Tahler one morning as he surveyed a group of six dead VC he and another sniper had taken at a creek bend. "And I turned my scope on this one," he told me upon his return, "and it was a girl. And all I could think was how beautiful she was."

The snipers were just one among many ideas I was experimenting with to make the 4/39 a real guerrilla battalion, that is, one that could "out-G the G"—out-guerrilla our VC guerrilla foe. Even before Colonel Hunt left, I'd managed to implement some changes, and by the time our new brigade commander, Special Forces Colonel John Hayes, was firmly in the saddle, the reorganization was almost complete.

Each Hardcore company specialized in a particular facet of guerrilla warfare as tailored to our needs. Alert and Claymore companies (formerly Alpha and Charlie) were the ambush elements, long range and short range respectively. Both Battle and Dagger (Bravo and Delta) were Ranger-like (Korean War vintage) guerrilla units, though Battle had the Vietnam-era luxury of airmobile assets when they were available to the battalion, while Dagger moved almost solely on foot once in its AO. The specialization of roles compensated for my soldiers' overall low skill level. It stood to reason that if a company did just one thing all the time, be it ambushes or eagle flights or whatever, it wouldn't take long to become truly professional at it. And not only did the changes improve the overall success of the battalion, they also did wonders for individual and team morale. For the first time the soldiers really knew *what* they were doing, *where* they were doing it, and *why*.

One tremendous blow to our ever-growing confidence occurred the night two platoons of D Company were attacked in their own ambush position by a VC element that (we conjectured later) had been watching them all day. The Dagger element was completely asleep at the switch, and its casualties were close to a score dead and wounded, including the new company commander (KIA). I was heartsick that this had happened to one of my units, and just thankful that my boss was not Hunt but John Hayes, a true warrior, who accepted probably better than I did that this sort of thing happened in war. I turned the remains of Dagger Company over to Captain Ed Clark, whose cherubic face belied his guts and nerves of steel, and in the days to come he brought the unit back to strength, both physically *and* in their heads (which was even more important).

The rest of the Hardcore, meanwhile, though sobered by word of D Company's debacle, picked it up as a "lesson learned" and didn't look back. The esprit of the unit was growing stronger every day, a combination of a number of factors, not least of which were the battalion's steady kill rate and the fact that the *Old Reliable* 9th Div newspaper, as well as *Stars and Stripes,* were beginning to write up some of the Hardcore's exploits. Such recognition did wonders for morale (and for producing cocky wise-asses en masse), and as I started giving back to the men many of the privileges I'd stripped away so savagely at the outset of my tour in order to shake off their dangerous complacency, I couldn't help but get the feeling the 4th Battalion, 39th Infantry, was on the verge of something big.

Ed Clark, new commander of Dagger Company, ran one fine guerrilla outfit. They were "up tight" (in the vernacular of Vietnam) and ready for anything when, in the early morning hours of 23 March, their listening posts spotted enemy troops slipping into attack positions. With the memory of his predecessor's last fight still fresh, Clark felt the VC knew all too well where his people were. He immediately moved his unit back a couple of hundred meters. Minutes later two companies from the Main Force VC 261 Alpha

Battalion launched an attack on Clark's old position, rocket launchers and light machine guns blazing.

When they realized their prey had slipped away, the VC moved slowly forward. I wanted to send in some artillery when Clark radioed his sitrep, but Dagger's CO said no, not yet; he wanted Charlie to get a little closer in. Then a VC tripped a claymore mine and it was on: the enemy's attack formations were gutted as U.S. machine guns and individual weapons tore into their ranks. In the light of popping flares, gunships placed effective fire on Charlie and his probable escape routes. Artillery crashed down, too, and the enemy broke off their attack before it had really begun, making for safety as best they could.

It was a good, good contact, and as dawn broke, I had tracker dogs flown in to follow the blood trails of the fleeing VC. Based on the confession of a Dagger prisoner taken during a sweep of the battle area (who'd said his battalion's base camp was not far away), the pursuit began in earnest, with Troop C of the Black Hawks tracking down the enemy in LOHs flown barely above grass level. We could see foot tracks trampled into the young rice in the paddies, and trails where sampans had slipped through the water. From time to time we'd find an isolated group of Viet Cong, and a platoon would be dropped off to deal with them.

Then, about two miles along, we lost both the tracks and the trails. They just disappeared in the shimmering plain of water-soaked rice paddies and mangroves. But then, out of the corner of my eye, I saw a black silhouette leaning against a tree. And somehow, in that instant, Charlie's entire configuration became clear to me. I could see his perimeter, I knew what he was thinking and how he was going to move.

"Swing it around," I told the pilot of my C&C, and

as the chopper whirled, I saw this Viet Cong slip into a hole. Then we saw other enemy soldiers moving to prepared defensive positions. The Air Cav CO sent his scout ships in. One of them blew away some foliage only to uncover a .50-caliber U.S. machine gun. The gutsy LOH pilot whose bird uncovered it immediately dived down and pulled that gun right out of the enemy's hole.

I put four companies in a loose net around the VC positions and called in tac air to pummel the center and blast any escape routes that couldn't be blocked by my infantry. In the middle of the inferno that followed, my pilot told the two door gunners on our chopper to spray down the lily pads floating along the canal we were flying over. I couldn't imagine why, but the guy had done a lot of flying in the Delta so I figured he must have a reason. As the gunners opened up, the tactic became quite clear: one by one the lily pads bled red, and soon bodies began popping to the surface. It was another Delta trick: to evade capture the VC would go underwater, grab a lily pad, and, using reeds to breathe, just float along until they were out of harm's way.

Thirteen air strikes later the enemy gave up the fight. I'd put Clark's troops on the most likely escape route, figuring Dagger deserved the honor of delivering the final blows to an enemy who'd made the lethal error of tangling with them in the first place. Sure enough, as Charlie broke out of the charred foliage that had once so adeptly concealed his base camp, he ran right into Dagger Company's waiting guns. That night, Alert and Dagger made some forty more kills as VC stragglers attempted to steal away in the dark, and when dawn came and a final count was made, the Hardcore had utterly demolished the 261 Alpha's base camp, killed 143 men, and captured the battalion colors. Our own casualties were eight WIA, none of whom needed immediate medical evacuation.

I was so proud. D Company had out-G'ed the G, no question about it, proving themselves to be guerrillas as dangerous and savvy as their opponents (who, until this fight, had moved relatively freely through the Delta for years). My reaction force, Alert and Claymore companies (4/39) and Alpha of the 6/31, had performed like total pros. There was much cause for rejoicing at FSB Danger that day.

After the fight, I sent Dagger Company back to Dong Tam, ostensibly to train but more so to stand down, drink beer, and savor their victory. Besides, I knew word of the action would quickly make the rounds at Division, and I wanted the rear echelon commandos back there collecting combat pay to know what real warriors looked like. The following day Hayes informed me an awards ceremony had been scheduled for the men of Dagger. I was happy to hear about it, but I didn't want to attend. The battalion had the assets, and I had a feeling of unease about going off to Dong Tam and leaving them on their own. Hayes insisted, however, so I briefed Nev Bumstead on what I had in mind for the day, which was to go back to the previous day's battlefield to get the VC I felt sure would return to pick up their dead. But, I told him, under no circumstances was he to get decisively engaged. Then Hayes and I flew off to Dong Tam.

The whole time I was away I was worried. Worry bordering on panic—I was *not* where I should have been, I could feel it. By the time the awards ceremony was over, I was frantic. Finally, finally we headed home, and the minute we got within radio range, I called the Hardcore. Nev reported we had a contact going; Hayes took me to the scene in his C&C, and immediately I knew why I'd been so concerned. All the while we'd been at Dong Tam, my B Company was having the shit shot out of it.

The unit was in the middle of a 300-meter paddy devoid of cover and concealment. Two men were lying on their backs, which meant they were dead. (A guy seldom lay on his back on the battlefield if he was alive. There was a psychological thing about keeping your belly close to the ground. Guys about to die, on the other hand, frequently flipped over on their backs, because they didn't care about protecting their bellies anymore.) I couldn't believe my eyes.

Hayes immediately dropped me off near the battle area, and Nev swooped down in my C&C to pick me up. Battle Company was being pinned down by four machine guns, a bastard of a sniper, and a continuous stream of rocket-propelled grenade (RPG) rounds. They couldn't effectively return fire for fear of hitting their own men, and each time Lieutenant William Torpie, the young B Company XO and acting company commander, tried to get them low-crawling to the safety of a ditch, they drew more fire. It wasn't that the men could not get out; it was just that they were seriously hampered by a simultaneous effort to extract a number of their severely wounded.

I took charge of the battle, but no matter what I did, I couldn't bust Charlie's ass hard enough to allow those kids to come up for air. I used tear gas, napalm, artillery, white phosphorus, air strikes, the works; I drew on all the combat experience and knowledge I'd ever collected—my entire bag of tricks—and nothing helped.

When I finally ran out of options, I decided to go in and get the wounded out myself. It was the only way I could think of to give Torpie room to maneuver. I asked the pilot and his crew if they'd volunteer, because I knew it was going to be a hell of a mess on the ground. I told the gunship commander to keep fire going on the wood line where the machine guns were blazing, hoping to persuade Charlie to keep his head down. My chopper crew were good men and with me all the way, and we soon landed, right in the line of fire of a machine gun, within thirty feet of the wounded men. The gunships, meanwhile, began to hose down the enemy positions that were in very close proximity to our ship. One by one they swooped down and blasted those positions, and they continued to do so the whole time we were on the ground. They were our saving grace.

Bullets punched through the chopper as Nev and I jumped out. Together we ran over to the farthest wounded guy, grabbed him, ran back, and tossed him into the bird. We picked up a second WIA the same way, and then a third (amazingly, without becoming casualties ourselves), but by the time everyone was loaded onto the helicopter, there was no room inside for me. I stood on the skids and put on my crash helmet with its internal mike, through which I could tell the pilot to take off (at the time he was just where he should have been given the circumstances—as close to the floor of the chopper as possible, using its console as cover). But I found I couldn't talk. I was so dried out, my tongue had welded itself to the roof of my mouth out of pure fear. I had to open my canteen and drink some water before I could even gasp, "Let's get this mother out of here!"

We took the wounded back to Danger and returned to the fight. Without anything to hold him up now, I couldn't figure out why Torpie didn't do something about getting his men consolidated outside of that paddy. He still kept saying he was pinned down. Finally I lost my temper. I really chewed his ass over the radio, demanding he get cracking and get those men out of that paddy, like NOW. Apparently the next thing he did was put down the radio, stand straight up, and begin running from man to man to get them to move back. He got mowed down right away, and died a short time later.

I thought I'd learned something from Jim Gardner's death at My Canh, but maybe I hadn't. I hadn't asked Torpie to stand up (he didn't need to in order to extricate himself, and it hadn't occurred to me that he would). But it was due to the force of my word as his commander that this inexperienced young lieutenant was sent to his death. Like Jim Gardner's, Torpie's death was a big guilt thing for me, and has remained so all my life.

Dark was coming. With the exception of one lieutenant, all of B Company's officers had been killed or wounded. I sent Nev in to get the unit organized and withdrawn from the paddy. As night fell, all the wounded were evacuated and the unit was safely out of the machine guns' reach. But it had been a defeat. A stinging defeat and a waste of good men's lives damn hard for me to accept, especially after our brilliant victory just two days before. But before I had a chance to figure out how to reverse our fortunes, my chopper, flying low over the now mostly quiet battle area, took a serious spray of machine-gun slugs in the belly. My artillery LNO got hit in the gut, and I took one in the leg. At first glance my wound didn't seem so bad, but the LNO needed immediate medical attention, so I called Hayes and told him I was going in. Hayes put my XO, George Mergner, in charge of the battalion, and Chum Robert, now the brigade liaison officer, came down to help until a replacement for the wounded LNO was found.

In the subsequent hours, the two tried to get something going with the enemy, but it proved an impossible task. On the one hand, the commander of Alert Company (which had been sent in to take the pressure off Battle and to salvage the fight) was about to go tilt in a bona fide nervous breakdown, and on the other, Nev Bumstead, though courageous by day, had had his bottle fill up and overflow three years previously during the 1/101's fight at Dak To, and as a result he seemed to become almost paralytic, operationally speaking, in the dark. Consequently there was no seal and no sweep of the area. The morale-shattered remnants of B Company—which had taken six dead and about eighteen wounded—and the leaderless men of A basically squatted in their holes until morning, during which time the VC ran away.

To make matters worse, one of our ammo resupply choppers, trying to negotiate an ill-thought-out, too-small LZ in the darkness, hit a tree and crashed to the ground, killing one of the door gunners who was pinned in the wreck and burned alive, and tossing exploding ammo all over the perimeter. Talk about a bad night.

My C&C was still operational after it got hit, so we bypassed Danger and flew directly to the 3d Surgical Hospital at Dong Tam to get my LNO looked at. There I found I wasn't walking too well myself, so two guys carried me in. At the door I ran into gutsy Charlie Wintzer, the HQ Company medic. He saluted smartly and said, "Hardcore Recondo, sir," and immediately a chorus of "Hardcore Recondo, sir" rang out from within the emergency room. The unwavering Hardcore spirit among these guys who'd just paid the price themselves was a huge boost for my morale, as was the appearance of most of D Company, under Captain Clark, who, still on their short vacation, had heard I was hit and stormed in to see me in the underground, reinforced bunker I was waiting in to go into surgery.

They brought beer and war stories and we swilled both down, talking loudly and ignoring the incredible mortar attack the hospital came under even as we spoke. The mortar rounds came crashing down outside, but when we were all in there together, it might as well have been rain.

Chapter 19
Warriors

★ ★ ★

In the Delta the VC generally hid all day to avoid our air surveillance and ground operations, and moved at dusk when the Americans traditionally stopped the war to eat dinner. So whenever I saw a chopper flying anywhere near Danger at the end of the day, I flagged the pilot down for a quick overfly of our area in the hope of catching Charlie on the move. The pilots were usually eager to oblige; it was well known that at Danger we made a point of providing such volunteers with souvenirs (like captured Soviet weapons) and other tokens of appreciation.

One evening a brigade loach came in to Danger flown by Warrant Officer Kenneth Carroll, one of the three pilots who flew for the brigade command regularly. Carroll was one of the best pilots I'd ever known, and I loved to fly with him because he had great courage and a sense of adventure, and whenever we got together (especially for these sundown hunting parties) something exciting seemed to happen. So on this particular evening, we took off and, as usual, started our visual recon from the outer strand of defensive wire that wrapped around Danger. Carroll flew along about twenty feet off the ground as I checked the wire for cuts and the surrounding area for tracks, bent grass, or other signs indicating enemy presence. As we slowly circled, I saw nothing unusual at first. Then, to my complete surprise, I saw a guy in a green uniform studying our position, lying motionless near the last strand of wire but exposed thanks to the blast of air created by the chopper's rotor blades, which flattened the grass all around him.

The first order of business was to find out if he was alone. I wanted this joker, but not bad enough to go down there and get Carroll and myself blown away if there were more VC concealed in the high grass nearby. We hovered right over him and I leveled my M-79 (so he knew the game was over). Then Carroll swung the chopper around and we did a quick but thorough search of the area. We found nothing, so we went back to the guy, landed, and I motioned with my weapon for him to get into the chopper. Not surprisingly, he didn't want to, so I got out and hoisted him into the backseat. I got in the front and poked my .38 Smith & Wesson through the cables between the front and back seats as a gentle reminder for the guy to stay put. I hoped he would. If I actually had to shoot him, the bullet would probably go right through his body and into the helicopter's transmission.

Our plan was to take him back to the fire base, but as the chopper lifted off, the VC started to panic. It was obviously his first helicopter ride. In the rush of things, I hadn't buckled him in; now he got up and started moving toward the door. We were up about thirty feet when he turned paratrooper and bailed out for his cherry jump. Fortunately, his chuteless self landed in a rice paddy, so he splashed rather than splattered on impact. We went down again and hovered over him as I motioned with my M-79 for him to get back into the chopper. Once again the VC refused to comply, but this time he grabbed a skid of the helicopter and began to shake it. And he shook it and shook it as if he really thought he could pull that bird out of the sky. Carroll took the aircraft up fifty feet or so, but the guy hung on, still shaking and kicking up a storm. Carroll took the bird down a little, and finally the VC fell off, only to make for a clump of bushes.

I didn't know what was back there, and I wasn't going to let us get zapped finding out. So Carroll spun the chopper around between the VC and the bushes, and I shot the enemy soldier at point-blank range. It was getting dark, so we only had time for a very quick look around the area to find out what the guy had been up to. We soon discovered a number of wooden arrows on the ground pointing toward Danger, which indicated to us that this VC had been a recon man, with the mission of designating enemy weapons emplacements for an imminent attack on our fire base. The attack was not so imminent anymore.

Still, part of me didn't feel very good about killing that VC. Besides the fact that I'd rather have taken him back as a prisoner, our one-on-one encounter had somehow connected us, and I admired his guts. Unfortunately for him, my job was not to admire his guts; I knew, too, that if he could have wasted me instead, he'd have done so in a second.

Some time later I got involved in a true David and Goliath drama with another, even more gutsy VC, this time in broad daylight. Ed Clark's D Company was in contact, and as I flew around the battle area I saw a squad of VC hightailing it away from Clark's maneuvering forces. We followed them in my loach, only to discover an entire *platoon,* all looking good in pith helmets and neat uniforms, wearing load-bearing equipment and carrying AK47s. It was one of the few times in the Delta I saw such a large group congregated together in daylight. I called for gunships and told Clark to move an ambush force in that direction. Meanwhile, to buy some time and to pin them down until the guns were on station and Clark made his move, we took the VC force under fire from the LOH. Instantly they scattered in every direction—all, that is, except one guy.

Far from running away, every time we made a pass in the chopper (with my M-79 blazing) this character would adopt the most perfect firing position Fort Benning ever dreamed of, and shoot at us with his AK47. On one knee, foot pointed toward the target and elbow under his weapon, this guy didn't even flinch as the chopper barreled at him. He was absolutely determined to get us, and his only problem was that I was just as determined as he was. But neither of us could manage a direct hit. The VC's slugs would come straight toward us, but then they seemed to hit the chopper's airstream and veer off at the last moment. On my end, I had to aim well in front of my opponent (using the wildest Kentucky windage imaginable), fire, and hope the airstream did the rest. And while the current did pick up the rounds and whip them around toward the guy, I could never get right on target. And no matter how close I did get, that VC just knelt there with his perfect bearing, firing his weapon at my chopper. Finally a close hit on my part knocked him over, and after a moment he took off. I didn't go after him, though. In fact, I wished him well. He was one courageous dude—probably the platoon commander of the unit I'd surprised—willing to take me on against near-impossible odds so the rest of his platoon could escape.

Perhaps the most exceptional Viet Cong of all that I encountered in Vietnam was the POW Gordie De-Roos's company took from the 261 Alpha Battalion, the unit Dagger had battered and the Hardcore had creamed in March. Despite being warned he was a belligerent, mean little bastard who wouldn't give me a word more than his name, rank, and serial number, I wanted to talk to the guy. Since March I'd been tracking the 261A as it rebuilt (both because there was little doubt they were the best in Dinh Tuong Province, and I had a feeling they had plans for my battalion), and I thought I could get some information out of him.

The S-2 brought him to me just as I was eating at the end of a long day. The prisoner was a first lieutenant, a recon company commander in his late twenties, as defiant as I'd been warned and even more banged up. The worst of his many battle scars was a leg that had a depression in it almost as deep and wide as my fist. A huge chunk of flesh had been blown out and never sewn up. It would have been a bad, bad wound even if medical attention *had* been available. Still, it had healed, and the guy had gone back to duty. This was one hardcore stud.

He didn't want to talk to me, so I pointed to the old wound in his leg and through an interpreter asked if he had been hit. He said he had. "No hospital?" I asked. The prisoner shook his head almost scornfully. Then I showed him some of my wounds, which provoked the first bit of interest from the guy. He asked if they were from Vietnam. "No, no," I replied. "Before. Korea. But this one," I continued, showing him my leg wound, "this one came from the VC here in the Delta." The wound was still red and raw, with big, vicious-looking stitch marks.

"Maybe I did it," said the VC lieutenant, and he roared with a huge belly laugh.

"Yeah, maybe you did," I replied.

The warrior-to-warrior exchange broke the ice. It

was a common bond that transcended patriotism or nationalism or causes. We laid down our flags and allowed ourselves to be friends.

"Look," I said, "I know you're a hardcore son of a bitch. I know you'd like to grab a weapon or a hand grenade and blow us all up. Let's not do it that way. Let's be honorable. I know you're not going to tell me anything about your unit's disposition, because I know you wouldn't get anything from me about my outfit. So I'm not going to ask. But I'm a soldier. I admire your army's skill, and your fighting spirit. So I want to know more about your army and your cause. Why you're fighting and why you believe as you do."

For the next three nights I'd come in from the field and the prisoner and I would get together for chow and a talk. For all my talk of honor, in the back of my mind I still hoped to break him down. I wanted to know where the 261 Alpha was and how it operated. But while we talked of many things, that subject was one he didn't say a word about.

Meanwhile, the Intelligence people at higher headquarters were starting to yell for him. I'd initially said I was hanging on to him because he was giving me hot stuff on the 261A, but after a couple of days, patience up above was wearing thin.

"Look, my friend," I told the POW, "the word is I've got to evacuate you. Since I can't get any decent intelligence from you, I'm going to have to send you to my division HQ, where you will be interrogated further, and then they'll turn you over to the 7th ARVN Division. Now, the first thing ARVN is going to ask you is to *chieu hoi*.* If you do, they'll send you to a reeducation center, and when you come out, you'll get a South Vietnamese uniform, a new M-16,

---

Chieu hoi, or Open Arms, was a program designed to encourage VC defections.

and be assigned to a South Vietnamese unit. Maybe you'll even come back here as a Tiger Scout so we can work together. So when you go to the 7th Division, tell them you're going to *chieu hoi.*"

"I'll never do that," the prisoner replied.

"But you've got to do it," I said. "Do you know what they do to people who don't *chieu hoi?* They shoot them!"

"Then I will be dead. I expect to die anyway, fighting for my cause, the freedom of my country Vietnam."

"My friend, you've put me in a very bad position. I like you. I respect you as a warrior. I know we're not going to convert you, but I do not want to see you get blown away. So do me one favor. Lie. *Chieu hoi.* I'll see if you can come back to my unit."

"No. I believe in my cause," he said, and began pointing to his mangled leg and his many other raggedly healed wounds. "I believed in it through all of these. I will never surrender. I will fight until I'm dead. If they ask me to *chieu hoi* I will spit in their faces."

It was a lost cause. Since I couldn't get the guy to *chieu hoi,* I turned to Plan B, which meant organizing for him to be flown back to Saigon to be turned over to an American POW camp. That way not only would he be spared ARVN's final solution (and the bamboo splinters under the fingernails, tiger cages, and electric shocks along the way), but he would not have to *chieu hoi,* and he would be allowed to live. And though I never saw him again, I have little doubt that he did.

Encounters like these only increased my enormous respect for the Viet Cong, our enemy. Unlike our South Vietnamese allies, who were far more concerned with what the Americans could do for them, give to them, or buy from them throughout the conflict, to the VC the war was a cause, not unlike the

American Revolution was to those who fought in it. Unquestionably, as warriors the VC were as welcome in the brotherhood as the best of "our" side; only on reflection does the double edge of that period seem so sharp: the better Charlie was, the more his focus and his tenacity drew me toward him, the more determined I was to best him, to destroy him at his game.

When I got hit on 25 March, I'd been just about to launch an attack on an area not far from Danger that was seeing a tremendous amount of VC traffic. At first I'd thought it was just a way station, but the more I watched, the more I'd felt a large enemy force was using it as a base camp. Why not? Each day we operated far and wide throughout our huge AO looking for Main Force units, and very seldom ventured into the relatively secure areas right on our doorstep at FSB Danger. Wasn't the safest place for a crook to hide on top of the police station? But when I got hit, my hunches had to go on hold, and I let the word go out that I didn't want anyone to go in there—I'd been watching the area for too long, and I knew it was not the time just yet.

I was not to have my way. A 1st Brigade attack was launched on "my" target while I was in the hospital, and the whole thing backfired. They went in with three complete battalions, an overkill tactic in any event, but one that was rendered entirely ineffective when part of the airmobile assault went off prematurely, tipping our force's hand. The VC cleared out, and the net result of the operation was zero. Was I angry.

But when I got out of the hospital and back to the Hardcore, and the intelligence profile on the area started developing again—the same activity, the same movement of people and supplies—I lost my anger and called on my guerrilla's patience to tide me over. And for almost six weeks I waited.

On the third of May a platoon in Clark's Dagger Company ambushed a couple of sampans, killing four VC and capturing several weapons not far from my "pet" target area. When a couple of enemy troops got away across the canal, the platoon leader, Lieutenant Dave Crittenden, grabbed a few of his men and dashed across as well, in hot pursuit. Unaware that they were virtually walking into the headquarters of the 261A Battalion, Crittenden's force came under fire from a well-defended VC bunker. Crittenden destroyed the bunker, and in the subsequent search came away with vital enemy documents, including the 261A's Order of Battle and attack plans.

It was a true windfall, giving focus to the picture my intelligence was piecing together, and shape to the enemy's intention. Among the documents was an attack plan against a nearby Regional Forces camp. If the VC were going for an RF camp, their objective was obviously not military. Instead, it was psychological, and targeted at the local villagers; that is, if an RF company could be destroyed under the nose of a U.S. battalion, how secure was the average peasant? Fortunately for us, the attack plan came complete with the locations of all the 261A companies' assembly areas, so as I watched enemy activity heat up on my own intelligence profile, I knew we were one up on our foe whenever they decided to launch.

Our target was perishable, but not so perishable that it was appropriate to bombard the VC positions with artillery or tac air immediately, or grab every chopper I could find for a hasty airmobile assault. If I intended to get a complete harvest of these jokers, the only way to do it was to out-G them, and for the moment I was content reinforcing the RF camp with a U.S. rifle platoon and two M-41 "dusters"* with twin 40mm cannons. I knew this would cause the VC commander to go back to the drawing board; the move would buy us time.

By 21 May the enemy activity we'd been monitoring was at frenzy level. There was no question that their attack on the RF camp was imminent, and it was time for us to make our move. I got my companies in the field turned around, all tasked to move at dark, by stealth, toward the objective area to set up ambushes along all the enemy's probable withdrawal routes from their encampment. Meanwhile, still in daylight, we made false helicopter insertions along these same routes (the same as real helicopter insertions, only no one got out of the birds, and upon lifting off, the doors were closed and the troops lay down on the floor), to make the VC think twice in case they got wind of our plan and had a mind to bug out. When dark came, more forces left Danger bound for other critical ambush positions, and by 0600, 22 May, the stage was set.

At 0700 Battle Company conducted an airmobile assault into the heart of the VC encampment. Their job was not to get decisively engaged, but simply to act as a beater. It proved one easy mission, for the VC, who only stood and fought when there was nowhere to go, immediately ran away through what looked like an easy escape route. Their only problem was that we had chosen that route for them: at the end of it, and every other escape route they tried, the Hardcore had an ambush ready and waiting. The scene on the ground was mass panic among the VC. Forced out into the open by U.S. air strikes, artillery, and gunship fire,

---

*A full-track vehicle, kind of a cross between a light tank and a Korea-vintage quad .50, designed for antiaircraft but used in Vietnam in a direct support role

Charlie bounced off one ambush right into the next, recoiling from one blocked escape route only to hit another and then yet another as he tried frantically to get away, each time leaving seven or nine dead behind. Besides swooping down and picking up each of my company commanders during the fight to let them see the scene from the air before the VC hit their units, all I did during the battle was sit in my chopper and call down to my leaders when the time came: "Heads up, Clark, they're coming your way, let 'em have it," followed by, "All right, DeRoos, they'll be in your position in about twenty minutes," as I watched the VC reel back from Clark's people and dash on to their next "avenue of escape." Jim Mukoyama, my new S-3 whom I brought in from the States, was stunned how the VC played right into our hands. "From the air it was like watching a game of pinball," he said. "Every time they moved, we thumped them."

It was the most satisfying operation of my career. Synthesizing guerrilla tactics with our enormous firepower, I'd had my wish: we'd beaten them at their own game. We'd used *their* book of tricks to fight them on the ground, and at the time that was to *our* advantage. The VC could not be destroyed by conventional tactics employed by the average U.S. battalion in Vietnam; only guerrilla tactics augmented by U.S. firepower (and our tremendous air mobility, when required) could defeat the enemy at a low cost in men and matériel.

In this battle, for example, when the VC realized they were trapped, many resorted to hiding in bunkers. But there they were only further pummeled by the seven air strikes, 500 rounds of artillery, and wall-to-wall chopper, minigun, and rocket fire we laid on them, until they either got up and fled to the ambushes or went to ground until dark, when they could try to steal away. In the latter case, they had no better luck. At the end of the day, when the rest of the battalion vacated the battlefield, Gordie DeRoos's C Company went into a hide position (after a false helicopter pickup) to police up any stragglers, and their nighttime ambushes added seventeen to the final tally of 113 enemy dead. In exchange for that number, the Hardcore took exactly four casualties, all just slightly wounded.

The next day Louis B. Mayer would have been impressed by the number of stars we had visit us at FSB Danger: the Deputy COMUSMACV, the commanding generals of U.S. Army, Vietnam (USARV) and II Field Force (the corps-level command headquarters under USARV), the 9th Div CG and his two assistants. All were there to congratulate us on our job well done. And it *was* a job well done—like a graduation exercise for the 4/39, after being transformed from a hard-luck battalion into the Hardcore, after months of becoming more and more skillful and sophisticated in fighting Charlie, after taking his initiative away and chasing his sweet ass ragged around the province. In our corner of the Delta, that birthplace of the Viet Cong and their longest and strongest of strongholds, we were cleaning their clocks.

The 4/39 was my last combat command, that perfect operation of 22 May 1969 my last fight. Soon after, to my great disappointment, I was personally yanked out of the battalion by General Creighton Abrams, Westmoreland's replacement as COMUS-MACV, when he discovered I'd been wounded four times in the previous three months.

Still, my experience with the Hardcore Battalion proved to me all my ideas and theories on how to fight the G that I'd ruminated on since I'd left Vietnam almost two years before. There was satisfaction in that—but much less in the fact that my success didn't make a dent in the way the war was prosecuted (even after General Abrams said that all his battalions should fight like the 4/39).

Ironically, what did was the debacle of Hamburger Hill, where eleven assaults were ordered up an extremely well-fortified, totally useless piece of real estate. Almost 400 American men dead or wounded later, the Americans *were* King of the Mountain, but within a week the objective was abandoned. The ensuing, horrified uproar among the American people and in Washington made sure Hamburger Hill was the last huge and costly battle fought by American troops in Vietnam. So I guess if no one learned how to fight the war from me and the men of the Hardcore, at least from Hamburger Hill they finally learned how *not* to.

But we were already four years into the war. And there were almost four more to go.

Postscript

★ ★ ★

David Hackworth would remain in Vietnam for two more years, in consecutive advisory assignments to the South Vietnamese Army. He was promoted to full colonel in March 1971. In June of that year, increasingly disgusted with the conduct of the war, Hackworth appeared in uniform on ABC TV's nationally broadcast "Issues and Answers," jettisoning his Army career with the public airing of impassioned views that condemned both the war itself and the American military leaders who managed it.

The recipient of more than one hundred awards, eighty-two of them for valor, including two Distinguished Service Crosses, ten Silver Stars, eight Purple Hearts for wounds sustained in combat, eight Bronze Stars with "V" (valor) device, and four Legions of Merit over a career spanning twenty-five years and two wars, Colonel Hackworth retired from the U.S. Army in September 1971 at the age of forty. Shortly thereafter, he moved to Australia, where in 1983

Postscript

he began work on his influential and controversial autobiography, *About Face: The Odyssey of an American Warrior,* which became a major *New York Times* best-seller.

He now lives in Montana.

Glossary

★ ★ ★

AA Antiaircraft

ADC Assistant division commander

Airborne The term used to describe a parachute-trained soldier, a parachute unit, or an operation in which parachutes are employed to drop personnel and equipment

Airmobile An operation in which personnel and equipment are moved by helicopter

AK47 A Soviet assault rifle, the standard individual weapon in Eastern bloc countries

AO Area of operation

APC Armored personnel carrier; a thin-skinned vehicle used to transport infantry to and around the battlefield

Arc-light B-52 strike

Arty Artillery

ARVN Pronounced "Arvin," the Army of the Republic of Vietnam (i.e., the South Vietnamese)

Assets Available helicopter and other fixed-wing aviation support

BAR Browning Automatic Rifle; the standard U.S. infantry assault rifle during World War II and the Korean War; considered by many to be the most rugged, reliable, and effective weapon the U.S. military ever fielded

Glossary

Battalion A military unit traditionally composed of 1000 men

Bird Slang for helicopter or airplane; the term is also used to describe a full colonel

Bird colonel A full colonel; the term "bird" refers to a full colonel's insignia, which is a silver eagle

Booby trap An explosive device normally employed in an antipersonnel role

Brigade A military unit that normally controls three maneuver battalions as well as supporting units such as artillery, armor, engineer, medical, maintenance, etc.

C-4 A plastic explosive; its most popular use on the battlefield in Vietnam was to heat water and C rations

C&C Command and control helicopter

CG Commanding general

Charlie Slang for Viet Cong or NVA personnel

Chieu hoi Meaning "open arms," a program designed to encourage Viet Cong and NVA surrender or defection; individual enemy soldiers who came in under the program were also called "Chieu hois"

Chopper Slang for helicopter

CIB Combat Infantryman's Badge

Claymore An antipersonnel land mine

CO Commanding officer; conscientious objector

Commo Slang for communications

Company A military unit traditionally composed of 200 men

COMUSMACV Commander, U.S. Military Assistance Command, Vietnam

Corps A military unit traditionally composed of three divisions as well as tactical supporting units such as artillery, armor, communications, engineer, signal, etc.

Counterinsurgency Military operations conducted against insurgents (guerrillas)

CP Command post

DEROS Date eligible return from overseas

Division A military unit traditionally composed of three regiments/brigades as well as supporting units

DMZ Demilitarized zone

DSC Distinguished Service Cross; the U.S. Army's second-highest award

Dust-off Slang for medical evacuation by helicopter; also known as "medevac"

Fart sack Sleeping bag

FO Forward observer; the FO accompanies infantry in the field, and adjusts artillery and mortar fires

Frag Slang for a fragmentation grenade; in Vietnam, the term also referred to a mutinous soldier's killing, or attempting to kill, a disliked leader with a frag grenade

FSB Fire support base; a permanent or semipermanent installation that houses artillery, infantry, command and control, and supporting facilities; its purpose is to provide indirect artillery support to infantry units within its AO

Guerrilla Also referred to as an "insurgent"; a member of an irregular (paramilitary) unit that employs unconventional tactics, usually in fighting a war of resistance

Guerrilla warfare Low-cost, economy-of-force, unconventional military operations conducted by irregular (guerrilla) and/or regular military personnel, generally against an established government or order

Gunship A helicopter designed as a firing platform to place supporting fires (machine gun and rocket) on the enemy

GVN Government of South Vietnam

Half-track The M16, a lightly armored vehicle with front wheels and back tanklike treads; used in World War II as C&C and to transport infantry, and in the Korean War as an infantry support system employing four .50-caliber machine guns

H&I Harassment and interdictory fire

HE High explosives

Huey Slang for any of the UH-series helicopters

I&R Intelligence and Reconnaissance platoon, also known as the eyes and ears of the regiment

Incoming Indirect enemy artillery and mortar fire that falls on friendly positions

Insert Deployment of any maneuver element by helicopter

Insurgency Armed activity directed against a constituted government

Kentucky windage An educated guess as to how to hold on a target to allow for such variables as wind and distance

KIA Killed in action

Klick Slang for kilometer

KMAG Korea Military Advisory Group

LD Line of departure

Leg A non-Airborne soldier

LMG Light machine gun; in World War II and the Korean War, the .30-caliber, and in Vietnam, the M-60

LNO Liaison officer

Loaded for bear Enough weaponry and/or ammunition of sufficient size to deal with any foreseeable threat

Lock and load To place a weapon on safety, and then ready it to fire by placing a round in the chamber

LOH Light observation helicopter, also called a "loach"

LP Listening post; an early warning element deployed in front of the main lines

LRRP Pronounced "lurp," long-range reconnaissance patrol; members of LRRP teams are also called LRRPs (lurps)

LZ Landing zone

M-1 U.S. .30-caliber semiautomatic rifle used during World War II and the Korean War

M4 The Sherman medium tank; thirty-six tons, with a 76mm main gun, the Sherman is the best tank the U.S. Army has ever fielded

M-16 Unquestionably the worst infantry weapon ever forced upon America's fighting men; the standard U.S. infantry rifle employed in Vietnam

M46 A U.S. medium tank with a 90mm gun, used during the Korean War

M-60 A U.S. light machine gun used during the Vietnam War

M-79 A U.S. infantry direct-fire weapon, commonly called a grenade launcher but which in fact fired 40mm HE and buckshot rounds; without doubt the most effective U.S. infantry weapon employed during the Vietnam War

MACV Military Assistance Command, Vietnam

MASH Mobile army surgical hospital

Glossary

Medevac Medical evacuation by helicopter; also known as "dust-off"

MIA Missing in action

MLR Main line of resistance

Montagnards The indigenous mountain people of Vietnam

MSR Main supply route

NCO Noncommissioned officer

No-man's land The contested zone between the main battle areas of two antagonists

NVA North Vietnamese Army

OCS Officer Candidate School; an accelerated program designed to produce officers from within the enlisted ranks

OP Outpost or observation post

OPCON A term used to designate the operational control of a unit over a subordinate unit

P-38 An infantryman's best friend: his inch-and-a-half-long metal can opener; the P-38 was also a World War II reconnaissance aircraft

P-51 A World War II and Korean War vintage tactical fighter aircraft

PAVN People's Army of Vietnam, known as the NVA after American forces were engaged

PF Popular Forces; the village-level South Vietnamese militia

PFC Private, first class

Platoon A military unit traditionally composed of forty soldiers

PRC-25 Pronounced "prick twenty-five," the standard U.S. infantry FM radio used in Vietnam

Punji stake The ultimate in low-cost antipersonnel weapons: a sharpened bamboo stake, partially buried by the VC in wait for unsuspecting counterinsurgents

Purple Heart A military decoration awarded for any wound sustained in combat

PZ Pick-up zone (used in connection with helicopter operations)

Quad .50 Four .50-caliber machine guns mounted on an M16 half-track

R&R Rest and recreation

Glossary

Recon Reconnaissance

Regiment A military unit traditionally composed of three infantry battalions

RF Regional Forces; the district- and province-level South Vietnamese militia

ROK Republic of Korea (i.e., South Korea); ROK also referred to the South Korean Army, members of which were called ROKs

ROTC Reserve Officers Training Course

RPG Rocket-propelled grenade; specifically, the Soviet B-40 antitank, antipersonnel weapon

RTO Radio-telephone operator

RVN Republic of Vietnam (i.e., South Vietnam)

S-1 Personnel and administration officer, or staff, at brigade/regiment/group or below; in general, the -1 designation always refers to personnel (the S indicates Special Staff, which is always found at brigade/regiment/group and below)

S-2 Intelligence (see S-1 for more details)

S-3 Operations (see S-1 for more details)

S-4 Logistics (see S-1 for more details)

S-5 Civil affairs (see S-1 for more details)

Sapper A soldier specially trained in infiltration and demolition; in the British forces, a sapper is an engineer

SCR-300 The standard U.S. infantry FM radio used in World War II and Korea

Search and destroy A military operation designed to destroy enemy formations and facilities, but not to hold ground

Second balloon Slang for second lieutenant

Sitrep (SITRPT) Situation report

Six Originally the radio identification for unit commander; popularly used as shorthand when referring to the CO, as in "The Six wants it done right now"

SKS A Soviet semiautomatic carbine

Slick A troop-carrying helicopter

SOP Standing Operating Procedure

Squad The basic infantry fighting unit, traditionally composed of approximately twelve men

Stand in the door An Airborne term referring to the moment before one steps out of the door of an aircraft; used in popular jargon to signal a total commitment on one's part to a belief, or one's determination to stand by one's word or commitment

Steel pot A soldier's steel helmet with plastic liner

Tac air Tactical air support

Tet The Vietnamese lunar New Year holiday period

TOC Tactical operations center

Top, Topkick First sergeant

USARV U.S. Army, Vietnam

VC Viet Cong

VCI Viet Cong infrastructure

Viet Cong Vietnamese Communist

Vietnamization The American program under Richard Nixon to turn the war over to the South Vietnamese so that America could withdraw from the conflict "with honor"

War of attrition The destruction of enemy forces and matériel at a rate that the enemy cannot sustain

Waste To kill

WIA Wounded in action

Willie Peter, WP White phosphorus

XO Executive officer

Zap To kill

4-F A World War II medical classification; 4-F meant not fit for military service because of physical or mental impairment or deficiency

Index

★ ★ ★

Index

Index

Index

Index

Index

Julie Sherman, co-author of *About Face: The Odyssey of an American Warrior,* was born in Harrisburg, Pennsylvania. Educated at Northwestern University and the American Film Institute, in 1981 she traveled to Australia to pursue a screenwriting career. In 1983, she was introduced to David Hackworth while writing a documentary film, and soon after embarked upon a five-year "career detour" that resulted in Colonel Hackworth's critically acclaimed best-selling memoir. *About Face* was Ms. Sherman's first book.

Author of numerous screenplays as well, Julie Sherman is currently a freelance writer in Los Angeles, California.

ADD THESE

ROGUE WARRIOR®

BOOKS FROM RICHARD MARCINKO, AND JOHN WEISMAN TO YOUR COLLECTION

Echo Platoon

Option Delta

Seal Force Alpha

Designation Gold

Task Force Blue

Green Team

Red Cell

Rogue Warrior

AND FROM RICHARD MARCINKO

Leadership Secrets of the Rogue Warrior

The Rogue Warrior's Strategy for Success

The Real Team

Visit www.SimonSays.com/rogue

Visit
❖ **Pocket Books** ❖
online at

www.SimonSays.com

Keep up on the latest new
releases from your favorite
authors, as well as author
appearances, news, chats,
special offers and more.

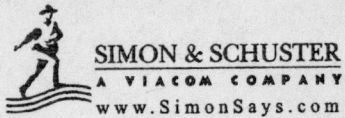

SIMON & SCHUSTER
A VIACOM COMPANY
www.SimonSays.com

Pocket
Books

2381-01